All Generations Will Call Me Blessed

Sermons *on the* Mother of God

Copyright © 2022 by Patristic Nectar Publications
ALL RIGHTS RESERVED
Printed in the USA

Illustrations by Predrag Ilievski. Drawings by Vladimir and Goce Ilievski.
All interior illustrations and artwork, Copyright © Newrome Press.

Publisher's Cataloging-In-Publication Data

Names: Filaret, Metropolitan of Moscow, 1782-1867, author. | Ilievski, Predrag, illustrator. | Ilievski, Vladimir, 1989- illustrator. | Ilievski, Goce, illustrator.
Title: All generations will call me blessed : sermons on the Mother of God / Saint Philaret of Moscow ; illustrations by Predrag Ilievski ; drawings by Vladimir and Goce Ilievski.
Other titles: Sermons. Selections
Description: [Riverside, California] : Patristic Nectar Publications, [2022]
Identifiers: ISBN: 9781735011646
Subjects: LCSH: Mary, Blessed Virgin, Saint--Sermons. | Russkai︠a︡ pravoslavnai︠a︡ t︠s︡erkovʹ--Sermons. | Sermons, Russian. | LCGFT: Sermons.
Classification: LCC: BX513 .F5522 2022 | DDC: 252.019--dc23

SAINT PHILARET OF MOSCOW

All Generations Will Call Me Blessed

Sermons *on the* Mother of God

Contents

Foreword vii
Introduction ix
1. The Devotion of the Virgin 1
2. The Silence of the Virgin 9
3. Miracles 19
4. The Foundation of God in Man 24
5. The Blameless Confusion of the Virgin 37
6. Jesus' Mother and Brothers 44
7. The Secret Virtue of the Virgin 50
8. A Sword in Her Heart 59
9. The Mystery of Godliness 68
10. The Dignity of Virginity 79
11. All Generations Bless Her 87
12. Grace 96
13. Obeying the Will of God 105
14. The Contemplation of Death 114
15. Martha's Earthly Cares 121
16. Following the Footsteps of the Mother of God 130
17. The Seed of the Woman 137
18. The Icon of the Dormition 145
19. The Beauty of the Heavenly Queen is Within 153
20. The Humility of the Virgin 160
21. The Translation of the Virgin 167

22. The Holy Seed of God 174
23. The Virgin's Unblinking Gaze into Eternity 181
24. The Exalted Faith of the Virgin 188
25. A Good Encounter with Death 194
26. The Consent of the Virgin 201
27. Death Rendered Into Sleep 208
28. Cultivating Pious Contemplation 213
29. The Inheritance that the Virgin Bequeathes 219
30. Secret Interiority: The Primary Law of the Virgin's Life 224
31. Lessons in War and Peace 230
32. The Incarnation of the Son of God 236
33. Vigilant Watchfulness 239
34. The Second Man 245
35. The Half-Night Vigil 250
36. God's Rights Over Us 257
37. The One Thing We Need 267
38. The Virgin's Humble Wisdom 272
39. The First Resurrection 279
40. Walking Behind the Virgin 288
41. Lessons from the Miracle at Cana 294
42. Heart-Attention to God's Word 299

Foreword

It is with continued great joy that Patristic Nectar Publications offers this third volume of St. Philaret of Moscow's homilies entitled *All Generations Will Call Me Blessed: Sermons on the Mother of God*. St. Philaret's fame as a preacher of the Word of God has resounded far and wide for the last 150 years. It is clear from his homiletical corpus that there is no subject to which the great saint dedicated his preaching prowess more than the subject of the Most Holy Theotokos. In these 42 homilies St. Philaret's great love for the Most Holy Virgin Mary shines forth as he reveals the virtue of our Heavenly Queen, and expounds upon the virtues of her whose "glory is within." Our Holy Father not only teaches us the significance of the Virgin's free collaboration with the Lord God in the mysteries of Jesus' Incarnation and saving deeds, but also sets forth the Holy Virgin as the model Christian, the example of faith and life for all Christians in all times. May the blessing of our Holy Mother Mary attend all those who read these sermons in faith.

Father Josiah Trenham
Patristic Nectar Publications

Introduction

In the beginning, God created man and destined him for a great purpose, that of becoming equal with Him by grace. The fall of our forefather did not bring to nought God's will for the creation of His reasonable creature, and for centuries He looked down from heaven upon earth, to see even one person who would *do righteousness* and be able to respond as His minister in the great work of regeneration of mankind. This person was the Most Holy Virgin.

cf. Psalm 14:2

We know that by one word of Christ, the whole universe came into being. *'Let there be light: and there was light. Let there be...'* and the whole creation. Due to the greatest virtue of the Holy Virgin, which is Her perfect surrendering to the will of God, She too, with Her one word, *'Be it unto me according to thy word'*, constrained the bowels of Him Whom nothing can constrain, God the Saviour, Who *bowed the heavens and came down* in order to fulfill the pre-eternal counsel of the Father and of the Son and of the Holy Spirit, and to become the Author of the great mystery.

cf. John 1:3
Genesis 1:3

cf. Luke 1:38

2 Samuel 22:10;
Psalm 18:9

In the name *Theotokos*, which was first given to Her by the Tradition of the Church and then consecrated by Synodal decrees, the whole mystery of Christ is contained. And whoever honors this name, fulfills the prophetic Spirit of the New Testament, which She expressed Herself in Her triumphal song after the Annunciation: *From henceforth all generations shall call me blessed.* All those who bless and magnify the Most Holy Virgin, are in the current of this prophetic Spirit, receive grace from God and become a new creature in Christ. Whilst those who reject this mystery, wage war against the prophetic Spirit; they are left desolate by Godforsakenness and scattered to the four winds because of their vanity.

As the Gospel testifies, the Holy Virgin was Virgin before giving birth. She remained Virgin as She was giving birth, because the Fruit of Her womb sanctifies, perfects and deifies by His grace whatever He touches. Therefore, virginity at birth was the requirement and the fruit of the Divinity of Him to Whom She gave birth. Virginity after birth is confirmed by the long Tradition of the Church. When they received even a slight touch of God's grace, clouds of holy monks forsook the vanity of the passions of this world and lived only by the spirit of grace, *perfecting holiness in the fear of God* unto their last breath. The Holy Virgin became the minister of such a great mystery, having the most perfect union with the Son of God, and Her grace exceeds the measure of all the Saints, being 'Holier than the Holies' (cf. The Akathist Hymn to the Mother of God, Oikos 12). Therefore, virginity after giving birth became a categorical imperative of Her spirit in order to preserve the unique grace She had been given. She now surrendered Herself of Her own accord to the will of God and to the ministry of the great and awesome work of salvation wrought by Him Who was Son of God and Son of the Virgin.

This mystery surpasses the mind of man, but he who is surrendered to the will of God, has the key of the uninterrupted and apostolic Tradition of Him Who remains *the same yesterday, and today, and for ever.* This key is none other than *the messianic key of David,* which was given to the Lord Jesus after His Resurrection, and through Him to all His disciples. This key opens the mind of man and strengthens his heart to have *the mind of Christ* and understand *what is the breadth, and length, and depth, and height* of this mystery, which is the humble love *unto the end* of the Saviour God. _{cf. Ephesians 3:18; John 13:1}

The Spirit makes the man on whom He descends, His mouth, and makes of his heart the psaltery of His creative word. Whereas the man whom He forsakes, *for that he is flesh* rendered useless by its own craftiness, the Spirit grinds him to powder and scatters him in the abyss of eternal oblivion. _{cf. Gen. 6:3; see 1 Corinthians 3:19}

The Russian land offered to God a cloud of Saints, Martyrs, Holy Ascetics, Hierarchs and Righteous, but only one Philaret of equal standing with the great and ecumenical Teachers, Basil the Great, Gregory the Theologian, John Chrysostom, Athanasius, Cyril, Epiphanius of Cyprus, Maximus the Confessor and other great Fathers of the Eastern Church.

This key of Tradition, which is the history of the holiness of God's people from the appearing of the Lord Jesus until the end of time, was granted by Christ to Saint Philaret. This great Hierarch not only mastered the Holy Scriptures, but, even more than that, he was able to interpret Scripture by Scripture, and to impart the grace of Christ's salvation by informing the hearts of all the faithful who inherited his teaching.

Archimandrite Zacharias
Holy Stavropegic Monastery of St. John the Baptist
Essex, England
2022

1

The Devotion of the Virgin

*Homily on the Annunciation
at the Ascension Church of the Chudov Monastery (1822)*

"Behold, the maidservant of the Lord!
Let it be to me according to your word." (Luke 1:38)

These may not seem to be great words. However, a great matter has been brought into existence through them.

It may be that we call ourselves "servants" often, even servants of other people (though perhaps not always in our actions). However, whether we do so or not, we often act in a subservient way to other people. Is it so difficult, then, to call ourselves the servants of the Lord? For it is entirely obvious that we are His slaves, whether we admit it to ourselves or not. By His word was everything created in the beginning, and until this day, whenever He sends His word down to this earth, that word cannot return back to Him in vain. For this reason, it is not difficult, it seems to me, for us to agree with the word that He sends down to us. *Let it be according to your word*—this should always be our answer.

Luke 1:38

As we examine this passage, many might miss the importance of Mary's words. But the great work that begins because of her words must awaken the attention of every person who meditates on this passage. During the days of creation, when God uttered His living and powerful word, *Let there be...*, material reality was brought into existence. However, on this unprecedented day in the history of the world, when the divine Mary uttered her meek and obedient *let it be*, I hardly dare to utter aloud what happened next, for the word of a creature draws down the Creator into His creation. And then God speaks His word: *Behold, you will conceive in your womb and bring forth a Son, and He will be great, and He will reign over the house of Jacob forever.*

Genesis 1

Luke 1:38

Luke 1:31-33

However—O inconceivable wonder!—the very word of God hesitates to act, stopped by Mary's word, *How can this be?* First, her humble *Let it be* was required, before God's mighty *Let there be* could act. What sort of mystical power was contained in the simple words, *Behold, the maidservant of the Lord! Let it be according to your word*, what power could bring to action such a wondrous thing? This mystical power is the most pure and complete devotion of Mary to her God, a devotion of will, thought, soul; a devotion of her entire being, her actions, her hopes and expectations.

Luke 1:34

Luke 1:38, Genesis 1

Luke 1:38

Christians! If each one of us could commune only a little bit with this Godly power, through the prayers of the most blessed Virgin! Behold, the servants of the Lord, and your servants, O Mother of the Lord! Let it be for us according to your example!

Brothers! Let the example of the most pure Virgin be our guide in true fidelity and devotion to God.

Devotion to God is a disposition of spirit in which a person offers everything that he has, everything that happens to him, to the will and Providence of God, so that he himself remains only a warden over his soul and body, since both belong to God. A person can train himself in such a disposition by attentively watching over his own efforts to make himself perfect and spiritually prosperous.

For example, let us say he desires to become wise, so he gathers his talents, he strains the powers of his mind, he strengthens himself through the powers of other chosen minds, he forms for himself a model of knowledge, and what then? While he tries to clarify for himself this or that aspect of knowledge, another darkens for him, ceases to exist, and fades away. The more he widens his circle of knowledge, the more the realms of the unknown appear vast and endless before him. The truth, which long ago was admitted to be reliable, is suddenly brought into doubt by truths newly acquired. The end of any self-directed seeking after knowledge, as the greatest of the ancient wise men admitted, is the revelation that man by himself knows absolutely nothing.

Let us say that he desires to become good. He seeks to know the law of justice. He arouses his heart to virtuous feelings; he begins to accomplish good deeds, and what then? Experience only proves that the desire to be virtuous is often weaker than the passions that incline one to sin. Virtue is often defeated by vice. Experience shows that the law offers virtue, but it does not give the strength to act upon it. Virtuous feelings coming from a cruel heart, like fire from flint stone, are difficult to bring to a steady flame, and they go out quickly. As for a soft heart, virtuous feelings may rise quickly, like a piece of linen catching fire, but they are destroyed just as quickly. Often deeds that seem virtuous on the surface prove themselves to be defiled by impure intentions such as avarice, desire for pleasure, and vanity. Human nature, as one of its newest and most zealous devotees was forced to admit, that so-called "moral reasoning" of man, often produces evil at its core. What can any self-directed efforts to make oneself virtuous hope to achieve in light of this bitter experience?

Where true good is lacking, naturally, no spiritual success can occur. The correct conclusion to be made of these experiences must be this—self-sufficient man will always lose hope in himself. If he does not want to perish—for a person will find nothing but failure if he has no actual success or hope—he has no choice but to raise his desires and hopes to God, and even though he cannot yet see or anticipate how his success will occur, he must offer himself to God as a ruin that he cannot repair himself.

Having begun to commit to God, man encounters other experiences that contrast completely to all experiences of self-sufficiency. Before, his own personal efforts to know the truth could barely produce a weak, evanescent light, quickly replaced by intense darkness. Now, from that very darkness in which he prostrates before the Father of lights, a sudden light is born for him, and if he is sometimes left in that darkness, he still comes to know the wondrous nearness of the One Who is the Light beyond all lights. Before, his own personal efforts to do good were either completely suppressed inside him by his own evil inclinations, or they were proved to be incompletely effectual. Now, when he commits his heart to the power of God, in that very weakness the power of God begins to be accomplished within him, destroying evil and creating good.

Before, his best-laid plans for his own success either never worked or were found to be insufficient. Now, he makes no plans for himself, but from day to day, he sees more and more clearly the great plans of Providence, according to which, in spite of all obstacles (save one, that is, his previous obstacle of stubbornness and unbelief) his own salvation is slowly built. Before, his successes puffed him up, while his failure plunged him into despair. The past left him with wounds of regret, the present only burdened him, and the future frightened him. But now, he greets all successes with pure joy, because he sees in them the mercy and gift of God, while all failure he greets with hope, because he sees in them the proof of his own unworthiness, an instruction to his humility, purification, and a preparation for a better future. Past remembrances no longer burn with regret, but fall like dew on the soul, because he has plunged all his sins into the blood and water that pour out of the rib of the Savior.

For such a person, there is no labor that is too difficult, for he has laid all his sorrows onto the Lord. There is no fear in him, because he lives under the protection of the Almighty. The past is not lost for him, the present is not dangerous, and the future is bright, for all are in the hands of the Eternal One. Before, even when he acted with the intention of pleasing God, he was filled with busyness like Martha in the Gospels, and he made a lot of noise, though through it he received no good gift from God. Now, like Mary, he is silent and still, remaining at the foot of the Savior. With every passing minute, he fills himself with the life of the word of God, and in the depth of his soul, he finds confirmation that he has *chosen that good part, which shall not be taken away from [him]*. *Luke 10:42*

Thus, fidelity to God, which begins as a conviction of the mind, grows into a living sensation of the heart. Man plunges himself irrevocably, like the widow's two mites, into the treasure-house of God, but he does so believing and hoping that there his offering will not be lost, that no matter how worthless it might seem, it will prove useful in building, together with countless other talents, a living temple to the living God.

Some say that this means that we should simply sit down, fold our hands over our lap, and await our salvation. Not in the least! If anyone has truly imagined that this is what fidelity to God is, and acts accordingly, he is in delusion. He is not devoted to God, but to his own laziness. A person who is not dedicated to God is not remarkable for his action, but rather for acting according to his own will, for hoping in his own reason. Likewise, a person who is faithful to God is not remarkable for his inaction, but rather for not acting according to his own will and reason. Just as one who is not dedicated to God can be inactive, so also fidelity to God does not exclude action, that is, action according to God's will and the Spirit of God. To place one's talent into the ground, without a doubt, is not the same thing as putting it into the hands of a capable merchant.

You have given your treasure into able and trustworthy hands. You have provided for yourself. However, you can do more: you can give the merchant your hands as well, so that he may use them according to his own ability and talent. Then, you will receive an even greater return on your investment. And so, he who desires to acquire his own soul will commit this treasure to the Redeemer of souls, and he will calmly trust in Him through faith, hope, and love. But at the same time, he will offer the cosmic Merchant all his ability and strength as tools to perform a great labor, through which that which is earthly, perishable, and worthless will be revealed to be heavenly, incorruptible, and divine.

If someone still finds it necessary to ask why fidelity to God is even necessary for self-perfection and human flourishing, then here is my answer. Man lost his perfection and his blessedness when he stole himself from God. God was his Master, not only by all the just laws of the Almighty, but He had also assimilated man to Himself, having placed His seal onto man, that is, His image. The personal will of the creature tore off a third part of heaven and lit the fires of hell in it. Self-will infected human nature with sin and death, and cursed the rest of the world as well. Man will not cease to produce all kinds of evil, until he will be completely dedicated to God, Who alone is strong enough to once again enter into that fallen nature through blessing, life, holiness, and heavenly blessedness.

Therefore, the word of God often reminds us of this need for devotion, both internally and externally, both temporally and eternally. *Commit your way to the Lord, trust also in Him, and He shall bring it to pass. Commit your works to the Lord, and your thoughts will be established. Therefore humble yourselves under the mighty hand of God, that He may exalt you in due time, casting all your care upon Him, for He cares for you. Our Father! Thy will be done on earth as it is in heaven.*

Psalm 36:5
Proverbs 16:3
1 Peter 5:6-7

Matthew 6:9-10

All the great things that Scripture offers us have occurred through great devotion to God.

Who does not know Abraham and his great sacrifice? How was he able to raise a death-dealing hand over his own son, concerning whom he had received a promise of descendants? How could he have failed to doubt God's word? How did he now say to God: was it not You, Lord, who promised that *in Isaac [my] seed shall be called*? Where will this seed be when my son Isaac will burn on the altar table? And yet, the patriarch did not have a single thought or desire or action of his own. He committed everything to God, *contrary to hope, in hope believed*, and in this way he was able to offer the desired sacrifice and not lose his beloved son and still increased God's blessing over him! As God said to him, *blessing I will bless you, and multiplying I will multiply your descendants...and in your seed all the nations of the earth shall be blessed, because you have obeyed My voice*. Thus, devotion is the greatest sacrifice one can offer God, and the truest pledge of His blessings.

Genesis 21:12

Romans 4:18

Genesis 22:17-18

Who has not heard of Job, whose virtue God Himself proclaimed before the assembly of the heavenly powers? But where is the power of his virtue if not in his devotion to God, to Whom he dedicated himself with gratitude, in spite of the inconceivable losses of children, riches, and health? Through this devotion, he made worthless all the efforts of the enemy of virtue and human blessedness. *The Lord gave, the Lord has taken away; Blessed be the name of the Lord*. Such fidelity to God is the surest bulwark against all temptations.

Job 1:21

Look now at Moses in that terrifying moment when the sea lay before him, while the hosts of Egypt came up behind him. The people cry out to God; they complain about their leader. And what of that leader? He doesn't prepare the people for battle, nor does he seek a way to escape, nor does he raise his miraculous staff, nor does he even utter a single prayerful word to God! What does this mean? He committed himself to God, and he leads his entire nation into this commitment: *The Lord will fight for you, and*

Exodus 14:14

you shall hold your peace. Here we can see that devotion to God is itself the most firm and active form of prayer.

However—to summarize for the benefit of every Christian—how did the great work of Christ begin? Through the complete devotion of the Son of God to the will of God His Father. Behold, I go *to do Your will, O my God.* This is what He said as he descended to incarnation. And how does this great work end? With the same fidelity: *Not as I will, but as You will. Father, into Your hands I commit My spirit.* Thus, devotion to God is both the beginning and the perfection of Christianity and our eternal salvation.

Let us conclude this teaching with an admonition that the Church places at the end of most of its prayers, the better to grow in us constantly this spirit of commitment that is the heart and soul of true Christianity: "Having called to remembrance our most holy, most pure, most blessed Theotokos and ever-Virgin Mary, with all the saints, let us commit ourselves, and one another, and all our life to Christ our God." Amen.

2

The Silence of the Virgin

*Homily on the Annunciation
at the Ascension Church of the Chudov Monastery (1824)*

"And Mary said: My soul magnifies the Lord, and my spirit has rejoiced in God my Savior. For He has regarded the lowly state of His maidservant; for behold, henceforth all generations will call me blessed." (Luke 1:46-48)

Finally, the silent Mary speaks, and her word, filled with the Spirit, flows like a river and swirls upward like sweet-smelling clouds of incense. Like lightning, this word illumines and brightens. This beginning of her triumphant speech, spoken in the presence of Elizabeth after she greeted her for the first time with the name *Mother of the Lord*, contains so much already! She glorifies God and raises to Him not merely her voice, but her entire soul: *My soul magnifies the Lord*. She rejoices, and she transmutes her joy into prayer and a spiritual sacrifice: *my spirit has rejoiced in God my Savior*. She is humbled, and yet she prophesies the descent of the Almighty One: *For He has*

Luke 1:43

Luke 1:46

Luke 1:47

Luke 1:48

regarded [my] lowly state. She prophesies, and her prophetic gaze pierces through all times even to the end of time: *henceforth all generations will call me blessed.* Thus, the one into whom the Word has descended became fruitful with her words. Before the Word came out of her as the fruit of her womb, He appeared within her as the fruit of her lips, confessing the Lord: *And Mary said…*

<small>Luke 1:48</small>

<small>Luke 1:46</small>

Wondrous is the word of Mary, but majestic also is her silence. Let us reverently attend to the depth of the wisdom of her words that we hear so often in the Church; let us especially pay attention to that which is not so obvious at first glance. Let us also listen in on Mary's silence and let us learn from her how to use the treasure house of our language more sparingly.

I will not speak of the silence in which the most holy Virgin grew up and was raised, because this is hidden by the silence of the holy evangelists. As for what holy tradition has to say about this period, we can say that she had a completely pious upbringing. It would be appropriate also to ask whether or not the distraction and freedom so willingly given children in our own time is conducive to her kind of blessed spiritual fruits.

The day of "annunciation," that is, the joyful announcement of the imminent incarnation of the Son of God, begins to reveal to us the hidden spiritual life of the mother of God. The words of the angel reveal in her the virtue of silence. He suddenly appears in her solitude, and he says to her: *Rejoice, highly favored one, the Lord is with you! Blessed are you among women!* How many questions must have arisen in Mary's mind at this moment! Who was this unknown visitor? What right had he to break into the solitude of a Virgin? What is the meaning of this unheard-of greeting, which announced her to be greater than all other women on earth? But nothing causes her to come out of her customary silence. She feels the movement of the Spirit; however, her lips are sealed. She does not hurry to answer this greeting. She remains

<small>Luke 1:28</small>

in silent and deep contemplation: *She was troubled at his saying, and considered what manner of greeting this was.* Luke 1:29

The angel, having calmed her spirit with a single word—fear not! (for the words of the heavenly powers have power in themselves, and so are never without consequence)—continues his greeting to her. In explaining why she was *highly favored*, he adds that she has *found favor with God*. Then he prophecies her conception, the birth of a Son, His salvific name, His divine dignity, and the coming of a wondrous, eternal kingdom. How many more reasons for her to answer or to ask questions! And yet, the most blessed one does not desire to test the mysteries of grace. The highly favored one does not dare to speak in many words about that which is beyond word and reason. Even now, she would not have broken her silence, had not her love for virginity forced her to speak these brief words: *How can this be, since I do not know a man?* Luke 1:28 / Luke 1:30 / Luke 1:34

In order to correctly understand this word, we must first assume, as tradition tells us, that Mary had already given a vow of life-long virginity. Otherwise, since she was already betrothed to Joseph, why would she have any reason to ask, *How can this be?* Secondly, we must consider the Law of Moses, according to which any vow of a virgin or a woman could be annulled by a single word of a father or husband, and only became legal when the father or husband heard it and confirmed his agreement with it. Therefore, we can conclude, also in agreement with tradition, that Joseph knew of this vow of chastity and confirmed it, and that he agreed to a betrothal with Mary only to be a protector of her virginity, which would have had to be hidden under the superficial cover of a marriage union, since the Jewish people at that time did not respect the moral heights of virginity. For this reason, even though Mary had no thought of disbelieving, or doubting, or contradicting the word of the angel, she was still forced to asked, *how can this be?* Luke 1:34 / Numbers 30 / Luke 1:34

It is as though she said, "Though I have a husband according to the conventions of betrothal, but I have no husband according to my vow of chastity. This vow was spoken aloud and confirmed; I no more desire to annul it than the law would allow such a thing, for the law says, *If a man makes a vow to the Lord, or swears an oath to bind himself by some agreement, he shall not break his word; he shall do according to all that proceeds out of his mouth.* The Lord does not break His own laws; therefore, how can it be that my vow of chastity will be preserved, and the law will be fulfilled, and yet a son will be born?"

Numbers 30:2

Can you see that it is only necessity that forces open the sacred bonds of her silence? Or, better yet, it is grace itself that pours out of her mouth; she reveals the mystery of her betrothal to Joseph, the better to hide another mystery, the more profound mystery of her betrothal to God Himself. Mary's rejection of an earthly husband gives the angel an opportunity to announce her worthiness to become a bride of God, a calling that has been foreordained: *The Holy Spirit will come upon you, and the Power of the Highest will overshadow you.*

Luke 1:35

The annunciation has been accepted. The angel has gone. The Word is incarnate. The Virgin conceived, and the signs of her pregnancy became evident: *She was found with child of the Holy Spirit.* However, Joseph did not know of the mystery of her conception by the Holy Spirit. For if he had known the mystery of the bride of God, then could he have worried about her becoming a *public example*? Could he have come to the conclusion that it would be better to *put her away secretly*? There are so many miracles of silence here that I do not know if we have enough words to describe this silence.

Matthew 1:18

Matthew 1:19

Matthew 1:19

Joseph sees something in Mary that he did not expect, and that he cannot understand. However, he remains silent and does not ask her. Mary sees herself in danger of becoming subject to vicious gossip, and even official sanction. However, she remains silent and does not reveal her secret. Where is the angel who announced the good tiding to her? Why is he silent, why does he not console her in this new confusion? Where is Joseph's own guardian angel? Why does he wait so long to appear to him, why does he not forewarn the righteous man when his pure soul could so easily have become darkened by an unjust thought, even a blasphemous suspicion? And—if it is not too brazen to ask such a question—why does He Who sends the angels wait for such a long time? Why does He wait so long to illumine His own beloved righteous man, or to save His beloved bride through whom the world will be saved?

Hear what St John Chrysostom has to say:

> For so far from punishing, he was not minded even to make an example of her. Do you see a man under self-restraint, and freed from the most tyrannical of passions? But nevertheless he was so free from passion as to be unwilling to grieve the Virgin even in the least matters. Thus, whereas to keep her in his house seemed like a transgression of the law, but to expose and bring her to trial would constrain him to deliver her to die; he does none of these things, but conducts himself now by a higher rule than the law. Hence also this man exhibited great self-command, in that he neither accused nor upbraided, but only set about putting her away.[1]

It is truly evident that the heart of this righteous man already had a premonition of Christ's future commandment to have a *good eye* and to *judge not, that you be not judged.* Therefore, though he sees signs of pregnancy, he does not want to have any suspicious thoughts about the Virgin. There is a law that gives full rights to the husband over the wife; however, he has no desire to judge the betrothed one. *Joseph, not wanting to make her a public example, was minded to put her secretly away.*

Matthew 6:22; 7:1

Matthew 1:19

---

1 Homily 4 on Matthew, chapter 7 (https://www.newadvent.org/fathers/200104.htm)

Can you see what exalted virtue is contained in Joseph's silence? But Mary's silence is even greater. His silence lessens the burden of another, while at the same time finding a way of lessening his own. Her silence is dangerous to her, and with each day, her silence only increases her danger. What does this inconceivable labor of silence signify? That Mary is the perfect vessel of grace. For as an earthly vessel is useless when it leaks, so a spiritual vessel is unworthy if it cannot preserve the grace poured into it through complete, humble silence, instead leaking through vain words or immodest language or impatient complaining. A good earthly vessel not only keeps liquids safe, but even contains the smell of the liquid without allowing it to escape. Such a good vessel would not be broken if you struck it or put it into the fire. Similarly, a perfect spiritual vessel is someone who *[holds] the mystery of faith with a pure conscience*, in peace of heart, and in the silence of his entire being, preserving the grace poured into him with such firmness that no blows can break him, no passions, no temptations can destroy him.

1 Timothy 3:9

If Mary spoke of her mystery with Elizabeth, it was only because Elizabeth herself had come to know of the mystery through revelation of the Holy Spirit. However, if she would have spoken of the divine mystery with Joseph, it would have been according to human trust or human fear, and consequently not by divine utterance. Now, she hides herself from the person who knew her heart better than anyone else, for she had chosen him to be the guardian of her virginity. She hides herself, though it is clear that this is dangerous for her, not only because she might be publicly accused, but, as Chrysostom makes clear, because she could have been judged and brought to death. This silence most reliably testified that she was firmly preserving the Word she had accepted into her womb, loving Him more than her chosen and betrothed husband, more than any earthly consolation, more even than her life. For this silence was a constant, pure, and great sacrifice to God the Word.

It is thus not strange that for a time divine revelation also remained silent, to allow such great virtues to ripen and bear fruit, the better to instruct all of us. The silent sacrifice of Mary was accepted; the thoughts of Joseph were justified in his dispassion; and only then did the word from heaven hurry down to crown their labors of silence, to put to end the difficulties of Mary, and to reveal to Joseph the great mystery of piety: *But while he thought about these things, behold, an angel of the Lord appeared to him in a dream, saying, 'Joseph, son of David, do not be afraid to take to you Mary your wife, for that which is conceived in her is of the Holy Spirit.'*   *Matthew 1:20*

If you have enough constant attention to follow Mary throughout her life, you will see a constant recurrence of this character of profound silence, this concentration within herself that was never distracted, in a word, you will see that her entire life was hidden within God Himself. Neither the greatest joys nor the worst sorrows could affect this most important characteristic of her spirit.

The Word is born, and the angels sing in praise. The shepherds prophesy. Is it not right for the mother of the Word also to sing and prophecy in word? But she remains silent, not wasting words, only preserving all she heard within herself: *But Mary kept all these things and pondered them in her heart.*   *Luke 2:19* Simeon pierces her soul with a terrifying prophecy; Jesus Himself, as a youth, abandons her, as though rejecting her, announcing that He *must be about My Father's business.*   *Luke 2:49* Even so, she does not contradict Him, but remains silent. *His mother kept all these things in her heart.*   *Luke 2:49, 51*

Finally, she stands before the Cross of her beloved Son, and the prophesied sword pierces her heart. Even strangers could not remain indifferent at His sufferings: *A great multitude of the people followed Him, and women who also mourned and lamented Him.*   *Luke 23:27* Even after His crucifixion, *the whole crowd who came together to that sight, seeing what had been done, beat their breasts and returned.*   *Luke 23:48* How much more might we expect the mother of the Crucified One to weep, wail, and tear her hair as she stood at the foot of His cross! But we see or hear nothing like this; the eyewitness himself gives not a single word of hers in his gospel. She suffered, without a doubt, as no one on earth has ever suffered, except for the Crucified One himself. But the abyss of her sufferings did not cause her to drown, for they constantly fell into the equally vast abyss of her patience, humility, faith, hope, and unconditional faithfulness to the judgments of God.

Look, O Christian soul, at this holy image of spiritual silence that the Gospel offers you, partly in the person of Joseph, but much more in the person of Mary. Look, and come to know the mystical, majestic beauty of her soul, which the prophet described thus: *the royal daughter is all glorious within...* Then you will love this spiritual beauty, and coming to love it, you will labor to acquire, at least in part, this beauty of the royal daughter, and to follow her footsteps to acquire her blessedness, for *her companions who follow her shall be brought to You.*

Psalm 44:13

Psalm 44:14

Are you confused by anything in the faith? Don't rush either to curiosity or to contradiction, but in silence listen to the word of faith, and patiently await the time when He who speaks to you in parables will find you worthy of receiving their interpretation through the living word and deed.

Do you see something strange or, as it seems to you, incorrect in the words and deeds of your neighbor? Don't hurry to accuse and condemn him if you do not hold the responsibility of a father, pastor, ruler, or instructor. Do not be righteous like the Pharisee, who found no other righteous people in the world other than himself: *I thank You that I am not like other men—extortioners, unjust, adulterers, or even as this tax collector.* Instead, be righteous like Joseph, who was good and meek.

Luke 18:11

Are you afraid that some action of faith or love will be subject to unjust condemnation or accusation? For that reason, don't trumpet your virtue aloud. By preserving its glory hidden, you will not lose its purity. Do not commit your actions to men with their vain words, but "trust" your prayer to Him, *commit your way to the Lord... and He shall bring it to pass.* *Psalm 36:5*

Have you been visited by good fortune, or does joy expand your heart? Don't also expand your lips for vainglory; but treasure the words of Providence in the gratitude of your heart.

Are you attacked by calamity, or does sorrow fill your soul? Don't increase your moans and groans, because in most of them you can hear the echoes of stubbornness and lack of submission to the judgments of the Almighty. Instead, *wait on the Lord; be of good courage, and He shall strengthen your heart; wait, I say, on the Lord!* *Psalm 26:14*

And never waste your words without discernment, O reasoning creature of the Creative Word! If God created all things by the Word, and if man is created in the image of God, then what majestic power should reside in the word of man! In actual fact, human words have healed the sick, raised the dead, called down fire from heaven, stopped the sun and the moon in their tracks, and, what it most important, having become the instrument of the incarnate Word of God, this word of man transformed human nature, corrupted by sin, into a new, pure, and holy creation. This is how the word of man acts when it is first firmly kept in the crucible of reverent silence, and, having been stoked by the mystery of internal prayer, becomes filled with the power of the Word of God and the Holy Spirit.

How horrifying, then, that we turn this mighty, creative, holy instrument to impure, corrupting, impious actions, to evil words, slander, blasphemy. How tragic that we flippantly break apart this powerful word into dust, throwing it up into the wind of vain and idle talking!

Someone once said of himself: *In my heart I have blessed nine suppositions, and I will mention a tenth.* This is how those who know the worth of the word protect it. At the very least, O Christian, *Do not be hasty with your mouth,* give yourself a chance to think *Sirach 25:7*

Ecclesiastes 5:1

whether or not your words will benefit you or someone else. Though this word may seem small or insignificant, it will survive until the final judgment, and it will stand at the judgment to witness either for or against you. Remember the counsel of the apostle: *Let no corrupt word proceed out of your mouth, but what is good for necessary edification, that it may impart grace to the hearers. And do not grieve the Holy Spirit of God, by whom you were sealed for the day of redemption.* Amen.

Ephesians 4:29-30

3

Miracles

Homily on the Sign of the Mother of God (1825)

But He sighed deeply in His spirit, and said, "Why does this generation seek a sign? Assuredly, I say to you, no sign shall be given to this generation." (Mark 8:12)

The Lord warned the corrupt and unfaithful people of Israel that they would not receive a sign. But we Christians, the new chosen nation, should we not instead hope that a sign for our benefit and salvation will be given us?

Yes! There was a time when Christians sowed abundantly not into the physical earth, but into the noetic heaven. Consequently, they received abundant fruits of heaven and the Spirit. They sowed in faith and received a harvest of signs and miracles, beneficial and salvific that fed and strengthened their spirits for eternal life. Reciprocally, God sowed signs and miracles from the heavens, and they brought forth abundantly on this earth, among mankind, fruits of repentance, correction, faith, hope, gratitude to God, and virtues of all kinds. God often performed miracles not only through holy people, but through holy signs or through visible signs and even images of the saints, such as the pure bodies of the saints and their holy icons. He performed miracles that were so obvious and majestic that the Church triumphantly commemorates some of them with distinct days on the Church calendar.

But today, do we only know of such signs by historical remembrance? Do we not seek them only as an extreme rarity? Or perhaps we search for them in vain?

In other words, does not the Lord once again lament about his chosen people? Perhaps he once again withholds signs from us with a threat? "Why does this generation seek a sign? Assuredly, I say to you, no sign shall be given to this generation."

The assertion that we no longer see miracles in our time is so commonplace, and often accompanied by such strange reasoning, that it would not be fruitless to contemplate why we do not see many miracles in our days.

Some say with conviction that we do not see signs and miracles because they don't exist, neither should we expect to see any miracles in our time. For the Lord, so these people say, uses miracles as a means to spread and confirm the faith. And since the faith in our time is quite widespread, and since it is confirmed among many, then miracles have ceased to become necessary.

I agree, if you will, with the idea that God uses miracles to spread and confirm the faith. But should we then conclude that our time is such a righteous time that miracles are no longer necessary? Let us consider this assertion dispassionately. Are there any who do not believe? If so, then we still need means to spread the faith. If there are still active persecutors of the faith or those who strain to destroy it, then any means we have to strengthen the faith would be useful. But since in our time there are still many unbelievers and many who attack the faith, to the sorrow and even danger of the faithful (unfortunately, even within Christianity, like a snake in the grass), then should we conclude, I repeat, that miracles are no longer necessary to spread and confirm the faith?

Now, lest we give too much credit to the self-assured wise of this world, let us more fully examine their proposition that God uses miracles as a means to spread and confirm the faith. There are indeed miracles that are clearly meant to propagate the faith. One of these, for example, is the giving of tongues to the apostles by the Holy Spirit, allowing them to speak and understand languages they had previously not known. Evidently, the intention of this specific miracle was to give all nations the best possible chance of hearing the teaching of faith. The history of Christianity shows that the gift of tongues produced incredible results in the early Church. Through this miracle, the faith reached out to all the nations of the world with the speed of lightning. However, after each nation that accepted the faith began to have its own native sons learn the teachings of the faith and become able to continue its spread, the miracle of tongues faded. In this case, it would not be incorrect to say that miracle was no longer necessary, and so it stopped.

However, there are other miracles that are not so closely connected with the spread of the faith. These miracles occur in places where the faith has already spread and been well established, and still, they can lead to the good and salvation of people. Such miracles include the gift of healing or the miraculous ability to heal sicknesses by prayer, by a word, by the laying on of hands, or by some other sign. For what reason was King Hezekiah raised from his deathbed through Isaiah and returned to life for another fifteen years? Was it so that word of this sign of faith would reach unbelieving Babylon, leading to a seductive and dangerous embassy that tempted Hezekiah's vanity and became the cause of a prophecy of coming doom? No, it was not for this that Hezekiah wept and prayed on his deathbed: *Remember now, O Lord*, he said, *I pray, how I have walked before You in truth and with a loyal heart, and have done what was good in Your sight.* And God answered

4 Kingdoms 20:3, 5

him through the prophet: *I have heard your prayers; I have seen your tears; surely I will heal you.* Thus, this sign occurred only because of God's unutterable love for mankind and his extreme compassion to Hezekiah, as well as a reward for his faith and virtues. In addition, such a sign could not fail to inspire other faithful Hebrews who were weak in faith to increase their faith and trust in God.

Why did Jesus Christ Himself raise the son of the widow of Nain? The evangelist gives no other reason than this: that the Lord had compassion on the widow. *When the Lord saw her, He had compassion on her.* Can it be that such miracles, occurring for such reasons and causes, ever be excessive? When Apostle James commanded the sick to *call for the elders of the Church, and let them pray over him, anointing him with oil in the name of the Lord,* he added the following promise: *The prayer of faith will save the sick, and the Lord will raise him up.* What does this mean, other than that he immortalized for the Church the gift of healing given by the Lord to the apostles in the beginning? Did the Lord Himself only give this law and this right as a temporary measure: *He who believes in Me, the works that I do he will do also; and greater works than these he will do?* He who believes will do. Consequently, while there are faithful people on this earth, the works of Christ must continue, and "greater works than these as well," including, without a doubt, signs and miracles of various kinds.

Let us say it even more directly. Just as God always is, so miracles always are. For if God always exists, then God always acts, and if He acts, there His works abound, and the works of God are miracles. *You are the God who does wonders.*

And yet, foolishly, the wise of this world are trying to steal from themselves this eternal benefit and expression of the might of the Creator! But is He the God who does wonders if we do not have an ardent desire for union with God? Truly did Apostle Paul accuse the Corinthians of an unworthy communion of the Body and Blood, saying, *For this reason many are weak and sick among you, and many sleep.* In other words, many have been struck by sudden death for defiling sacred things. It seems to me that for many of us it is in fact nothing short of a miracle of God's mercy that we are not similarly struck for our careless approach to the sacred.

Brethren! Let us instead approach our Lord Who works miracles for the salvation of each one of us, and all of us, and let us exclaim together with the apostles, *Lord, increase our faith!*. And then, together with David, *Show me a sign for good, that those who hate me may see it and be ashamed, because You, Lord, have helped me and comforted me.* Amen.

Luke 17:5

Psalms 85:17

4

The Foundation of God in Man

Homily on the Annunciation of the Mother of God (1826)

Nevertheless, the solid foundation of God stands, having this seal: "The Lord knows those who are His," and "Let everyone who names the name of Christ depart from iniquity." (2 Timothy 2:19)

It seems to me that today I see this foundation of God that the apostle describes as being sealed, that is, as being known only to God. What can the foundation of God, on which all of God's creation stands, be other than the Son of God, Jesus Christ?

Colossians 1:16-17

For by Him all things were created that are in heaven and that are on earth, visible and invisible, whether thrones or dominions or principalities or powers. All things were created through Him and for Him. And He is before all things, and in Him all things consist. If one must raise up again those creations of God that have fallen, *no other foundation can anyone lay than that which is laid, which is Jesus Christ.* This foundation of God today is borne by the Holy Spirit from the heights of heaven and is placed in the depths of earth. It is borne

1 Corinthians 3:11

from the glory of the divine and is placed in the secret places of the human, hidden by more than a single seal—the seals of virginity, humility, and silence. Truly, who other than the Lord could know You, O You Who are One in Essence with Him, in this inconceivably lessened state in which, all the same, the God who is all in all was hidden, when You were placed, as the foundation of our salvation, into the womb of Mary, in a way that no one can explain. *1 Corinthians 15:28*

Let us wonder at the glory of the creative works of God. Let us wonder also at their secrecy. Let us deepen our attention a bit more into the foundation of God that the apostle speaks of. I hope that we will find a hidden treasure there.

Part One

The solid foundation of God stands, having this seal: *The Lord knows those who are His*. *2 Timothy 2:19*

Though it is true that *the beginning of the creation of God*, or the foundation of that creation, is Jesus Christ, the Son of God, we should take note that the apostle here speaks of the foundation of God not in terms of all of God's creations, but in terms of the chosen ones whom the Lord knows and calls His own (*The Lord knows those who are His*). *Revelation 3:14*

2 Timothy 2:19

In this narrower sense, what does the *foundation of God* even mean? Without a doubt, it means that on the Son of God, as on a universal foundation, the human race is specially created. It means that every single Christian soul is built in Jesus Christ, as on a foundation. Let us say it even clearer: the apostle is here speaking of the Church that the Son of God established. This foundation is the grace-filled and salvific gift of God in man, the faith itself, whose author and confirmation is Jesus Christ. *2 Timothy 2:19*

This foundation of God is firm or even impossible to destroy, as the apostle says, for the Lord Himself said of His Church in general, *I will build My Church, and the gates of Hades shall not prevail* *Matthew 16:18 against it;* and of its members in particular: *neither shall anyone snatch them out of My hand.* [John 10:28]

From ancient times, it was customary for signs on buildings to indicate their importance or to whom they belonged. Similarly, the apostle sees a sign on the spiritual building of God that distinguishes its invincibility from the easily-destroyed foundations of human buildings. This sign also protects those inside it from the attacks of cunning or boldness, of ignorance and anger. "The solid foundation of God stands, having this seal."

What is this seal or sign? The apostle continues: *The Lord knows those who are His.* [2 Timothy 2:19] What a truly wondrous seal! You see that it is a sign, for it is made of words, and not without reason does the apostles call it a seal, for it does not so much make evident and reveal as it hides and closes. This is the nature of a seal.

The Lord knows those who are His. [2 Timothy 2:19] Can it be that people do not know those who are God's? Yes, it is so. Very often, maybe most of the time, such people are not well-known. Let us consider Moses, who put down the might of Egypt, who rescued Israel, who sealed his feats with wonders of air, water, earth, tree, stone. Could anyone fail to know that He was God's? And yet, evidently, his own people didn't know this well enough, for they murmured at him often and even raised rebellions against him. Joseph was raised by the path of prison and slavery to the heights of the throne. He was glorified by his knowledge of God's mysteries. He was invested in might. And yet, his own brothers did not immediately recognize that he was God's man; He was forced to reveal it to them himself: *Do not be afraid, for I am God's.*[1] [Genesis 50:19]

Who does not know the angelic life and heavenly teaching of John the Baptist? But how many knew that he was called an angel by the Lord Himself? (*Behold, I send My messenger,* i.e., angel) [Malachi 3:1] And when Jesus asked the question, *The baptism of John: was* [Matthew 21:25]

---

[1] It seems the Russian Bible has a different reading of this verse from the English Bible, which sounds like this: "Do not be afraid, for am I in the place of God?" However, in context, both readings essentially mean the same thing.

it from heaven or from men? the chief priests and elders, who were the intellectual elite of their people, were not ashamed to declare their ignorance of the answer.

And You, O Eternal One, Who is one in essence with the Father, even after You spoke as no man has ever spoken , even after You performed miracles that no man can perform *unless God is with him,,* did they know You, from Whom the only true knowledge proceeds as light from the sun? If they knew, they would never have spoken so irreverently: *Is this not the carpenter's son?* They would never have rejected You so flippantly: *As for this fellow, we do not know where he is from. Had they known, they would not have crucified the Lord of glory.* If these blind people could not see the stars in heaven or the very Sun Himself, if they did not recognize men who were clearly sent by God and even incarnate Wisdom Himself, then it is not so strange that the world does not recognize those who belong to God. God's Providence does not reveal His chosen to the world, and their own humility hides them from their fellow men. *John 7:46 / John 3:2 / Matthew 13:55 / John 9:29 / 1 Corinthians 2:8*

The Lord knows those who are His. According to the apostle, no one other than the Lord has this knowledge; and so, can it be possible that even those who are God's don't know that they are His? Truly this is so. This is the only conclusion we can make from the words of the apostle. *The Spirit Himself bears witness with our spirit that we are children of God,* if we are truly so. According to another apostle, *He who believes in the Son of God has the witness in himself,* but what sort of a witness is it? *This is the testimony: that God has given us eternal life, and this life is in His Son.* However, since this life of the faithful, until the revelation of the sons of God, *is hidden with Christ in God,* then it may happen that they themselves do not fully know what sort of divine treasure they contain within the fragile vessels of their own humanity. And is not the Spirit that witnesses to their spirit the same Spirit that *2 Timothy 2:19 / Romans 8:16 / 1 John 5:10 / 1 John 5:11 / Colossians 3:3*

John 3:8 — *blows where it wishes, and you hear the sound of it, but cannot tell where it comes from and where it goes?*

Acts 9:15 — Did the Lord Himself not choose Paul as a *chosen vessel*, having laid in him His divine foundation and having built in him a divine habitation that led to not only many people being converted, but to many great Churches in many lands and among many nations being founded? And yet, what do we see? Even so, Paul does not know if he has acquired a perfect level of assimilation to God: *Philippians 3:13-14* — *Brethren, I do not count myself to have apprehended; but one thing I do, forgetting those things which are behind and reaching forward to those things which are ahead, I press toward the goal for the prize of the upward call of God in Christ Jesus.*

Truly, only God Himself knows who are His. But why does He hide them from other people, and to a certain degree from themselves? Why should they not know more clearly that they are God's, for their consolation? Why should others not come to know them, for their instruction? Sometimes, this does happen. After all, the seal of God cannot be completely invisible, nor should it be without benefit to others. However, in this case, as in others, more is hidden under the seal than revealed by its visible sign.

The grace-filled foundation of God is hidden in man because it is laid in the very depths of the soul, so that deeper than it, nothing human remains that might weaken the firmness of the divine foundation. This, according to the apostle, is the *hidden man of the heart*. You can find him neither in the roadways nor in the mirror.

1 Peter 3:4

The foundation of God is hidden from the world at least partially not intentionally, but rather because of the natural consequences of its carnal formation. The world cannot see the saints, just as blind men cannot see the light.

The grace-filled foundation of God is hidden in people partly by the intention of the Providence that preserves them, so that the forces of the enemy might not attack them as often, for they can lead to their destruction. In the same way, the foundation of earthly buildings is hidden underground, lest, being revealed to the destruction effects of the elements, it become weak and the building itself collapse.

Finally, the foundation of God in man is hidden from man himself, lest he *thinks himself to be something, when he is nothing,* lest he delude himself and become puffed up, destroying by pride within himself the foundation of grace that lies firmly and safely only within the depths of humility. *Galatians 6:3*

These and similar thoughts might lead us to understand why the foundation or the building of God, though visible in its whole, is hidden with mystery in its particular parts and in its internal composition, for the Lord Himself alone knows who are His.

Let us feel reverence before the mystical judgments of God. Let us arouse profound attention within ourselves to seek men of God, and the foundations of God within them. Let us not brazenly judge our neighbors, for we do not know them as God does.

Part Two

The solid foundation of God stands, having this seal: 'The Lord knows those who are His,' and *Let everyone who names the name of Christ depart from iniquity.* *2 Timothy 2:19*

Up to this point in our examination of the seal or sign on the foundation (or building) of God within man, we have only examined its first half. The second follows: *Let everyone who names the name of Christ depart from iniquity.* *2 Timothy 2:19*

If the building of God within man only had the first half of the seal, we could only read the first sign: *The Lord knows those who are His.* In other words, only God truly knows those who, according to their living faith and unrelenting love, eternally belong to Him and to His Church (both earthly and heavenly). This first half alone could both console and terrify us. It could console us *2 Timothy 2:19* by the thought of the firmness of God's foundation that no one can undermine, of the indestructibility of God's seal, and of the safety of those who are hidden in the mystery of the face of God. It could terrify us with its obscurity, for no one can ever be assured of being among God's chosen. For if the Lord knows His own, then who are they among whom we live and with whom we converse, whose instructions we follow, whose examples we emulate? Who are we ourselves? Are they God's? Are we? God knows! What a horrifying word, in that case! If God alone knows those with whom I live and those who lead me, then how can I know if I am being led in a false spirit? Do I live among God's enemies? Am I in danger then of being and remaining apart from the true, grace-filled assimilation to God? What a horrifying state of unknowing!

O Lord Who knows His own! You are righteous and wise to hide them from the world that is not worthy of knowing them, a world that would misuse their fame for evil means. However, be equally beneficent to those who, though they might not yet be Yours, desire to become so and to remain so forever. Show us a sign by which we, who do not know, may come to know the true, good, grace-filled, holy, that is, all that is Yours within man, so that we might come to love all that is Yours even more, to seek what is Yours even more, to be instructed by what is Yours and follow it, to be united to what is Yours, and through union with those who are Yours (that is, with Yourself as well) we may have a blessed expectation of being Yours unchangingly and eternally!

The king's seal hides the mystery of the king, while at the same time indicating to whom it belongs, ensuring its contents remain safe and true. Similarly, it is necessary for the mystical seal by which God indicates those faithful ones whom He has chosen for Himself, as known only to Himself, to be signed with some faithful mark by which the attentive might be able to distinguish God's chosen from those who are trying to fool us, or themselves, by declaring themselves to be God's. This is the reason for the second sign that the apostle noted in the spiritual foundation of God within man: *Let everyone who names the name of Christ depart from iniquity.* *2 Timothy 2:19*

It is a great benefit for us on this earth, and a great hope of heavenly blessedness to come, to be able to name the Name of the Lord in faith. Our divine Savior comprises nearly all the work of His salvific embassy from heaven to earth in this one thing: that He made men capable of naming the Name of the Lord. As He approached the limit of His earthly life, He called in prayer to His heavenly Father: *I have finished the work which You have given Me to do.* What is this work? *I have glorified You on the earth,* or, in another way, *I have manifested Your Name to the men whom You have given Me out of the world.* *John 17:4* *John 17:4* *John 17:6*

This makes it clear that those to whom the Name of the Father in heaven has been manifested, i.e., those who "name the Name of the Lord," are Christ's. They are God's. *Therefore ... no one can say that Jesus is Lord except by the Holy Spirit.* And whoever speaks by the Holy Spirit must be Christ's and God's, for the Spirit of God is not given to anyone else. Another apostle says, *Whoever believes that Jesus is the Christ is born of God.* And whoever is born of God is God's in the most intimate sense. *1 Corinthians 12:3* *1 John 5:1*

And so? Can we not then make the following conclusion? We ourselves name the Name of the Lord; we name the Lord Jesus; therefore, we must truly be God's! Truly, the kingdom of God is within us already, and we will be in the kingdom of God in its own time! According to the life and deeds of some, we can truly see that they have such thoughts and sensations, upon which they establish their hope both of heaven and eternity. However, this means that their building has only one half of the sign: *Let everyone who names the Name of Christ depart from iniquity.* Not the other half. *2 Timothy 2:19*

Let us be very careful. This is a broken seal. This is an incomplete sign. This is not a firm foundation. For not everyone who names the Name of the Lord is truly and completely confirmed in the Lord and in His kingdom. The Lord Himself said, *Not everyone who says to Me, 'Lord, Lord,' shall enter the kingdom of heaven, but he who does the will of My Father in heaven.* And His subsequent words are even more terrifying:

<blockquote>

Many will say to Me in that day, 'Lord, Lord, have we not prophesied in Your name, cast out demons in Your name, and done many wonders in Your name?' [23] *And then I will declare to them, 'I never knew you; depart from Me, you who practice lawlessness!'*

</blockquote>

_{Matthew 7:21}

_{Matthew 7:22-23}

What a terrifying surprise! They called the Lord, being sure that they knew Him and believed in Him. They had prophesied, cast out demons, performed miracles, meaning that their faith was not weak, but stronger than most. And yet, the Lord did not accept them in His kingdom. Not only this, but He does not even know them! O, what a horrifying success of evil and human corruption! Can it be that the life-giving knowledge of the One true God and the One Whom He sent, Jesus Christ, can be without faith and life?

And yet, we must admit this to be true, for there are people who *profess to know God, but in works... deny Him.* Can it be that the faith that was provided for the salvation of man might be fruitless? Yes, truly, it can be fruitless, as Apostle James said, *What does it profit, my brethren, if someone says he has faith but does not have works? Can faith save him?* Can it truly be that even the actions of the Spirit of God in man, such as prophecy, casting out demons, miracle-working, can be intermixed with the qualities and deeds of corruptible, carnal man? The heavenly flame, once catches fire within man, is supposed to raise man up to the heights. Can it be that this flame will be snuffed out in the dust of the earth? Can it be that once it has begun to illumine man, it can still abandon man to the outer darkness? If there were no such danger, then the warning would not have been spoken: *Do not quench the Spirit!*

O Christ our Lord! If not everyone who names Your name will enter Your kingdom, then who among them will? The Lord answers: *He who does the will of My Father in heaven.* And why will some of them not enter the kingdom? He answers again: *You... practice lawlessness.* *Matthew 7:21* *Matthew 7:23*

O Christian! You believe with your heart; it could be that your faith is righteous. But God alone knows this. For the Lord knows those who are His. While the seed lies in the ground, who knows if it will be a tree or a good fruit?

You may profess the Name of the Lord with your lips and with your faith; however, if you confessed as the holy confessors and martyrs did, amidst the horrors of persecution, while being threatened with death for your faith, your confession would not be a mere frivolous word, but it would also be a powerful deed. Then it would be clear that you confess the Name of the Lord unto salvation. But without that, who can know if the confession of his lips comes from true internal strength or from living faith? In the spring, some trees bud that will never bring fruit, for whether their roots are shallow, or they don't have enough sap, they will wither and fade. What if your tree will only bear small and bitter fruits? What if your apparent faith, which calls itself Orthodox and may even present itself as miracle-working, is actually accompanied by a carnal and sensual lifestyle, by deeds of iniquity and unrighteousness? In that case, no matter how impressive the buds, no matter the abundance of flowers, you cannot hide the fact that the tree is not cultivated, but wild. *For every tree is known by its own fruit.* These are the words of the Gardener Himself. *Luke 6:44*

No matter how much you might trumpet about your faith, no matter how much you decorate it with words of confession, your unrighteous deeds and impure life reveal what you are in actual fact. And so, do not delude or be deluded. You do not belong to the good, cultivated trees of the garden of Christ, but to a garden where *every plant which My heavenly Father has not planted will be* *Matthew 15:13 uprooted*, unless the plants be cultivated with new spiritual deeds of righteousness and holiness.

Do you want to be a good tree in the garden of Christ, a tree that will not be cut down or uprooted? Then bring forth good fruits! Do you want to be a true building of God, an eternally living temple of the Holy Spirit? Do not only *name the Name of the Lord* in faith, but also *depart from iniquity*. 2 Timothy 2:19

There is only one firm foundation for blessed hope, only one building of eternal salvation, only one *having this seal: let everyone who names the name of Christ depart from iniquity*. By this seal you may discern those who are truly God's from among those who merely name the name of Christ. St Basil the Great offers this most trustworthy sign of a grace-filled state: a hatred of untruth. "How can a soul come to know that God has forgiven her sins?" He asks, then answers, *If the soul sees in herself the same disposition as the one who had the power to say: 'I have hated and loathed untruth.'*

> 2 Timothy 2:19
>
> Psalm 118:163

O Christian soul, you house of God! Attend to yourself: does your internal disposition have that true seal that confirms and protects you? Does it protect you from the abyss, from death, from the gates of hell? Do you depart from untruth?

Let us look at the foundation of our deeds. Are they sealed with a desire that the world come to know us? Do we wish to please the world? If so, then our deeds are not founded on God's foundation, and the Lord does not know us.

Let us test our life. Is it founded only on the crude senses of the body? Does it rise only to the heights of the stormy reason? Oh, how unstable is such a foundation and such a building! It will crumble with the storms of the world, and then what will we be left with?

Let us stop building ostensible good things on the sands of the world, let us destroy all trust in ourselves, let us establish our hearts in the Lord, and let us begin the secret work of prayer in the heart, the work of faith, love for God, all of which would properly guide our current good deeds. Then, we can dare to hope that the world will know us as His own. Amen!

When we see on the building of God the first seal on which is written, *The Lord knows those who are His*, that is, when we come to know that God alone can properly know... *2 Timothy 2:19*

But wait. This is not everything. This seal is not complete. This foundation is not stable.

Can you not hear how loudly all of Jerusalem proclaimed the Name of the Lord?[1] Not only the disciples of the Lord, but the people of the city as well, and you may even think that this is a manifestation of a stable "building of God," that perhaps it is not God alone who knows those who are His, for the entire cosmos can see the entire city accepting the Lord, consequently presenting itself as the city of God Himself. But wait! Let pass a few short days, and something else will become obvious. The same people who proclaimed Christ as King, now proclaim a new king with much more fervor: *We have no king but Caesar.* There will *John 19:15* come an hour when all of Jerusalem, which today is filled with triumphant exclamations directed at the Lord, will fall silent for all words save this: *Crucify Him!* *John 19:15*

O miserable nation and city! How could such a sudden and terrible change have overcome you? Thus: you did not walk away from iniquity, even though for a time you named the name of the Lord with some reverence. The chief priests, the scribes, the princes, the Pharisees did not depart from the iniquity of ambition and envy; the people did not depart from the iniquity of superstition and willing servility. This was no foundation of God, and so it was not firm, but was destroyed, and not merely destroyed, but cast out to the four winds.

---

1 Note: This sermon was originally meant as two different sermons. Part one was spoken on Annunciation, while part two was intended for the Feast of the Entrance into Jerusalem. However, St Philaret was ill on that day and did not read his homily, so it was later published as a single homily in two parts.

O Christians, you new chosen nation of God! Be warned by the sorrowful example of the ancient nation of God. Let all who name the Name of the Lord depart from iniquity as from an abyss, as from death, as from the very gates of hell.

Amen.

5

The Blameless Confusion of the Virgin

Homily on the Annunciation of the Mother of God (1827)

> *"But when she saw him,*
> *she was troubled at his saying." (Luke 1:29)*

You who hear these words, are you also troubled that I want to speak of the confusion of the most blessed Virgin Mary, as though this feast of hers has no more exalted subjects for contemplation? How many virtues, how many perfections, how many miracles, how many mysteries offer themselves to the mind at the invocation of the name of Mary, at the remembrance of her angelic annunciation! Truly, the short and small confusion of her peaceful and quiet soul nearly passes by unnoticed.

But I am not put off by such objections. Miracles are glorious without words; mysteries often are better contemplated in reverent silence rather than a brazen attempt to explain them; virtues and perfections—oh, if only it was enough for us only to speak of virtues and perfections! If only we did not need to remind ourselves of imperfections and even of sins! However, I believe many will agree with me when I say that every day, if not several times in a day, we are brought to confusion by this or that word or event, and that this confusion often extends to our own words, actions, and relations with others. Such confusion ruins our calm and dims the clarity of our soul.

And so, this is no small reason to examine with especial attentiveness this seemingly unimportant event, when even a soul that has been blessed by the peace of God falls to confusion. Let us then also see how she resolves this confusion, so that by her example our own—primarily self-inflicted—confusions may be lessened and corrected. Perhaps we may even find true peace for our own souls.

Luke 1:29 — *But when she saw him, she was troubled at his saying.* Who is it that brings into confusion her who must be filled with peace, *Ephesians 2:14* — for she is called to give birth to *our Peace*? Is this a man with a hostile disposition of spirit? Is it a hostile spirits perhaps, the eternal enemy of any peace, who himself can never have peace? Is it the spirit who usually sows confusion and trouble because he himself lives in constant rebellion? No! What a wonder that the source of Mary's confusion is an angel, a peaceful servant of God's peace! Can it be that the form in which he appeared to her was terrifying? No, this is not apparent. The angel quietly enters *Luke 1:28* — and speaks: *having come in, the angel said to her...* So what is it that disturbs her? Was his word stern in any way? On the contrary, it was a message of joy and blessing: *Rejoice, highly favored one, the Luke 1:28 Lord is with you; blessed are you among women!*

Let us more deeply examine these words of the angel to help us find the hidden reason for Mary's confusion. Up to this moment, no human being had ever heard such a greeting from heaven. Notably, heavenly messengers generally do not lavish greetings on human beings, for pure heavenly truth is just as unfamiliar with excessive affection as with unnecessary asperity. "Peace be with you," the angel said to Gideon, but only to calm him, for

Gideon, according to the beliefs of his time, assumed all angelic appearances to be harbingers of death. However, the word "rejoice" is missing in all ancient appearances of angels. *The Lord is with you*—the angel greeted Gideon with these words as well, for the same reason: to inspire strength and courage in him for a miraculous victory over his enemies and for the salvation of the nation of Israel. *Judges 6:12*

God generously blessed Abraham many times, as in this example: *Blessing, I will bless you, and multiplying I will multiply your descendants as the stars of the heaven and as the sand which is on the seashore; and your descendants shall possess the gate of their enemies. In your seed all the nations of the earth shall be blessed, because you have obeyed my voice.* And in another place: *Abraham shall surely become a great and mighty nation, and all the nations of the earth shall be blessed in him.* But nowhere does God say that Abraham is blessed among men, that is, the greatest of all living men. As for Sarah, though she participated in bringing this blessed seed into the world, no word of blessing is given to her. Yes, the Lord did once say concerning Sarah, *I will bless her*, but it is worth noting that this short blessing is spoken not in her presence, but in her absence to Abraham directly. *Genesis 22:17-18* *Genesis 18:18* *Genesis 17:16*

Evidently, it was God's judgment that a woman, who before man lost the blessing of God in Eden, would now contain within herself the beginning of the returned blessing to the earth cursed by the Fall. Doubtless, the Virgin Mary understood this, both from reading the Scriptures and because of her own humble contemplation of God. And so, when she heard that the unexpected visitor greeted her not only with peace, but with joy, that he ascribed to her grace not as a gift but as something that belonged to her intrinsically, that he announced to her a blessing as to one greatest among all women on earth—her soul was disturbed as a quiet lake stirred by a strong wind.

There is nothing impure in this confusion; however, that moment of distress does not have that spiritual quiet that preceded it. When a wind disturbs the surface of water, it often lifts it from the place of its calm rest, and then even pure water trembles and appears to be turbid for a moment. In the same way, the soul of Mary was not only lifted from her natural self-abnegation by the praise of the angel, but was raised up beyond all that is created, and so she was filled with pure terror, and her constant striving to the depth of humility, disturbed by this exaltation, led to a state of confusion and distress.

We see how the holy and dispassionate soul is distressed. But let us see if she remains in this state of confusion or how she resolves it.

Luke 1:29 *She was troubled at his saying, and considered what manner of greeting this was.*

When an event causes confusion in a soul that does not immediately end, but continues, becomes more powerful, and eventually overwhelms inner peace, then we hear impatient words, notice erratic movements, see disorderly actions. But nothing like this happened to the most holy Mary. Her confusion did not force her into any action, nor did it push her to speak a single word. From this, we can clearly see that the distress that occurred naturally within her did not control her for a single moment. But as soon as she felt herself overcome by this confusion, she immediately turned to abandon it, and her first weapon against her confusion was silence.

Luke 1:29 Another weapon she used against her inner distress was this thought: *she...considered what manner of greeting this was.* The evangelist does not elaborate concerning these considerations, though they were of course as pure as her soul, as exalted as her spirit, as powerful as the grace given to her. The evangelist did not find it necessary to include this detail. He wrote of Mary's confusion only the better to inform everyone who is also subject to confusion that the way she left it behind was through a rooted and careful consideration. If she needed the consoling word

Luke 1:30 of the angel (*Do not be afraid*) to complete the restoration of her inner peace, then she needed her own calming thoughts, which were enlivened by prayer, just as much, to prepare her for the subsequent words of the angel. Heavenly influence brings complete peace to the soul, but only to a soul that is already steeled against inner and outer storms, a soul that raises the thoughts of the mind to contemplation of God. Only such a soul can accept the exalted and generous influence of heaven.

Let us now compare our typical inner confusion to the blameless confusion of the most blameless Virgin.

Mary is confused by a word of praise, even though there is no word of praise capable of worthily extolling her, for no praise could be too great for her. But is this how we encounter praise when it enters our ears? Do we think that though the words seem to be coming from an angel, it might still be a false word of temptation? Are we ashamed of undeserved praise, do we abhor passionate praise, do we fear even justified praise, lest it put to sleep our virtue or taint it with impurity? Does not our careless heart swallow praise whole like a sweet morsel, though it might be a sweetened poison? Does not our insatiable self-love reach shameless levels when begging for praise or when simply ascribing it to ourselves? Without any shame, some say of themselves: I am a good Christian; I am a true son of the Church. And they remain calm when speaking these words! But I must admit that I would prefer if they had a bit of dubious self-doubt instead of excessively careless and overconfident calm that might end with a much more terrible confusion down the line.

Mary is confused by a word that clashes with her humility. But are we not, on the contrary, often distressed by words that clash with our pride? Not only words that are actually hurtful or actions that are truly insulting cause us to abandon our patience, but even trivial inconveniences, inadvertent words, or justified and temperate rebuke distress us to the core of our being, so that we are irritated and angered. A soul that has not been purified of the passions brings up mud and silt from its depths, like impure water, at the slightest provocation. And this external distress is joined by much more serious internal darkening.

Mary is confused, but she does not wait to put down that confusion by containing it with silence. But many of us, every time our displeasure boils on the inside, are transformed into a bursting vessel of sour wine or a belching volcano that explodes lava and rocks on everything around us. As soon as a spark of disturbed displeasure smolders inside you, immediately take care not to give it any more air, lest the smoke turns into an open flame, and you become a conflagration. No matter what the cause of your inner disturbance, close your vessel carefully by silence, and let it stand in patience until the restless fermentation calms and your wine becomes pure again.

Mary is confused, but she defeats her distress with contemplation. Let us also take up this weapon with her to use in our internal battles. No matter how different the manner of attack, a word of wisdom, especially one refined by the word of God, is like a two-edged sword that can slash in all directions and keep us safe from enemies on all sides. Who is it that stands up against you and disturbs the peace of your soul? Is it reproach? Stop and think: is it justified? If not, then the arrow has already passed you by, so why are you acting as though you have been wounded by it? If the reproach is justified, then do not be upset at the one reproaching you, as though he were your enemy, but rather thank him, for he is your physician, revealing your seeping wound and urging you to heal it.

Have you been upset by a workplace insult? Think about this: is it better to insult or to be insulted? Without a doubt, it is better to be innocent rather than guilty. Continue the thought process: is it better to be irritated or patient? Irritation can suddenly make you guilty and even more miserable than before, while patience preserves blameless behavior and lessens misery as well.

Are you distressed by your own shortcomings or by failing to address your faults? Has a sudden fall into sin or other internal distress led you to confusion and despair? Think of this: confusion by itself solves no problems, nor does it lead you to better yourself, while despair saps internal strength. And so, you shouldn't linger in pointless confusion, and you should quickly rise from despair, and through continual labors you will eventually acquire victory over the passions and lusts, and with that victory will come peace of soul and the joy of salvation.

May the grace of the most holy Mary be with every Christian soul in all unexpected distress. May she help us as we calm confusion with silence and completely stop it through contemplation and prayer, so that the angel of peace may speak directly into our hearts, which will then grow the *fruit of righteousness* that is *sown in peace by those who make peace.* James 3:18

Amen.

6

Jesus' Mother and Brothers

Homily on the Nativity of the Mother of God (1828)

*"But He answered them, saying,
'Who is My mother, or My brothers?'" (Mark 3:33)*

Why was the righteous Elizabeth—when she saw the Virgin Mary come to her and heard Mary's entirely mundane greeting—immediately filled with such joy that it also filled the child in her womb, causing him to jump, and causing her to proclaim and bless the Virgin? As Elizabeth herself explained, it was because she recognized that Mary was the Mother of the Lord. *But why is it granted to me, that the mother of my Lord should come to me?*

And why does the Church also rejoice at the most holy Virgin Mary, magnifying her with such enthusiasm? Why is even her birth and childhood given such a triumphant feast, which we celebrate for no other holy man or righteous one? It seems to me that we need look for no other answer than the answer of Elizabeth: Mary is the Mother of our Lord.

Luke 1:43

SERMON 6. JESUS' MOTHER AND BROTHERS, 1828

But look at this unexpected turn of events in the Gospel. The Mother of the Lord, who has already been shown to us by Elizabeth, suddenly hides. And see how the Lord Himself asks, *Who is my mother?* We cannot, of course, imagine that He either didn't know His mother or wanted to reject her. And yet, to ask, *Who is my mother?* means either lack of knowledge or rejection. Mark 3:33
Mark 3:33

Are we then making a mistake when we magnify the blessed Mother of God, thinking that by doing so we are gratifying Him, coming closer to Him through her, since He seems to be separating Himself from her?

Do not be distressed, all you who sing praises to the Mother of God, by this difficult thought. It will lead us to secure contemplation that will only increase our confidence in her divine glory, as well as instructing us in discerning the holy teaching of her Son and our God.

The evangelist Mark tells us, *A multitude was sitting around Him; and they said to Him, 'Look, Your mother and Your brothers are outside seeking You.' But He answered them, saying, 'Who is My mother, or My brothers?'* Mark 3:32–33

That he might not want to know His own brothers might not be that surprising. At that time in his life, they deserved to be rejected, since, as St John the Evangelist notes, *His brothers did not believe in Him.* But even aside from the fault of their unbelief, His stance might still be justified because they were not Jesus' actual brothers: they were the sons of Joseph, who was only called the father of Jesus. Thus, by rejecting his brothers, who were no brothers in actual fact, the Lord was not denying any earthly truth, but only confirming the heavenly truth of His divine birth. John 7:5

But how did the mother of the Lord receive the same treatment as His brothers? She is not a mother only in name, but His true mother by human birth, and this exalted dignity in no way was lessened by any amount of unbelief in Him as the true Son of God. That faith alone through which she accepted Him before His earthly conception and birth, during the annunciation, already surpasses the faith of all other faithful. When Jesus, being still a child in the manger, was admitted to be the Christ and Lord by the shepherds, what inspired her, other than faith, to *keep all these things and ponder them in her heart?* Before He *manifested His glory* through miracles, leading to His disciples *believing in Him*, the mother of Jesus already believed so fervently in His miracle-working power that it was she who asked Him to perform His first miracle in Cana of Galilee. Thus, she believed before all others and more completely than all others, and she acknowledged Him to be the Son of God. But no sooner does He utter the beloved name "mother" than He seems to refuse even to see her: *Who is my mother?* Or, when He does see her, He does not call her by the name "Mother": *Woman, what does your concern have to do with Me?* And later, *Woman, behold thy son.*

Luke 2:19;
John 2:11

Mark 3:33
John 2:4
John 19:26

Lord! We do not investigate Your actions, but rather we desire to learn from Your salvific wisdom. Do not find us guilty of testing the scriptures, but instead give us the grace of discernment.

Must I warn you, O Christians, lest you think that the Lord did not fully honor His all-blessed Mother? I hope not. For you should know the universal refutation of such assertions, which He Himself spoke to the Jews, when He said, *Do not think that I came to destroy the Law or the Prophets. I did not come to destroy but to fulfill.* Thus, there can be no doubt that He did not destroy but fulfilled the following command of the Law: *Honor thy father and thy mother.* And truly, even when He was a young man, though He was filled with the significance of His own divine calling when speaking with the elders in the Temple, He was still *subject to [His parents]*. Finally, when the suffering on the Cross was tearing apart His body and soul, when He hung heavily on nails, wavering between life and death as the whole world hung on His shoulders over the abyss in expectation of salvation, nothing—not the pains of hell, not His care of the world, not the entirety of all time and eternity—could diminish within Him the sense of His lawful responsibility for His mother. He passed this

Matthew 5:17

Exodus 20:12

Luke 2:51

responsibility, which was about to be cut off together with His own earthly life, to John, whose virginity and love made him the most worthy servant of the Virgin Mother. Through this action, He showed us a perfect fulfillment of this law (and the entire Law), which maintained that respect for parents, and care for them, extends to all circumstances of life until the grave, and even beyond the grave.

If the Lord demonstrated, in such difficult circumstances, such complete respect for His mother, then doubtless we must conclude that in a situation when He apparently distanced Himself from her, He did so not because He desired to stress His greatness over her, but only in deference to other exalted responsibility of His earthly service. Let us remember His own teaching: *He who loves father or mother more than Me is not worthy of Me. And he who loves son or daughter more than Me is not worthy of Me.* [Matthew 10:37] Since He taught thus, He had to act thus as well, and He had to give an example of the power of this teaching, according to His own rule that *whoever shall be called great in the kingdom of heaven must [do] and [teach].* [Matthew 5:19] Thus, the Lord Jesus had to show in deed how He loved His earthly mother completely, but not more than His Father in heaven. He showed how human, filial love must be brought as a sacrifice to the work of God that He accomplishes.

Now look at how this sort of mindset can help explain Christ's actions when at first they seem hard to understand.

The mother of Jesus asks that He miraculously transform water into wine at a wedding. But miracles are intended not to please a mother but to reveal the glory of God. And so here it seems proper to offer Mary's desire as a sacrifice to God's work; thus, to make this sacrifice perfect, even the thought of motherhood and the name mother is sacrificed: "Woman, what has your request to do with Me?" However, the hour for the revelation of God's glory, which had not yet come before this sacrifice, immediately followed it. And so, the miracle, in which it seems at first that He rebuffed His mother, in fact occurs the next moment.

The mother of Jesus and His brothers come to take Him away from the house where He is preaching heavenly truth to a multitude of people. They did this with a good intention, believing Him to be in danger, because His enemies were publicly proclaiming Him to be either mad or possessed by the prince of demons, and were considering how to put Him to death. But if at that moment He had submitted to the will of His family, then He would have harmed the work of God, not only because His preaching would have been cut off prematurely, but also because His enemies would have used the interference of his family as proof that He was dependent on their care (i.e., prone to fits of madness). And so, here also He had to offer His desire to please His mother as a sacrifice to God, and this sacrifice again was a whole-burnt offering, that is, the Lord offered as a sacrifice all of His love for His most-beloved Mother, and even the very thought and memory of her: *Who is my mother?*

Mark 3:33

It is as if He were saying, "Why do you wish to use the will of my earthly mother to distract me from the fulfillment of the will of my heavenly Father? When these two wills go in different directions, I know, and will immediately show you which one you must follow, and with what conviction. I leave behind my earthly birth and relationships, as though I have forgotten them completely, as though they never were, for I am completely dedicated to the will of my heavenly Father, to His work, and to His kingdom. But even here I also seek familial relationships: *Who are my mother and my brothers?* Who are they? *Children of God... those who believe in His name: who were born, not of blood, nor of the will of the flesh, nor of the will of man, but of God*, or, put another way, *whoever does the will of My Father in heaven is My brother and sister and mother.*"

Mark 3:33

Matthew 12:50

Do you see, O Christians, that the Lord in no way deprives His mother, who is worthy of all veneration, of any attention or honor? Rather, He teaches us righteousness and truth by word and by example. Be attentive and learn from Him; notice what He does and imitate it.

When your parents, relatives, instructors, superiors require of you something that is contrary to your thoughts, your inclinations, or your taste, but is necessary or beneficial or at the very least harmless, then you should offer your thoughts, your inclinations, your taste as a sacrifice to the requirements of obedience. Remember Jesus, the Wisdom of God, Who *was subject to* Joseph the carpenter.   *Luke 2:51*

When your parents, relatives, neighbors, ask for your help, consolation, service when you yourselves are also in need or in sorrow or in sickness, gather the dregs of your strength, forget your sorrow for the sake of their sorrow, share your last crumbs and your last drops with them. Remember Jesus, in the midst of the suffering on the cross, Who worried about the state of his mother.

However, when the unfortunate example or desires of your parents, relatives, honored elders and beloved friends distract you from the fulfillment of your holy responsibilities before God, leading you to actions contrary to the Law, to the breaking of the peace of your conscience, to the detriment of the true benefit and salvation of your immortal soul, then ask them, in the words of Jesus, *Who are my mother or my brothers?* Remember   *Mark 3:33* that you have a better and more exalted relationship, that God is your Father, that the Church is your mother, and that all who do the will of God, all the saints are your brothers, or at least wish to become your brothers. Do not demean yourselves before such exalted relations; do not abandon this good and wonderful family. Do the will of God instead of the will of man, so that the Lord Himself may point at you and say, *Behold, my mother and my*   *Mark 3:34* *brothers.* Amen.

The Secret Virtue of the Virgin

Homily on the Dormition of the Mother of God (1832)

> *"Do not appear to men to be fasting,*
> *but to your Father who is in the secret place;*
> *and your Father who sees in secret will reward you openly."*
> *(Matthew 6:18)*

At the tomb of the most-holy Virgin Mary, the Church aids us today in a pious contemplation. For what is a feast of the Church if not a pious contemplation, in which our spirit rests from the labors of the body and gathers strength for the working days of our life?

What do we see, then, being placed here before the tomb of the most holy Virgin? An incomparable sight! Usually, before the tomb everything is light and clarity, but after the tomb everything is darkness and obscurity. But here, the opposite is true. Before the tomb: what exalted dignity and virtue hidden in a profound mystery of obscurity! And after the tomb: what light and glory, what a triumphant reward for that dignity and virtue!

SERMON 7. THE SECRET VIRTUE OF THE VIRGIN, 1832

It is not very difficult to prove that the moral dignity of the most blessed Virgin Mary is greater than all other human beings. This is evident from the dignity of the service for which she was chosen and uplifted. If some virtue could be found greater than hers, then it would not have made sense that she was chosen, from among all others, to be the home, the throne, the mother of God the Word. But in the judgments and acts of God, there can be no mistake. Consequently, it is absolutely true that Mary is blessed among women, that is, she was blessed with the greatest blessing possible among all other women. It is equally true that her virtue is the most exalted, the purest, the most perfect, even though it is also true that she is pure and perfect only through the help of the same Christ Who became the reward for her purity and perfection.

But let us see how many knew or saw this exalted dignity of Mary before her death.

Who could have known her better than the one who was found worthy to guard this treasure of the world, this sealed treasure-house of heaven? But Joseph knew so little at first concerning the proper respect due to her, that he considered it possible even to "make her a public example," though he had no desire to do this. Joseph was about to cast aside a priceless treasure if not for its preservation by more illumined protectors, the angels. *Joseph... was minded to put her away secretly. But while he thought about these things, behold, an angel of the Lord appeared to him in a dream...*   Matthew 1:19-20

O wondrously-silent Virgin! Would it not have been easier for you yourself to tell Joseph what the angel finally told him? Why did you wait for this distant messenger from heaven? Why did you not hurry to help the righteous man who nearly fell into injustice. Doubtless it was *not to appear to men* with your virtue,   Matthew 6:18
with your grace, with your dignity, *but only to your heavenly Father*   Matthew 6:18
who is in the secret place.

This mystery of the Virgin Theotokos' exalted dignity was revealed more or less by the angels, the star, the magi, the shepherds, and Simeon. But the angels returned to heaven; the magi to the east; the star hid itself; Simeon was allowed to leave this world in peace; the light of Bethlehem's glory was put out by Herod's angry breath and the blood of children; Mary herself hid first in Egypt, then in Nazareth, and her dignity and fame she hid in her own heart. *But Mary kept all these things and pondered them in her heart.*

Luke 2:19

The time came when the glory of the wisdom and power of Mary's Son shone forth in Judea and Galilee. It would have been natural for a reflection of this glory of the Son to illumine the face of the mother as well. One time, it seemed that this was soon to be the case. Another woman—perhaps herself a mother, or one strongly desiring to be a mother—expressed the joy of the blessed mother more vividly than any other, and in the hearing of the multitude, she gave free rein to her exaltation, in which she praised both Jesus and His mother. *A certain woman from the crowd raised her voice and said to Him, 'Blessed is the womb that bore You, and the breasts which nursed You!'* But look: she speaks in a roundabout way, praising the womb and the breasts, but not uttering the name of the one whom she praises. Why? Doubtless, this is because she did not know who she was, neither her face nor her name.

Luke 11:27

Others knew Mary by face and by name; indeed, they could not fail to do so, but in spite of this, most people remained strangely ignorant of her. Listen to what the neighbors and fellow citizens of Jesus and Mary say: *Where did this Man get this wisdom and these mighty works?* (In other words, they can hear Jesus' wisdom, see His miracles, admit them to be real, and are trying to understand everything concerning him through these facts). *Is this not the carpenter's son? Is not His mother called Mary?* Can you see that they cannot even say: Joseph, son of David and Mary, daughter of David? They only know what their eyes tell them: Joseph is a craftsman, and Mary is… Mary. How could they not know what all the Jews so carefully tried to know about themselves and oth-

Matthew 13:54

Matthew 13:55

ers? How could they not know Mary's lineage? We can explain this no other way than this: the most holy Virgin, in no way desiring to *to appear to men*, never seeking any human comfort, did not want to comfort herself in her poverty by declaring before others the dignity of her lineage. And so, she spoke neither of her lineage nor of her virtues and grace. *Matthew 6:18*

But why should we be shocked that strangers, whether near or distant, did not give glory to her who would be called blessed by all generations? Her own Son—I hesitate to say this, if not that it were spoken by Truth Himself—her own Son seems to refuse to honor her before people even as His mother. *Who is My mother?* He asks. It is as though He seeks someone to give that name, that glory and honor due to His own mother, remaining silent about the one who deserved all such honors by giving Him birth. *My mother and My brothers are these who hear the word of God and do it.* Speaking this way, the Lord does not reject His earthly mother, as we have already mentioned in the preceding homily. However, the Lord exalts by these words all who hear His words and act upon them, thereby inspiring His listeners to salvific action. Secondly, when He spoke like this, He was merely following His own mother's rule not to appear so before men. She sought as much as possible to avoid the glory of her fellows, seeking the glory of God. And so, He hesitates, puts off revealing to others the fullness of her honor and glory, though she be "more honorable than the Cherubim, and glorious beyond compare than the Seraphim." *Luke 1:48* *Matthew 12:48* *Luke 8:21*

I pass further into the earthly life of Jesus and Mary. Wherever His glory is most revealed, there Mary is simply absent, such as at His triumphant entry into Jerusalem. And wherever she does appear, no glory greets her, as for example here: *There stood by the cross of Jesus His mother, and His mother's sister, Mary the wife of Cleopas, and Mary Magdalene.* *John 19:25*

Let us follow the Crucified One through the doors of His tomb, into the region of the glory of the Resurrection. By now, not just the first, but the last of the apostles has glorified His divinity: *My Lord and my God!* By now, a new divine glory of ascension has followed the glory of the Lord's resurrection. And I still seek a person, an action, a word in which, even now, the glory of *the mother of my Lord* would be revealed, and I do not find it (though it is true that very early, without any witnesses, and with no consequences, Elizabeth did praise her once).

<small>John 20:28</small>

<small>Luke 1:43</small>

Then, it was written of the apostles that *these all continued with one accord in prayer and supplication, with the women and Mary the mother of Jesus, and with His brothers.* What an unusual method of expression! The writer seems to have barely remembered *Mary the mother of Jesus* after mentioning all the apostles and even some unnamed women! What is going on? Can it be that the writer of the book of Acts did not venerate the Mother of God? God preserve you from such a thought, for it is insulting not only to the most pure Virgin but to the holy evangelist Luke as well. So what does it mean? It means that the holy Luke simply describes, in the book of Acts, how the most holy Virgin acted among the apostles. Though she invisibly, in her exalted grace-filled spirit, presided over the assembly of the apostles, because of the humility of her heart, in her flesh, visibly, she never allowed herself any external glory, she never insisted on any advantages, being content to remain among the other women, teaching them through her example that which later the Apostle Paul would teach them as well: *Let your women keep silent in the Churches. Let a woman learn in silence with all submission. And I do not permit a woman to teach or to have authority over a man, but to be in silence.*

<small>Acts 1:14</small>

<small>Acts 1:14</small>

<small>1 Corinthians 14:34; 1 Timothy 2:11-12</small>

I will quickly say here that I would earnestly desire that of our wandering brethren, who, before the judgment of Christ, have abandoned the priesthood, look at the example of the mother of God. For they have punished themselves through the willful abandonment of priesthood to complete chaos, allowing themselves to be guided by women in services, women who are doubtless not wise but foolish! For what Virgin other than a foolish one would dare put on herself, within the Church, that which the most holy Virgin Theotokos herself did not dare assume?

Now let us look at a different spectacle, also too immense in space, but now visible because of the light that revealed itself after the death of the mother of God. As soon as she died, the entire assembly of apostles, as pious tradition tells us, was gathered from all direction by the Spirit of God, not to lament her passing, but rather to celebrate her burial. As once before the doubt of Thomas became proof of the resurrection of Christ, so now the dilatoriness of Thomas becomes the means of glorifying the ascension of the mother of God, which to that point was hidden, just as her life on earth was hidden. Having accepted the glory of God in the heavens, from that moment she no longer rejected human glory on earth, which up to that moment was not appropriate for her humility, and which now has become beneficial and useful for all who live on earth.

Her glory had its enemies as well, just as Christ's glory did, but this would only serve as a greater means of revealing the divine power of grace, for all her enemies are less a hindrance than a means for her to accomplish her goals. What did the heretics accomplish when they so cunningly and boldly tried to steal from her the exalted name "Theotokos"? Only this: the Orthodox Church, careful to avoid their cunning and boldness, began to glorify the most holy mother of God with even greater zeal than before. And for this reason, now, there is not a single day or service in the ecclesiastical calendar that is not decorated with her divine glory. And this is not simply a polemical device against heretics but is rather the continuation of the spiritual war, and the complete victory of the power of Christ over the strength of His adversaries. For the lips that glorify her would have tired over the centuries if she herself did not visit her faithful ones with her mighty aid, in answer to prayers and doxologies, bringing to pious souls Christ Himself with His grace, just as she sometimes appears with Him in her arms in our holy icons. *Rejoice, O you who are full of Grace! Your divine glory shines bright with Godlike miracles!*

This, brethren, is what I see today in the rites of the Church and in my responsibility of service, standing guard at the tomb of the most pure Virgin Theotokos in contemplation. But what is the purpose of this vision? For any pious contemplation must result in action, not idle speculation. And so, I see that the example of her secret life can help us to know, to accept, and actively fulfill the teaching of Christ: *Do not appear to men... but to your Father who is in the secret place; and your Father who sees in secret will reward you openly.* And so, labor diligently, do good, serve God, but be careful lest your labors, your virtues, your piety become obvious to people without need, willfully, self-indulgently, vainly. Have God as the lone witness of your conscience, and He will reward you for everything that you have done for Him or endured for His sake, unnoticed by your fellow men.

The Lord commands this secrecy, first of all, for all deeds of mercy to others: *But when you do a charitable deed, do not let your left hand know what your right hand is doing.* Secondly, He commands it for all deeds of piety: *When you pray, go into your room, and when you have shut your door, pray to your Father who is in the secret place.* thirdly, He commands it for all deeds of self-denial and mortification of the flesh: *Do not appear to men to be fasting, but to your Father who is in the secret place...* Consequently, He commands this mystery of meekness and humility as a responsibility for every person toward God, toward his fellow man, and toward himself, for all virtues and all deeds of the Law.

Some might say: but how then can this word of Christ be fulfilled: *Let your light so shine before men, that they may see your good works and glorify your Father in heaven.?* Do not worry about that. The word of God will be fulfilled by its own power; it doesn't need your help. After all, the phrase is *let your light shine*, that is, let it do so as a natural quality, as all light shines. He does not say: show off your light so before men. Good deeds are light-bearing by their nature. Do them secretly, and the light will still shine whenever God the Giver of light commands it. The calamity is when you do deeds of darkness and evil, from such, of course, no light will shine, and God will never be glorified by them.

Some may continue to say: well, how are we to pray or preach in Church if all our works of piety must be done in secret? To answer this, I remind you that in that same sermon in which the Savior speaks of secret prayer, He also speaks of the gift brought to the altar: *if you bring your gift to the altar...* And this can only occur in public and triumphant worship. Therefore, we see that the command concerning secret prayer does not cancel the need to take part in the common worship of the Church. But even here there can be a degree of care applied to our behavior, lest we vainly show off to others during prayer. Instead, we should stand in humility before our heavenly Father who is in the secret place. If you stand in Church and perform all the proper actions of piety common to all, but you try to restrain them or make them unnoticeable, especially when you are moved by an exaltation of grace that leads to sighing or weeping or tears, then in this disposition you will remain, even in the midst of a large congregation, standing before your Father who is in the secret place.

Matthew 5:23

Let us think, brethren, how ignoble and onerous and pointless it is to live only for effect, as many do, both in their moral, social, and personal lives. They show everything off, they trumpet themselves, they announce the most insignificant of their deeds like a hen clucking after it lays an egg. But even the clucking of the hen is more profound, for she announces the arrival of an egg that was truly born and will persist, while the vain announce that which does not exist, or by announcing it, destroy it. For example, let us say that you performed a deed of charity. Good, at this point, your action exists. But if you begin to boast about it, then the good deed disappears. For now, it becomes clear that there is nothing good in your heart, but there is only vanity there. There is no good in that deed, for nothing that is produced by vanity can be a virtuous deed. Naturally, there can be nothing good here in the eyes of God. He rejected the vain when He said, *Assuredly, I say to you, they have their reward.*

<small>Matthew 6:2</small>

O Christian! Be, and do not seem to be! This is one of the most important rules for your life. Know the incomparable dignity of a meek, quiet, secret virtue. For it is natural for virtue to be secret on earth, because it has a heavenly birth, and it exists for heaven alone. And so, be virtuous in secret, and preserve your virtue from the eyes of men, which are often impure and pass on their impurity to the actions of others. Instead, carefully and constantly offer your virtue to the pure and purifying eye of God. *And your Father who sees in secret will reward you openly.* Amen.

<small>Matthew 6:18</small>

8

A Sword in Her Heart

*Homily on the Day of the Mother of God
at the Monastery of the Passion (June 2, 1834)*

"Yes, a sword will pierce through your own soul also." (Luke 2:35)

Tragedies in the life of pure and good people are one of many difficulties that the world offers to intelligent, reasoning people. Seeing the suffering of a good person, a person who himself is good also suffers, since he experiences fellow-suffering, and that leads to another conundrum: for what reason does this second person also suffer? Someone who is weak in faith sees both these conundrums and is often plunged into doubts about the faith. Someone who is easily inclined toward sin sees this conundrum and resolves it thus: what is the point of being virtuous? Someone who tends to unbelief sees this conundrum, and he offers as an answer yet another conundrum, which is even more difficult to resolve, when he says: the world and human affairs are ruled by nothing but chance.

O blessed among women! O most pure of all daughters of mankind! The most wise elder Simeon did not doubt, but shared with you this terrifying riddle: *Yes, a sword will pierce through your own soul also.* The riddle of this prophecy was answered to you on a sorrowful and horrifying day, but a day that was also salvific. The thorns of Jesus' crown, the nails of His crucifixion, the spear of His piercing, His wounds, His pained groaning, His dying gaze—these are the swords that pierced a mother's heart as deeply as her love is perfect, as her purity is without peer. Now, when you abide in the divine glory of your Son, the conundrum of this incredible event has been resolved. Now you see everything in God's light, you can understand why your own pure soul had to be pierced with a sword and how this accords both with the endless wisdom, righteousness, and goodness of divine Providence and with your own endless blessedness.

Luke 2:35

O mother of the world! Send down a spark of light from the mind of Christ, so that we might come to know the mystery of tragedies and sorrows on this earth, not to satisfy our idle curiosity, but for the sake of our peace and salvation.

There would have been no evil on earth, and no tragedies among people, if there was no sin. *Through one man sin entered the world, and death through sin.* That death contains within itself the cessation of all tragedies and evils. For sin, man was cursed to labor in blood, sweat, and tears instead of in ease and comfort: *In the sweat of your face you shall eat bread.* For sin, man received sicknesses: *In pain you shall bring forth children.* For sin, man received death: *For in the day that you eat [of the tree of the knowledge of good and evil], you shall surely die.*

Romans 5:12

Genesis 3:19

Genesis 3:16
Genesis 2:17

When man lost the experience of his original pure state of being and the world, he lost his understanding of both. As a fish that swims in water knows no better or more perfect form of life, such as the land animals live in the air, so the miserable human soul, plunged into the crude and perishable world of the elements, living in it like a fish in water, knows nothing of the subtle and imperishable world of paradise. This is what leads to the doubts of the self-willed reason concerning whether such a primal life ever existed, and what sort of a life it might have been. I will offer you only one such doubt as an example of their worthlessness. The reason considers that if all people were born and never died, then eventually the multiplication of people would eventually become incompatible with available space on earth; for this reason, the limited space of the world demands that people be mortal, so that those who die might clear a space for their constantly-increasing progeny.

To these narrow-minded misers of human life, one might confidently repeat the word of the Lord to the Sadducees, who somehow managed to extrapolate a proof for the non-existence of life after death from the laws concerning marriage: *You are mistaken, not knowing the Scriptures nor the power of God.* Who told you that this earth would eternally be a prison for human immortality? Do you honestly believe that before the earth was cursed through the deeds of men it needed to be measured in units of ten for the sustenance of every human being? *You are mistaken, not knowing.* Man, before sin blighted him, depended an infinite amount less on the food of the earth than he does today. And the earth, even without his labors, was infinitely more generous for his sake in all its produce. Having lived for a certain time on this earth, he would have ascended to the heavens as easily as the angels on the ladder in Jacob's dream: *the angels of God were ascending and descending on it.* [Matthew 22:29] [Matthew 22:29] [Genesis 28:12]

We saw, in part, the potential of such passage to heaven in the lives of Enoch and Elias. Do not be afraid! The incorrupt life of a sinless person had been much better accounted for by divine Providence than life on this earth now, for the eternal Providence had foreseen, before the ages, even the fact that the most exalted and necessary gift of freedom would be used by man for evil, thereby ruining the original order of man and earth. But there is no doubt that Providence wisely and beneficially accounted for the subsequent intermixing of good and evil that so confuses and confounds us.

After the general question of why human suffering exists in a world upheld by divine Providence (the answer to which was given above), the doubting mind offers two more particular objections. First of all, why do the innocent suffer, and secondly, why do the guilty not suffer in a way that accords with the level of their guilt, or, put another way, why do the innocent often suffer more than the guilty? We will answer both objections.

In order to do this, let us look at humanity not with our superficial human gaze, but with the profoundly piercing gaze of people who have been illumined by heaven. How did these saintly people see mankind? *All have sinned and fall short of the glory of God,* says St Paul. *Who can bring a clean thing out of an unclean?* asks Job. *No one! Since his days are determined, the number of his months is with You; You have appointed his limits, so that he cannot pass. I have been conceived in iniquity, and in sins did my mother bear me.* This is what David said, not fearing by these words to destroy the law of honoring one's parents. What does all this mean? This: all human beings have sinned in Adam, who, since he began to have children only after the fall, could not pass on to them what he no longer had—sinlessness and incorruption—and so naturally he passed on what he did have—sin and corruption. What if one of us would dare to ask, "Why are we held accountable if we unwillingly inherited sin and corruption from Adam?" If we are attentive to ourselves, we will notice that our own conscience answers this question, closing our rebellious lips, for it can point out to us many instances in which we were not faithful to our own good intentions, though we were strong enough to do so, in spite of our inherited weaknesses.

If our heart condemns us, God is greater than our heart, and knows all things, and so He sees in us those subtle moral impurities that even our conscience, which has become more or less insensitive because of our sins, cannot see. Therefore, *if thou shouldest mark*

Romans 3:23
Job 14:4–5;
Psalm 50:7

1 John 3:20

Psalm 129:3

iniquities, O Lord, O Lord, who shall stand? This resolves the question of why the innocent suffer, and not only resolves it, but obliterates it, since, according to strict logic, there are no innocents on this earth, and so all who suffer do so as those who are more or less guilty, except for a single One *Who committed no sin, nor was deceit found in His mouth.* And so His sufferings, mystical in the most exalted manner, offer the best possible explanation to our doubts, for *He was wounded for our transgressions, He was bruised for our iniquities; the chastisement for our peace was upon Him, and by His stripes we are healed.* He lifted and carried a weight that crushed us in order to raise us up from our fallen state.

1 Peter 2:22

Isaiah 53:5

Now the question: why do people who, though perhaps not sinless, but still by all obvious metrics are innocent, suffer more severely than the guilty? But I ask you: who can accuse Providence of such a thing? If we admit that the one who suffers is not without sin, and if we know that every sin is a rebellion against the Law, then consequently any revolt against the will of God, the establisher of the Law, is mutiny in the kingdom of God. It is an insult to the might of God to claim to have the ability to decide which kind of temporary suffering is too great for a specific sin.

I do not argue that all sins are equally heinous, that there are degrees of guilt even in the same kind of sin; however, who among us can accurately measure that degree of difference? To do this, we would have to put on the scale not only the visible deed, but also the invisible desire and the hidden intention and the secret thought, strength and weakness, knowledge and ignorance, aids and hindrances, seduction to evil and encouragement to good, lack of attentiveness to what has not been experienced or infidelity to lived experience, repetition of sins and repentance of them, hardness of heart and compunction of heart. But who could possibly know all this except the One who tests hearts and reins, Who encompasses all and knows all? There are also other considerations to keep in mind, such as: the degree of the sufferer's sensitivity to pain, the presence or absence of comforting realities that could counteract the suffering, and many other things that cannot be measured or even seen by the superficial viewer. So how can we speak of the inequality between the suffering and the sin, except by guessing?

God acts on the temporal life of a person who has been damaged by sin not only as a judge (that will be His prerogative at the end of times) but rather mostly as a physician, for this is the time for healing. For this reason, sometimes He administers to each person a degree of suffering and tragedy that is not a calculated recompense for committed sins, but rather as medicine that can overcome the power of the illness of sin. This is a completely different kind of calculation. There are certain illnesses that superficially seem insignificant or not dangerous, but against which a well-experienced doctor may find necessary to use very painful means of healing. Moreover, the heavenly Physician does not always begin to heal a spiritual illness at its external manifestation; His gaze pierces into the depths of the soul, depths that the soul itself is unaware of, and there He finds a tiny embryo of sin, passion, self-will, self-pampering, a tiny admixture of evil and impurity even in good inclination and dispositions. By teasing out these embryonic tendencies, even painfully, he makes them manifest early, the better to heal them. He does this to lead the soul to ever greater heights of purity.

Have you not seen people who are prosperous in life and in that prosperity eagerly run to God? Sometimes when such people lose something that they loved, such as a child or a spouse, or earthly honor and glory, or land and wealth, they abandon themselves to such sorrowing that they focus their entire attention on that one sorrow, having no strength left to bolster themselves with thoughtful discernment, having no ability to gather themselves in the prayer that before they found so sweet. Faith, love for God, fidelity to the will of God—now these are no more than familiar words or sounds, while before this calamity they sensed their power and activity their own lives. What does this mean? It means that they loved that which they lost too much, more than God, even though they did not recognize this themselves. It means that their children, or their spouse, or honor, glory, riches were the idols of their heart. And what could the Knower of hearts and the Lover of souls do, except to take away that idol, to tear out that incorrect love for created things from the soul, even though the process be painful? For He wishes to fill that soul with His own divine love! He loves, purifies, has mercy, heals, and prepares us for blessedness; but we look at Him and say, "How difficult is His love!"

Finally let us all agree that there are tragedies when one simply cannot ask questions like "Why?" but only questions like "For what purpose?" In such tragedies one has no reason to accuse the sufferer, but only to learn how to justify and come to love Providence. Such sufferings include those of Job, the prophets, the apostles, and the most holy mother of God. We have not reached this exalted state of spiritual growth and life when the sufferer himself is able to be nourished by the fruits of his cross. We are in our spiritual childhood—God grant that we are at least children in the faith! —and so we can only speak weakly and indistinctly about the paths and labors of those who would have reached full adulthood in Christ.

What does Job say? *The Lord gave, and the Lord has taken away; blessed be the Name of the Lord.* What do the apostles say? *For as the sufferings of Christ abound in us, so our consolation also abounds through Christ.* Can you see how out of place we sinful people are when we think we are interceding for the righteous, daring to rise up against Providence itself for the sake of their sufferings? The righteous sufferers themselves do not accept our thoughtless service, for they do not complain at their bitter fate. They do not want it to leave them; they rejoice! They bless God; they are happy. It is we who do not understand their joy, thinking that

Job 1:21

2 Corinthians 1:5

it might be possible to complain about something that they are grateful for.

If you would like to at least understand that which you have not yet attained, then look at earthly things, but think of divine and heavenly realities. You love your friend, and he loves you and supports you. Ask this: is your mutual love, even if it is pure and full, sufficient? I think that if you are honest, you will answer no. You may think, perhaps, "Is my friend assured of the sincerity of my love for him? Perhaps he thinks that I love his financial support more than him?" Now let us imagine that a situation arises when you might be able to bear some difficult or sorrow or danger to help your friend. If you are a noble soul, you will run to do it! And having borne this difficulty for the sake of your friend, will you not rejoice that now he will not be able to doubt the sincerity and purity of your love? Now apply this example to those who love God while they are prosperous. They are sure that God knows their grateful heart, but they might not trust themselves, and they would be right. They might, and in some sense must, think carefully about whether their gratitude to Him is complete or not, whether their love for Him is pure or not, whether their hearts might not be attached with a secret passion to the benefits, not the Giver, and whether the love fed by temporary good things might not disappear as soon as that nourishment runs dry.

And so, a test comes and offers this invitation: sacrifice your beloved Isaac to me. Endure deprivation, for the sake of God, of that which you love more than anything in the world after God Himself. Endure persecution, dishonor, suffering for the name of your beloved Jesus. A God-loving soul would be given wings at such a chance. It is ready to enter the crucible of martyric endurance, to throw itself into the fires of testing. For it wants to see how firm it remains in the fires of testing. And how comforted it is at the thought that finally it can offer a worthy sacrifice to God that is not cheap! What a comforting and assuring proof is given by the conscience when the fires of testing do not melt away the gold of love in the crucible of suffering, when love for God only grows brighter, when through external mortification the internal life of grace flourishes, and heaven confirms the soul's hope of heaven in clear signs. Believe me, you who are still inexperienced in such things, they who speak of joy in sufferings do not lie. In the fires of tragedy, they sing and praise God with the same freedom and joy as the three youths in the fires of the Babylonian furnace.

Christians! Who among us on the path of our earthly life does not encounter, rarely or frequently, various troubles? We have carefully avoided all such encounters, but some at least are inevitable; consequently, we must train ourselves in advance to encounter them in a noble manner. Let these thoughts that I have offered you today incite us to greet our troubles not as enemies or torturers, but as just punishers of our sinfulness, as a physician for the illnesses of our spirit, as messengers of grace from God Himself. *For whom the Lord loves He chastens, and scourges every son whom He receives.* Amen. — Hebrews 12:6

9

The Mystery of Godliness

Homily on the Annunciation of the Mother of God at the Chudov Monastery (1835)

"Without controversy great is the mystery of godliness: God was manifested in the flesh, justified in the Spirit, seen by angels, preached among the Gentiles, believed on in the world, received up in glory." (1 Timothy 3:16)

Piously do we remember and celebrate today that unique day in history, that great moment when the most exalted of all mysteries—God in the flesh—not in word only, but in the power of the Almighty, is brought down by the Archangel Gabriel to earth, is hidden in the pure heart and ever-Virgin womb of the most blessed Mary, and is confirmed by her humble silence. Afterwards, this *mystery which has been hidden from ages and from generations* turned into a cosmic glory, but nevertheless it still remains a mystery. *Great is the mystery of godliness: God was manifested in the flesh.*

Colossians 1:26

1 Timothy 3:16

Without a doubt, the heavens themselves marveled at this mystery when it was revealed there, when Jesus Christ, having resurrected and ascended to sit at the right hand of God His Father, revealed Himself to the angels the previously unseen glory of the God-Man. This heavenly amazement is wondrous, as are all heavenly things. The angels marveled at the mystery and the glory of the God-Man, but they were not disturbed by it. They asked each other, *Who is this King of glory?* but they did so not out of idle curiosity, for they did not doubt. They wanted to know so that they could properly reverence, and before they received the answer to their questions, they already accepted Him as the King of glory, for they exclaimed, *Lift up your heads, O you gates! And be ye lifted up, you everlasting doors! And the King of glory shall come in.* The more inconceivable the mystery, the more the angels accept it as worthy of the incomprehensible God, the more they revere and glorify God, the more they are illumined by His glory and receive blessedness for it. In that heavenly place, knowledge and glory do not contradict or envy mystery, and mystery endlessly increases their glory and light. *Psalm 23:8* *Psalm 23:7*

But does the earth accept the wondrous mystery of God in the flesh in the same way, this earth for whom the mystery was conceived and hidden and revealed and brought down and raised up and given up to humiliation and finally glorified? Truly blessed among women is the only most-pure Virgin who glorified herself by becoming a worthy treasure house of the mystery that came from heaven, lest it be turned back, as a ship filled with treasure must turn around from a shore with no safe landing place. Having been raised up to the loftiest rank of Theotokos, she never allowed her thoughts to rise from the depths of her humility, not even a hair's breadth. She was capable of encompassing the limitless Word of God with a tiny human word: *Behold the maidservant of the Lord! Let it be to me according to your word.* *Luke 1:38*

After her, let us also glorify those who *believed on [the mystery] in the world,* who accepted it with faith, preserved it faithfully, *1 Timothy 3:16* and preached it to all nations, through whom this mystery, in unchanging purity, in unabated power, reached us even to this day. However, these are those who though *in the world* are still *not of the world*. What of the world itself? It did not want to accept this salvific mystery of God; however, at the rumor of this mystery, it rose up in terror to put the mystery down, to darken it with lies, to confuse it with myths, to cover it with dishonor and slander, to block its passage with a sword, to pour out the blood of its witnesses, to bury them in the earth, to burn them in fires, to drown them in water, to destroy it by any means necessary.

John 17:11, 14

It was not successful! In spite of all the efforts of the world, the mystery of God in the flesh transformed, as I have already said, into a cosmic glory. But even now, how many people still remain ignorant of this mystery or, having come into contact with it, have rejected it! And what is even more sorrowful, even some of those who have accepted the mystery from their fathers and forefathers either remain or become once again like those who are ignorant of what to do with this incomprehensible mystery. They dissemble, either with idle curiosity (Why is such an incredible means used for the salvation of mankind?) or with doubt (Was such an extreme method really necessary to save people?). And where there is idle curiosity, pure knowledge is lacking; where there is doubt, faith is incomplete.

This mystery disperses curiosity merely by the fact that it is a mystery. It calls not for knowledge, but for faith. All the same, the mystery does not forbid the use of humble discernment to help doubters leave their path of stumbling blocks.

Therefore, if I dare now to speak about the necessity of the incarnation of the Son of God for mankind's salvation, the faithful may be assured that at the foundation of my discourse are the words of Jesus Christ Himself.

Matthew 11:27

Here is the first word: *No one knows the Son except the Father. Nor does anyone know the Father except the Son, and the one to whom the Son wills to reveal Him.* No intelligent person will doubt that salvation and blessedness is impossible without knowledge of God. However, the treasure of this knowledge of God is hidden within the Divinity, unattainable by His exaltedness, and the only way anyone can take this knowledge for salvation is to become one "to whom the Son will reveal" it, while and at the same time the Son of God, Who is the only One who can reveal the Father, is known to no one but the Father! What a conundrum!

It is thus necessary that the Son of Himself, unknowable in His divinity (which is beyond all conceivable forms), become knowable, so to speak, in a form conceivable to creation. For this reason, He is called *the image of the invisible God*. But what sort of form? Naturally, it must be a form close to the divine, a spiritual form. Let us start there. Through this, it becomes a bit more understandable how God Himself reveals the heavenly, angelic world. However, the earth is not the heavens. Man is not an angel, especially in the current state of both earth and man. For the heavens and the angels have been cut off from the earth and mankind; consequently, this revelation of God, appropriate to heaven and the angels, is not attainable for earth and mankind. Therefore, it became necessary that the Son of God, when He desired to reveal the salvific knowledge of God to fallen man, came down even lower than the heaven of angels, and took on a form conceivable to mankind. *[Colossians 1:15]*

The Word of God, without ceasing to be the Word of God, desired to enter into the form of a human word; *the image of the invisible God*, without ceasing to be Who He Is, desired to take on a form visible for the physical eyes of earthly minds. And so, He appeared first in passing forms (the revelations and visions of saints) and finally in an abiding form—behold, the incarnation of the Son of God! *[Colossians 1:15]*

Here is the second word: *No one comes to the Father except through Me*. What does it mean to come to God, to the God Who *alone has immortality, dwelling in unapproachable light, whom no man has seen or can see* in His essence? Naturally, no human being can come *[John 14:6]* *[1 Timothy 6:16]* to God with his feet on this earth or with wings in the air. So, what does it mean to come to God? One can only come to one from whom one has been taken away, but how can one be taken away from the omnipresent God? *God is Spirit,*" and so this coming to God must also be spiritual. A spiritual taking away and approaching occurs primarily in the will. With a sinful, evil will, man departs from God, as it is written in Scripture: *Your iniquities have separated you from your God.* With a repentant and good will, man approaches God. However, this approach cannot exist without the incarnation of the Son of God, as He Himself told us: *No one comes to the Father except through Me.*

John 4:24

Isaiah 59:2

John 14:6

If you ask, "Why can a person not approach God with his will alone, for it is a free will?" Here is my answer: "All in good time! You can certainly attempt this approach. But if you are attentive, then without a doubt you will find and admit this truth that others, better than you and me, have revealed for themselves: *'To will is present with me, but how to perform what is good I do not find. For the good that I will to do, I do not do; but the evil I will not to do, that I practice.'*

Romans 7:18-19

No matter how strange this contradictory reality of human nature may appear to the eyes of the mind, it has long been obvious even to those who did not yet become Christian. And if we delve more deeply into the reason for this, we will be assured that there is no other way. The source of good and of good will is God alone. If man stands in virtue, and therefore is in communion with God, then he still constantly draws power to continue in virtue from God alone; this is the only reason that it is so easy for him to desire good and act in virtue. However, if he allows sin to approach him, he breaks off communion with God; the more he departs from God, the more his ability to draw of God's power wanes. And so, even when his will, which is by nature free, makes an about face back to virtue and God, he no longer has the power to accord his actions to his good will, as did primal Man. Thus, man cannot approach God by himself alone without a special, extraordinary gift of power from God himself. He cannot approach God without this divine mediation, which encompasses both parties with total unity: God and Man. This mediation, or rather this Mediator, is the God-Man.

Here is a third word: *For God so loved the world that He gave His only-begotten Son, that whoever believes in Him should not perish but have everlasting life*. God can do nothing excessive or unnecessary, for this would contradict His wisdom. Therefore, since God gave His only begotten Son to the world, it was a necessary gift. For what purpose? As the Son of God Himself says to us, *That whoever believes in Him should not perish but have everlasting life*. Does that mean that if He did not do this, the world itself would perish and not have eternal life? Evidently, yes. But why? In order to make this as understandable as humanly possible, let us raise up our thoughts to the beginning of creation. *John 3:16* *John 3:16*

In the book of Wisdom, it is written, *God did not make death*. One can copy this sentence from the book of divine wisdom without effort into any book of human wisdom, at least as long as it is not lacking in an understanding of God the perfect Creator. God is the pure source of life. Creation, as creation, is subject to changeability; however, these changes, in creation and under the direction of the perfect Creator, can be rightly ordered toward perfection without suffering, without any crude or impure destruction, even in cases when things need to be reduced to their constituent parts with ease (we can even see this in the imperfect state of the world after the fall), such as when incense is pleasantly broken down into smoke. *Wisdom 1:13*

But what then is the source of the disorder, deformity, impurity, suffering, destruction, corruption—in a word: death? In my opinion, natural human reason can find no other answer to this than the answer given by God's revealed scripture: *Through one man sin entered the world, and death through sin*. Sin, as separation from God, is at the same time *being alienated from the life of God*. Consequently, death is temporary for physical, temporal, *Romans 5:12* *Ephesians 4:18* corruptible beings but is permanent for spiritual, indestructible, eternal beings, for there can be and never will be any other source of life than God.

For this reason, sin and death vouch for each other's presence in the world, so to speak. Do you see sin ascendant in the world? You could say that the world is on the path of death. Do you see death in the world? You could just as easily say that the world has sinned and is hurtling toward destruction. Whoever is not so blind that he cannot see the domination, in this world, of both sin and death can certainly see how much this world needs to be saved from destruction, to be given eternal life once again. For this reason, God sent His only-begotten Son. Death and destruction will come to every human life, both as a natural consequence of being separated from God and as the action of God's justice over sin. Thus, mankind needs, first of all, to satisfy God's justice (the reason for this is simple: no aspect of God can lack its corresponding activity, and so were God to declare arbitrarily that all would be forgiven or not punished, mankind would simply continue further on the road to sin, hurtling not toward salvation, but destruction). Secondly, mankind must once again be led into the life of God, which would then defeat and destroy the dominion of death over man.

These requirements are very difficult to accomplish; in fact, they are impossible for any creature. To satisfy God's justice, strictly speaking, would mean to send sinners to eternal death, not allowing them any possibility of eternal life. After all, how can the sinful life of a person approach the life of the all-holy God? Such a huge disparity threatens the inevitability of the destruction of unworthy creation, like straw in a furnace. It gives no hope of salvation. And so, what does the God of miracles do? He takes His own hypostatic life, the life of His only begotten Son, and places It into a small lot of human nature, long prepared by mystical activity for this fate, protected by His own grace from the admixture of sin, and He united divinity and humanity into a single hypostatic union of God and Man. He then led this divine-human union, which includes all of human nature save for sin, even into suffering, weakness, and death itself. And what happened?

The justice of God is completely satisfied, because in the person of the God-Man mankind as a whole received a just death, and received it fully, for all times, because the moment of the death of the God-Man, by virtue of the presence of eternal divinity, is equated to eternity. It is on the satisfaction of God's justice that the Redeemer has the power to forgive a repentant sinner without the dangerous hope of non-punishment for those who do not repent. At the same time, the life of God, having descended deep into human death, but not being contained by that death in His essence, from the depth of death shines forth for all mankind that has been brought to death through sin, and so He leads into eternal life all souls that open themselves up to that light through faith and do not repel it with unbelief and hard-heartedness. This is how God loved the world.

These thoughts of mine naturally lead to questions from you: how did mankind live or do good or even know God before the incarnation of the divinity? How do people who do not use the fruits of the incarnation also continue to live, do good, and come to know God? These questions are worthy of attention. For those who have not yet fully probed the mystery of God in the flesh to see its light from within, to sense its salvific power, the answers to these questions might at the very least demonstrate the greatness of the mystery from the outside.

How did the human race live before Christ? It lived in the primal purity of man's creation, through the mediation of direct communion with God the Word, in Whom *was life, and the life was the light of men.* As for the time after the fall until the coming of Christ, if man, already *dead in trespasses* internally, was still externally alive, this life was nothing but the remnants of life given to him by God in the beginning. It is similar to the life of a

John 1:4

Ephesians 2:5

branch cut off from the tree. It can continue to survive while the sap remains inside it, but unless it be grafted to another tree, it will shrivel up and die. Secondly, mankind after the fall continued to live only through the glimmers of Christ's life that could be found before the Annunciation in Nazareth and the manger in Bethlehem, for at the moment that our primal life was damaged by sin, God found it necessary to administer the medicine of Christ. This was done by the word of the first annunciation of the incarnation of God the Word: *the seed of the woman shall bruise the head of the serpent.* From that moment, that medicine continued to be administered and to act through grace, as we can see in the life of the Patriarchs and prophets. As for the natural life of man after the fall, how can we fail to notice (both in the lives of the ancients and in our contemporaries) how it never tends toward progress but rather to destruction and death? How it has shortened the lives of people with every passing age? How it has led some nations and tribes who do not know Christ to live in the lowest possible manner, more similar to the lives of irrational animals?

Genesis 3:15, reworded by St Philaret

How did man come to know God and do good works before Christianity and without Christianity? I have one answer. If they knew God, they knew Him only through the leftover glimmers of the original light of their creation, through the help of pious traditions. And if they did anything good in any sense, then it was only because of the remainders of their original good wills given them at their creation. By man's fall into sin, the image of God in him was shattered, though not completely destroyed. The eternal Sun set in his soul, but a few rays of the coming dawn still touch the tips of the soul's peaks. And in this diminished light, *His invisible attributes are clearly seen, being understood by the things that are made, even His eternal power and Godhead. For when the Gentiles, who do not have the law, by nature do the things in the law, these, although not having the law, are a law to themselves, who show the work*

Romans 1:20
Romans 2:14-15

SERMON 9. THE MYSTERY OF GODLINESS, 1835

of the law written in their hearts, their conscience also bearing witness, and between themselves their thoughts accusing or else excusing them.

But perhaps you will ask: if a certain degree of knowledge of God is natural for the human race, as well as a certain degree of virtue, then could not man be raised and made perfect and saved through natural means, by constant labor? The answer to this question is not difficult, for there are many examples. The human race, before Christianity, for several thousand years had plenty of time to try out its natural abilities. And what did mankind do? Despite the fact that the most ancient traditions spoke of one God and the pure Edenic state (which in the pagan world was called "the golden age"), they all devolved into polytheism, idolatry, vice, and evildoing, some of which horrify by their unnaturalness, including not only sanctioned murder but the murder of children, fathers, and even cannibalism. When the pagan world, pathetic in its ignorance, rises to an educated state, it becomes abhorrent in decadence, the two of which often go together. What did pagan philosophy accomplish? Did it lead even one pagan city or village into the knowledge of the one God? Did it not, on the contrary, concoct all sorts of doubts concerning the existence of God and of virtue?

During the time of Christianity, human reason could accomplish great things in the sphere of natural knowledge, because it was illumined with the light of divine revelation. But even in our times, when natural reason tried to act without Christ, it deprived itself of even the glimmers of spiritual light, resulting in a level of ignorance not even seen among the pagans, that is, a state-sanctioned atheism![1] Perhaps some will call this the vagary of chance, a temporary disorder, a misuse of reason by a small group of people who were led by their passions. I will not argue that fact, but if this is a misuse, a disorder, an illness, then where is the proper use, the order, and the health of natural human rea-

---

1 St Philaret seems to be speaking of the French Revolution.

son when it is not led by the revelation of the physician-Christ? Show me, if you can, any such society where human reason has led the human race to perfection and blessedness! And who can claim that the disorder, misuse, and illness will not return again and again in new situations, with even greater severity? To what awful depths will human reason lead mankind if you declare it the savior of the human race without any good reason? Truly, there are enough miserable examples in history that prove that man's self-salvation through natural means and the power of reason are nothing more than the mad delusions of a spiritually ill mankind.

The best use of human reason for the salvation and blessedness of mankind is this: to dispassionately assess and measure one's own abilities, means, limitations and to slowly approach the great mystery of godliness, to lay down one's weapons and crowns at the foot of this mystery, and to give oneself up to noble captivity to it, to a willing obedience of faith in the God who appeared in the flesh.

O Christians! Children of the faith, inheritors of the revelation, preservers of the mysteries of God! Let us bless the God of mysteries and revelations. Let us glorify the God-Man, the author and finisher of our faith. Let us preserve the mystery of God that has been given to us with such condescension. Let us consider how inappropriate it would be to preserve this mystery of godliness in a soul and life dedicated to impurity. We must preserve the holy and divine treasure in a vessel made of pure gold— *holding the mystery of the faith with a pure conscience.* [1 Timothy 3:9]

Amen.

10

The Dignity of Virginity

Homily on the Entry of the Mother of God into the Temple (1836)

"For the grace of God that brings salvation has appeared to all men, teaching us that, denying ungodliness and worldly lusts, we should live soberly, righteously, and godly in the present age." (Titus 2:11-12)

Remembering the lives and acts of the saints naturally leads us to contemplate the virtues and perfections that marked their lives. That being the case, what could be more appropriate, on this triumphant remembrance of the dedication to God of the most blessed and most pure Virgin Mary, than to contemplate virginity and chastity?

For did she not lay the most firm of foundations for virginity? Did she not raise this virtue to unheard-of heights?

The world of the Old Testament was zealous for childbearing, and therefore for marriage, for everyone was hoping to give birth to the Savior of the world. This world understood and honored virginity so little that it was a matter of sorrow, not joy. The daughter of Jephthah the Gileadite, who was supposed to die not having known a man, not only *went with her companions and bewailed her virginity upon the mountains,"* but even after her death, *"the daughters of Israel went yearly to lament the daughter of Jephthah the Gileadite four days in a year.*

Judges 11:38, 40

The life of John the Baptist, and before him of the prophets Elias and Elisha were early indications that virginity was honorable, but even these were not understood in their own time, because more often the Hebrews saw prophets who did not avoid the married life, such as Moses, Samuel, and others. From the beginning of the world, there have been men of God, but the first virgin of God is the most blessed Mary. Having been dedicated to God in the purity of her childhood, she became the first foundation, never to be shaken, of the angelic life on this earth.

She revealed the dignity of virginity to be even higher than the heavens. From Eve until her, women as well as men served the law of marriage in expectation of this reward: sooner or later one of them would produce the blessed Seed that would *bruise the head* of the hellish serpent, in which Seed *shall all the nations of the earth be blessed*. However, that reward was not predestined for marriage. Marriage can only produce people. Virginity alone is worthy of giving birth to the God-Man.

Genesis 3:15
Genesis 22:18

Before I say something more about virginity for you who hear me today, I fear the thought that perhaps may repel this word concerning virginity from your hearts: "The virginity of the most pure Theotokos, who was chosen to be the vessel for the incarnation of the Son of God, is the only person in the human race who had neither models before her nor emulators after her." It is true that there will never be another incarnation of the Word of God, nor another Mother of God. However, my brothers, this does not mean that we should conclude that the virginity of the most blessed Mary does not offer us any example for emulation or a lesson for life.

If the Virgin Mary was found worthy of being chosen by God for a most exalted role, then consider: why was this done? You might say it was because of a special grace of God, perhaps? I will not argue the point. But consider further: can the grace of God contradict God's righteousness? No, without a doubt not. If even in a human being an internal contradiction is considered foolishness, then how much more must there be complete agreement of qualities and actions in God, as appropriate to a most pure essence. And so, if the Virgin Mary was found worthy of the highest calling because of the grace of God, she was equally found to be so by God's righteousness. She was raised higher than all others by being specially chosen, because she was more worthy than everyone else of this election in her spiritual qualities and dispositions, but also, it must be said, by her most pure virginity. In this virginity, she rose like the sun, evidently higher than the entire ancient world before her, as well as the world to come after her. For this reason, we must conclude that if the most blessed Mary reached the highest level of election by God because of her pure virginity, though it be impossible to emulate her exactly, still those who emulate her virginity as much as possible may, through the righteousness of God, hope for a special grace of God, a special election, a special closeness to God. If virginity alone made her more honorable than the Cherubim, and beyond compare more glorious than the Seraphim, then her emulators can at least become equal to the angels. If her virginity alone made her the tabernacle of the Holy Spirit, the mother of the Son of God, then virginity can make other souls to become daughters of God, chosen ones of the King of heaven, brides of Christ. This is what the mystical psalm tells us in the words: *the virgins her companions that follow her shall be brought unto thee.* [Psalm 44:15]

If my conclusions seem to you not trustworthy enough, and if the words of the prophets are not clear enough for you, then perhaps you would listen to the Lord Himself concerning the angelic dignity of virginity? Hear His own word: *For in the resurrec-* [Matthew 22:30] tion they neither marry, nor are given in marriage, but are as the angels of God in heaven. Or, in the words of another evangelist: *They are equal unto the angels.* The state in which one neither marries nor is given in marriage is, of course, perpetual virginity, and the Lord calls it a state equal to the angels.

Luke 20:36

Would you like to hear a divine word concerning virginity, that it is not only attainable by many, but should be desired by all? Hear the words of the Apostle Paul to the Corinthians: *For I would that all men were even as I myself.* What does "even as I myself" mean? He explains this later in the same epistle: *Have we not power to lead about a sister, a wife, as well as other apostles?...Nevertheless we have not used this power; but suffer all things, lest we should hinder the gospel of Christ.* In other words, he deprived himself of the help and consolation of the marriage state, the better to serve without hindrance at the spread of the Gospel. Consequently, the apostle wishes that everyone else might also dedicate themselves to the service of God and the virtue of virginity.

1 Corinthians 7:7

1 Corinthians 9:5, 12

Would you like to see the great lot prepared for virginity from God Himself? Look with the eyes of the seer John:

Revelation 14:1-3

> And I looked, and, lo, a Lamb stood on the mount Sion, and with him an hundred forty and four thousand, having his Father's name written in their foreheads. And I heard a voice from heaven, as the voice of many waters, and as the voice of a great thunder: and I heard the voice of harpers harping with their harps: And they sung as it were a new song before the throne, and before the four beasts, and the elders: and no man could learn that song but the hundred and forty and four thousand, which were redeemed from the earth.

Revelation 14:1-4

Who are these people, do you ask? John answers: *These are they which were not defiled with women; for they are virgins. These are they which follow the Lamb withersoever he goeth. These were redeemed from among men, being the first fruits unto God and to the Lamb.*

Do you see the exalted lot of virginity? Perhaps you might now be curious to know what virginity is and how this virtue is accomplished?

Each person knows through his own personal experience that virginity is the natural state that precedes marriage, that has not tasted the mysteries of marriage, and has not been awakened to that knowledge of those mysteries. However, this is only the incomplete beginning of what we now discuss. It is still only the stem of the lily, not the flower. It is only the leaves of the apple tree, not the sweet-smelling fruit. The virginity of childhood, since it is simply a natural state, is not the work of free will, not the work of labor, and so there is no virtue in it yet. It is accurate to call it a state of innocence because there is no guilt in it; however, this state still lacks the exalted dignity that belongs to perfect virginity.

Virginity as a spiritual labor, as a virtue, as a flower of purity, as the fruit of chastity, as the path of perfection appears when a person, in mature age that more or less inclines him to marriage, does not follow the inclinations of his nature, does not become enamored of the customs, examples, pleasures, and needs of a married life, and instead makes a decision not to marry, but to remain a virgin for all time.

But just as a laborer will not be crowned if he labored unlawfully, so also he who makes the choice to begin the labor of virginity must know, always remembers, and keep the most important rule of this labor, which is that the labor of virginity is attempted and accomplished solely for the sake of God. *Eunuchs for the kingdom of heaven's sake* is how Christ Himself, the establisher of the rule of virginity, describes this state. The apostle continues in the same vein: *He that is unmarried careth for the things that belong to the Lord, how he may please the Lord…The unmarried woman careth for the things of the Lord, that she may be holy both in body and in spirit.*

2 Timothy 2:5

Matthew 19:12

2 Corinthians 7:32, 34

Pleasing God by sanctifying the spirit and body is the goal of those who labor in virginity. Whoever runs to the virginal life without this intention runs not to a crown of victory. The virgin avoids marriage to prevent an excessive inclination to earthly things from holding him back or turning him aside from the path to God. By striving with all the powers of his mind and love toward the Lord, by directing all the activity of his person to pleasing him, the virginal soul becomes worthy of being called a bride of the heavenly Bridegroom.

From this most important rule of virginity, it is not difficult to notice that the bodily avoidance of everything that is natural to the married state is not complete virginity, but only its lowest form. For striving toward, and approaching God as a Spiritual essence can only be done properly in spirit; bodily virginity merely takes away the obstacles for spiritual striving and cuts off all contrary striving. It is from this reality that the many more detailed laws concerning virginity are derived.

Matthew 5:28   The Lord said, *Whosoever looketh on a woman to lust after her hath committed adultery with her already in his heart.* Therefore, just as there is the adultery of the heart, there must also be an opposite virtue to this vice: the virginity of the heart. He who labors in this virtue must preserve his heart pure of all carnal desire, from all thoughts that are contrary to chastity. Any unwilling approach of impure thoughts must be cut off without fail. This means a constant, careful vigilance over the movement of one's thoughts and desires, an active preservation of the mind and heart by exercise in the word of God or attentive, internal prayer.

Since the Lord demonstrated that the eye is a tool for the adultery of the heart, we must learn to train our eye to serve virginity, that is, to turn aside our gaze from all seductive objects, and if any such things present themselves to our eyes without our ability to look away, we must look without passion, without thought, looking without seeing, as it were, and to cut off this dangerous vision as quickly as possible. This is what it means to mortify the

Matthew 5:29   sense of sight, as the Lord Himself commanded: *If thy right eye*

offend thee, pluck it out, and cast it from thee. This is the source of the eremitic and solitary life.

However, if it is necessary to mortify the sense of sight for the preservation of virginity, then, by comparison, we can come to understand that we must also mortify the rest of our senses: the ears from hearing immodest and seductive words, the tongue from tasting, the hand from touching, things that incline one to satiety and decadence. For this reason, we train ourselves in silence, fasting, eating food without oil, simplicity and severity in the style of clothing, house, and bedding. In all things we seek to mortify the body with labor, prayerful vigil, and prostrations.

If we were to summarize virginity in a single image, I offer this wonderful utterance of the holy Golden-mouth: "The root and fruit of virginity is a crucified life." (*On Virginity*, chapter 79).

But perhaps we have already spoken too much on a subject that many of my listeners will think does not concern them? It is indeed true that the Lord Himself warned us that not all are capable of the virginal life: *All men cannot receive this saying, save they to whom it is given.* He Himself called only those who were capable of it to this labor: *He that is able to receive it, let him receive it.* Since virginity is not for all, then you may even ask: "Why are you speaking of this one thing to everyone?" I acknowledge the question. It will lead me to my point and to the end of my homily.

I speak to all concerning virginity because there are some among all to whom this saying is given, and this saying seeks, among you all, those whom God has called to hear it and achieve it. Often, the person does not even know he is being called yet.

I speak to all concerning virginity so that even the married may know that there is a state higher than marriage, so that they might begin to think more humbly of marriage, and so that, by honoring virginity in others, and by thinking humbly of marriage, they might receive a blessing on their marriage that is close to the blessing given to virginity.

Matthew 19:11

Matthew 19:12

I speak to all concerning true virginity so that you all may avoid the false path of the foolish virgins, who, with unlit lamps of the mind, without the oil of the heart, wander about far from the bridal chamber, and instead of heavenly love for the heavenly Bridegroom, only feed themselves with enmity against the blessed state of marriage. For even in the apostolic times, *Now the Spirit speaketh expressly, that in the latter times some shall depart from the faith, giving heed to seducing spirits, and doctrines of devils; Speaking lies in hypocrisy; having their conscience seared with a hot iron; Forbidding to marry.*

1 Timothy 4:1-3

Finally, I speak to all concerning virginity so that both those who are married and those who are unmarried may distinguish with a careful and diligent eye the unseemliness of the state that is neither the golden coin of virginity nor the silver coin of marriage in terms of the spiritual labor of cultivating one's gifts according to the will of the Lord. Marriage and virginity may not be for everyone, but chastity certainly is. *For the grace of God that brings salvation has appeared to all men, teaching us that, denying ungodliness and worldly lusts, we should live soberly, righteously, and godly in the present age.* What does it mean to live soberly? It means that whether we live in purity of virginity or the honorable state of marriage, in both cases, we must live by the *abstaining from fleshly lusts, which war against the soul.* Only in this way can we who live in this age expect *that blessed hope* of the future. Amen.

Titus 2:11-12

1 Peter 2:11

Titus 2:13

11

All Generations Bless Her

Homily on the Dormition of the Mother of God
(1838)

"He has regarded the lowly state of His maidservant; for behold, henceforth all generations will call me blessed." (Luke 1:48)

Who among you, who are attentive to the services, does not recognize the frequently repeated hymn in honor of the most holy Virgin Mary: *All generations call thee blessed, O Virgin Theotokos*? If we contemplate where this hymn came from and what its words indicate, then our spirit will be offered food for wondrous and endless contemplation. In the distance of past times, do you see that from Nazareth of no renown a poor and unknown virgin travels to another little-known town in the Judean hill country to visit her relative. She greets her with a typical greeting, but suddenly her relative is incited by a prophetic ecstasy within her, and she greets her as the *Mother of my Lord*. Having been carried away in a similar ecstasy, the Virgin herself begins to prophecy concerning her-

Luke 1:48

Luke 1:43

self: *Behold, henceforth all generations will call me blessed.* This voice is heard by nations, ages, the ends of the earth, and the nations, ages, and ends of the earth answer her: "Behold, we fulfill your word, we and all generations bless thee, O Theotokos."

This temple, this feast, and this holy and triumphant gathering also belong to the fulfillment of the prophecy of the most holy Virgin that she will be blessed by all generations. In her, even that which has always been a source for woe—the end of human life—is also blessed.

Let us examine, brothers, the great dignity of the words of the most holy Virgin: *Behold, henceforth all generations shall call me blessed.* These are not simply the words of joy, not a guess that accidentally appeared in the form of a premonition. This is a prophecy in the most exact meaning of the word. It is the word of the Holy Spirit on the lips of Mary; it is an announcement of the determination and will of God concerning her fate, and our rightful responsibility to continue to bless her for all generations.

Let us also examine the importance of the tradition according to which the Orthodox Church constantly and zealously blesses the most holy Mother of God in every service. This is not a simple human tradition, not just a rite begun through willful zeal, but the thought of the Holy Spirit passed on to people. It is us following the edict written by the finger of God, the fulfillment of which is just as holy as it is right and beneficial for Christianity.

Apostle Peter described the law that determines what is a true prophecy in these words: *for prophecy never came by the will of man, but holy men of God spoke as they were moved by the Holy Spirit.* Two signs must unite to determine if a prophecy is genuine. First of all, the foretelling must be something that cannot be determined from known circumstances by the use of human reason. Secondly, the foretelling must be fulfilled exactly. If the event prophesied can be predicted by human reason or explained from natural causes, then this is nothing more than a good guess, not

God-inspired prophecy. If the foretold event did not occur exactly as it was foretold, then it is a false prophecy, or at least a prophecy that cannot be fully understood. This is how the prophets themselves assessed prophecy: *As for the prophet who prophesies of peace, when the word of the prophet comes to pass, the prophet will be known as one whom the Lord has truly sent.* Jeremiah 28:9

Let us now apply these criteria to the prophecy of the most pure Virgin.

The Virgin, who was poor and unknown by the world, could hardly have been able to make an educated guess that not only her contemporary world, but all generations for all future times would come to know her and glorify her. Yes, she was a descendant of kings, but the glory of that line had long passed. She herself was betrothed to a carpenter, and of course the distance from that social rank to universal glory is far too great. Could the Virgin perhaps have made a prediction based on the fact that it was already foretold to her that she would give birth to the Christ? But if she had considered this thought according to the established wisdom of the time (as the apostles continually did, even with Christ among them), she would have considered it in the light of the return of the kingdom of Israel. But this would have hardly resulted in a hope that all generations of mankind would come to know her, now and in the future! After all, who of the kings of Israel was more famous that David? And whose memory among the Hebrews was greater than that of Abraham? But the mothers of Abraham and David not only were not blessed by all subsequent generations, but we don't even know their names. Could the mother of the Messiah expect much for her own self, judging by human reason and the presuppositions of her nation and her time?

Add to this the fact that we must remember her own profound humility. Whoever thinks much of his own worth, his own virtues, such a person can fool himself with inflated hopes, but the disposition of her spirit was not like this at all. At the same time as she glorified God for being chosen to the high calling of being the Mother of the Lord, she still saw herself only as a slave, capable only of speaking of her unworthiness: *For He has regarded the lowly state of His handmaiden.* How, then, suddenly, from such a profoundly humble frame of mind, could she then naturally produce such exalted phrases concerning herself: "Behold, from henceforth all generations shall call me blessed"?

Luke 1:48

It should be clear that these thoughts did not arise from the seeds of her own human reason and heart. The Holy Spirit, to whom she dedicated herself in the ecstasy of prayer, illumined her mind at this moment, opened her lips, and she spoke that which He Himself predicted concerning her, that which the world-wide Church would fulfill for her sake, under the guidance of the Spirit's Providence.

Just as the prophecy of the most holy Virgin shows all the signs of the word of God speaking through her, so also the circumstances of this prophecy accord with the signs of God's activity, not only because the prophesied event came to pass exactly as predicted, but especially because the fulfillment of the prophecy occurred in a way that did not accord with the usual course of nature or the work of human hands. If someone who desires the praise of his fellows finds it, or does everything he can to take advantage of circumstances to glorify himself, that is clearly the path of the world and the work of human hands. However, if someone who avoids plaudits still becomes praised by other people, then it becomes clear that this is not the path of the world or the work of human hands. Here we see the paths of God, the finger of God at work.

I do not receive honor from men, said the Son of the Virgin Mary, and still His glory covers the earth, making it clear that this is "the honor that comes from the only God." He prepared the same kind of path to glory for His mother. It seems that she needed to expend no great effort to avoid the glory of men, the same glory that she predicted for herself, but nonetheless she constantly avoided it and shunned it. When the people were ecstatic from the divine words of Jesus; when they glorified Him for His miracles; when they greeted Him as a king, triumphantly; we never see His mother near him at such moments to share in His glory. On the contrary, we see her hurrying to Him with motherly concern only when He was dishonored by those who said that He was *out of His mind*. We see her at the foot of His cross, sharing His suffering and shame. The Lord Jesus Christ Himself never hurried to reveal the glory of His mother, lest it seem to be the result of human efforts, human love, instead of something that came about as a result of exalted grace. Therefore it is not surprising that even the apostles did not fully understand the due level of honor and respect that was proper to the mother of the Lord, and it was necessary for Christ Himself to begin to instruct His beloved disciple in this proper care from the Cross: *Behold thy mother* This is how far the most holy Theotokos was from the glory that awaited her, in accordance with her own humility, as well the time when *Jesus was not yet glorified*. *Mark 3:21*

John 19:27

John 7:39

But be attentive and see how even in this time, her glory was beginning to shine forth. As a lightning bolt from a cloud, she was suddenly praised by the lips of a certain woman, who, in evident spiritual ecstasy from the divine words of Jesus, *raised her voice and said to Him, 'Blessed is the womb that bore You!'* The unknown woman of course did not hear the prophecy spoken thirty years before in the presence of Elizabeth alone: *all generations shall call me blessed*. But how accurate was her response to this prophecy, not only in thought, but in word as well: *Blessed is the womb!* Can we not fail to see the path of God in the fulfillment of his prophecy, only the breath of the Spirit of God that is beginning to move all generations to call the ever-Virgin mother blessed? *Luke 11:27*

Luke 1:48

Luke 11:27

When the crucified Lord was glorified by His resurrection and ascension into the heavens, then the glory of His divine mother appears, not like a shining bolt of lightning that quickly disappears, but, as Solomon put it, rising "as the early morning." She who is "beautiful as the moon," reflecting the glory of the Sun of righteousness, remained on the earth among the eleven and twelve stars (the apostles) as one who was *choice as the sun*. As the Book of Acts tells us, *These all continued with one accord in prayer and supplication, with the women and Mary the mother of Jesus, and with His brothers*. Do you see that she who was never seen among the apostles during Jesus' life is now inseparable from their assembly? What does this new arrangement mean? Though it might be explained away simply by the desire to be in common prayer and the common expectation of the descent of the Holy Spirit, if we examine this more deeply, we can reveal something special, something more mystical. If a vessel that used to contain aromatic oils continues to smell pleasantly even after the oil runs out, in a certain way continuing the action of the now absent oil, how much more must she who became the vessel of God Himself in the incarnation be for all ages anointed with the sweet fragrance of the divine, even after the departure of Him whose *name [itself] is ointment poured forth*.

Song of Songs 6:9
Acts 1:14

Song of Songs 1:3

Therefore, it was natural for her, as it were, to attract, through her presence and her prayers, the blessed presence and salvific action of the One Who at one time abode inside her body, and Who always abode within her spiritually and divinely. The apostles naturally sensed this communion with the mother of the Lord as beneficial to them in their hearts, all the more so since they thirsted strongly to fill the lack of visible communion with the Lord Who had ascended. Thus, she became a profound focal point of their unity, in spite of the fact that by her humility she continued to avoid all appearance of domination over the assembly. *These all continued with one accord in prayer and supplication with Mary the mother of Jesus*.

Acts 1:14

Finally, miraculously and triumphantly did the grace of the one "choice as the sun" appear as a focal point of the Church's power when she, by the law of mortality, having recognized the

Occident of her time on earth, saw the dawn of her own unending day in heaven. For the Holy Spirit revealed this moment to the apostles, dispersed throughout the known world for the preaching of the Gospel, as the final moment of earthly communion with her. And the impetus of the Spirit united all of them around her deathbed, her life-giving tomb. From that moment, according to the Church's expression, "her divine glory shines forth through God-like miracles" (second sticheron on "Lord I have Cried" from the feast of Dormition).

Pointless is the dark philosophizing of those who improperly tried to dim her glory: they only sharpened the zeal of the Orthodox to praise her. Neither the increase of the Church's spread nor the passage and vagaries of time have lessened the light of her glory. No matter how far our own times are from personal communion with her, this does not hinder our faith from seeing her, our prayer from reaching her, especially with the help of her holy icons. And she herself, through mystically imparted signs and images, descends to meet us in faith and prayer, extending her proper grace and beneficent power on all the works of the Church, which consequently glorifies her universally, not only because it is appropriate to the mother of the Lord, but from an outpouring of a sense of faith, devotion, and gratitude.

Christians! The more completely we are assured that the glorification of the most holy Theotokos in the Church is the work of God, the more we know that our responsibility to praise her is God's own command, the more assiduously, the more faithfully must we fulfill this responsibility.

We bless the ever-Virgin one. But do we do it sincerely? Or do we do it with a desire for fair return? Such base flattery is abhorrent even among those who live on earth, who are rarely fooled by it, for all that. But it is impossible to delude her who lives in heaven, who sees through the all-seeing God. Can it be possible, you may ask, to flatter in a situation when even the most exalted praise remains insufficient for the object of adoration? We flatter falsely if we praise that which we do not respect. In other words, though we glorify the ever-Virgin, do we also honor virginity? Do we praise chastity? Do we preserve our own purity? Do we abhor impurity? Do we have zeal for our own purification?

We may praise the most blessed Mother in Church, but do not some of us do the opposite in our own homes? Do not some children offend the blessed name of father and mother by their lack of submission or lack of respect for their parents? As for parents, do you not do the same by disdaining your parental responsibilities and virtues?

Here, in this Church, we praise Mary, who was exalted in humility and profound in silence. But do we not hold on to our pride, our vanity, our busyness, our distractedness, and our tendency toward idle talk? And does not the hubbub of our passions dispel the praises of our lips from our hearts?

Luke 1:45 — Together with Elizabeth, we bless her *who believed* and who through that faith led the Author of our faith into the world. We marvel at her who was blessed by God. We glorify her miraculous mercies. But how carefully do we preserve the priceless pledge of our own faith, which could bring even us to a similar blessedness? Do we seek grace—I do not say the visible grace of miracle-working that is not given to all and is not beneficial for all, but the grace that comes alive within, fashioning in us a pure heart, renewing within us a spirit of righteousness, making us new creations in Christ? Do we not rather live carelessly and negligently in the corruption of our nature, in the old man, in the works of the flesh, in the cares and the pleasures of the world, with a faith in name only, with a fruitless love bereft of good deeds, incapable of giving birth within us to that inner blessedness of heaven?

Sirach 15:9 — *Praise is not proper in the mouth of a sinner.* If we desire to worthily bless the most holy Theotokos, then let us come to love her accomplishments and her virtues with our whole heart. Having come to love them, let us find the zeal to follow her whom we glorify with our lives as much as we can. And may she whom we glorify establish us in such a disposition, by the grace given to her and by the powerful prayers she directs to her own Son and our God, only-begotten and equally praised with the Father and the Holy Spirit unto ages of ages. Amen.

12

Grace

Homily on the Dormition of the Mother of God
(1842)

"The angel said to her, 'Rejoice, highly favored one, the Lord is with you; blessed are you among women!' But when she saw him, she was troubled at his saying, and considered what manner of greeting this was." (Luke 1:28-29)

I am not surprised that even you, O Mother of the Creator of the world, were troubled at the words of the heavenly messenger. The news was too incredible, too early comes this greeting that only an angel could utter, that you alone could hear and accept with faith.

Luke 1:28   To experience the state of *the Lord is with you* not only through grace-filled spiritual presence, but through physical incarnation within you—this is a favor that is incomparably exalted! This is a joy that is endlessly bright! But what darkness clung to you, O living and life-bearing tabernacle of Light! He had not even come out of your womb yet, and already around you arose a storm of doubting thoughts that, having darkened, almost defeated the protector of the light, Joseph. And when the divine Light shining from a manger was reflected in the heavens, and a heavenly song of glory resounded on earth, when He illumined the simple shepherds and the far-seeing Magi, Herod and all Jerusalem with him rose up in a deadly attack against the weaponless child. And you, O mother of the Light, had to flee into the darkness of Egypt. You even feared to return into the fatherland of the Light, Judea, and had to move to *Galilee of the Gentiles: the people who sat in darkness...in the region and the shadow of death.* Matthew 4:15-16

The righteous Simeon, one of only a few, not only saw, but knew, and took into his arms the *Light of revelation to the Gentiles.* Luke 2:32 But what happened then? As soon as the Light illumined the future for him, with the sword of the prophetic word he pierced the soul of the mother of the Light, foretelling that she would be pierced by the sword of sorrows at the foot of the Cross: *Yes, a sword will pierce through your own soul also.* Luke 2:35

Were you given sufficient joy by the divine proclamation of Jesus at the Jordan, at His outpouring of light on Tabor, at the triumph of His teaching and miracles? We do not know. What we do know, both from the Scriptures and from our own human sympathy (though it cannot compare with the love in your heart), was just how prolonged, varied, and profound your sorrows were concerning your divine Son, Who, though divine, had clothed Himself in all of humanity's weakness. You saw Him either in exhaustion from his labors or in contentious argument with the crowd, in danger from his enemies and finally in their clutches. You saw him when they raised cries and blasphemies against Him, when they struck and wounded Him, your own heart was stricken. You were with Him when He gave you another son instead of Himself, when You saw His final gaze, heard His final utterance. You did not abandon Him when you accompanied His dead body.

The light of His resurrection, without a doubt, illumined you more than all others, but was not the rest of your earthly life like a night made dark and sightless by the passage of lighting, when He hid Himself in ascending into the heavens? And is not this the lot of the one *blessed among women*—to be first an orphaned mother after the death of her son on the Cross, then orphaned once again, being left on earth by her Son who rose and abides always in heavenly glory?

But now, a new time comes. It is revealed that the seed of the heavenly word, though it does not always sprout quickly, always brings a much more abundant harvest. Now, not only the gaze of heaven contemplates your high favor, not an angel alone secretly wishes you joy, but the entire Church proclaims your grace and joy. The entire race of mankind blessed you who are *blessed among women*. Your own divine glory, like the glory of your Son and God, shines forth from your tomb. The miracles of your Dormition revealed that your God-borne soul departed directly to God, and the emptiness of your tomb the next day showed that even in your body, death found nothing to feast on, nothing infected by sin, nothing that could be corrupted. The life of the age to come, which we now only await with expectation, for you has become truly eternal life in the highest degree of glory. In the bridal chamber of heaven, like a queen according to grace, you were brought *to the King in robes of many colors*, you are a *woman clothed with the sun*, clothed in the uncovered and perfect (as I believe) light of Christ. You stood by the king not only to remain in His light and enjoy it, but to rule in that light, to be a witness that *the virgins, her companions who follow her*—the souls of the chaste or those who became newly chaste—shall also be brought before Him. Today you may truly rejoice, *you who are full of grace*, and from now until all ages you may rejoice without cease, not only rejoice, but also be blessed, for you are not only highly favored, but most glorified!

And if an exalted degree of light and goodness, grace and blessedness, is a state of perfection that overflows onto all that is like and similar to it, then send down, O greatly blessed one, from your abundance, a drop of the same grace to us who believe in and glorify it. It will be like the dawn of light, like the source of goodness, like the pledge of blessedness.

Forgive me, brothers, if I seem to be standing here for a long time thinking aloud, as though not speaking to you. In such days as today, one can completely forget the world in converse with heaven. And it would be good if we conversed more eagerly and more often with heaven, and less eagerly and less frequently turned back to the earth, not least because, having encountered our own limitations and needs, we find it necessary to all the more fervently run to the abundance and generosity of heaven.

Indeed, brothers, turning from this contemplation of the grace that Mary received from God, which raised her to such an exalted glory through such miraculous paths, we turn back to ourselves. Doing so, we must think of how much we ourselves require the same grace. If Mary alone is full of grace because of her perfections, then, on the contrary, no one can remain without grace without becoming completely immersed in evil and perdition. We need at least the smallest drop of grace to reach at least the next level of blessedness. *Luke 1:30*

Grace—if we want to fully exhaust all possible meanings of the word—is a gift from the Good One, a good gift, a gift given only freely, without any right or deserving or worthiness on our part. If we consider that, according to the word of the Lord, *No one is good but... God*, Who is consequently the source of all that is good in the creation; if we consider that we should never seek anything good outside of God alone; if we consider the pure goodness of the Gift-giver, Who never acts in retribution, for good or ill (for *who has fist given to Him and it shall be repaid to him?*), we might come to the conclusion that everything that man has both in himself and around him—being, life, body, soul, the ability to *Matthew 19:17* *Romans 11:35* learn, desire, act—comes from God's grace alone. However, since the good that God placed into people by the act of His creation has been given to them as though it were their own essential property, then that which was a gift of grace in the beginning, in its continuation became the essential nature of those born of man. In contrast to this, *grace* has come to mean all that the all-good God gives to man above his nature and essence. This is how the word of God uses the word "grace," meaning two things: 1) "the gift that gives universally" (that is, divine power that pours forth grace-filled influence on man: *For the grace of God that bring salvation has appeared to all men*) "the gift that is offered particularly" as we see in the following words of the apostle: *To each one of us grace was give according to the measure of Christ's gift.*

Titus 2:11 & 2

Ephesians 4:7

When there was no sin in the world, everything was transparent for the light of grace. It poured out into nature without hindrance, and constantly filled it with goodness and blessedness, preserving it in indestructible perfection and deathlessness even in the substance that hid within itself the possibility of corruption: the body of man. But when sin entered the world through the seduction of the devil and man's misuse of his free will to turn away from God's will to his own, the original connection between nature and grace was broken. Even though the light of grace, since it is divine (and therefore impossible to be hindered by any created thing), did not cease to shine, it no longer shines always and on all things. But nature, defiled, darkened, made crude, infected by sin, became unworthy and incapable of accepting the pure, bright, subtle, incorrupt influence of grace. Therefore, spiritual death entered the world with sin, and after her came bodily, temporal death, followed by eternal death. And if man managed to preserve some of what he originally received through grace, of course it was not possible for him to return, without the extraordinary help of grace, to return what he lost.

See Romans 5:12

And so, we discover the extreme need for an *abundance of grace* given in a miraculous fashion. For man, who had torn himself

Romans 5:17

and fallen away from grace, it would have become natural to fall all the way to the depths of hell, if the provident, eternally merciful God had not extended His protective and restoring hand. He wondrously united that which receives the grace and Him who gives it—divinity and pure humanity—in the single hypostasis of Christ the Lord. In His word and life, in His body and blood, in His baptism of water and Spirit, he renewed the super-abundant sources of grace that once again flow into our nature, which had cut itself off from grace without becoming completely foreign and incompatible to the Incarnate One. This outpouring of renewed grace purified that which was defiled by sin, illumined that which was darkened, gave spirit to that which had become crude flesh, healed that which had corrupted, raised that which had fallen, justified that which was condemned, enlivened that which was dead, and saved that which had perished. And this is not my own thought, but the teaching of the Gospel: *The God and Father of our Lord Jesus Christ...made us accepted in the Beloved. In Him we have redemption through His blood, the forgiveness of sins, according to the riches of His grace.* [Ephesians: 1:1, 6-7]

The apostolic word often turns to the thought of grace, and everything in Christianity is founded upon it. When this word wishes to remind us of the beginning of our salvation, it raises our minds to grace: *The grace of God that brings salvation has appeared to all men.* [Titus 2:11] When this word wishes to speak of our salvation as already accomplished, once again it references grace: *By grace you have been saved.* [Ephesians 2:5] When it wishes to show how the Church produced apostles, prophets, messengers of good news, pastors, teachers—all those whose work of service aided the salvation of other people—it points to grace as their teacher: "But to each one of us grace was given according to the measure of Christ's gift." When it wishes to strengthen Christians in their labors, it does so through grace: *You therefore, my son, be strong in the grace that is in Christ Jesus.* [2 Timothy 2:1] When it wishes to warn against sin, it does so using grace: *For sin shall not have dominion over you, for you are not* [Romans 6:14] *under law but under grace.* When it wishes to arrange our proper activity, it does so through grace: *Let your speech always be with grace, seasoned with salt, that you may know how you ought to answer each one.* When it wishes to greet and bless, it calls grace to its aid: *Grace to you and peace from God our Father and the Lord Jesus Christ.*

<small>Colossians 4:6</small>

<small>Romans 1:7</small>

Do you not see, O Christians, that in Christianity everything exists through grace, and nothing does without grace? And so, let every one of us strive to acquire grace for ourselves.

And may no one be flattered by the thought that in our salvation, grace accomplishes everything, and so we need not worry about our salvation any longer. No, you are fellow laborers with grace! Powerful and active grace is called and given to us to strengthen our weakness, to give courage in despair, to inspire our good deeds, not to increase our idleness or put us to sleep in inactivity. *We then, as workers together with Him also plead with you not to receive the grace of God in vain.*

<small>2 Corinthians 6:1</small>

But wait! Can grace, salvific for all mankind, truly be received in vain? Evidently, this may happen, since the apostle himself warns of it so assiduously. The grace of God is salvific in nature, but it will not save us without our cooperation. It is not received in vain when it is received with faith, when it is used and preserved faithfully, when we turn its riches to our life and actions. But it is received in vain when our faith grown weak, when our life and activity offend the grace of God, driving it away from us. Grace is that talent of the master of the house that enriches the good and faithful servant, but condemns the lazy and unfaithful servant, and is taken away from him. Thus, *We then, as workers together with Him also plead with you not to receive the grace of God in vain looking carefully lest anyone fall short of the grace of God.*

<small>2 Corinthians 6:1</small>

<small>Romans 12:15</small>

Let us also avoid another thought inimical to grace. Some think that they live well enough if they live according to nature alone, and so they do not labor to raise up the level of their life to live according to grace. This is a very dangerous thought. We have already shown that even original man, uncorrupted by sin, did not live by nature alone, but found blessedness in grace. That being the case, how can a life according to nature be good enough when it has been damaged by sin and not corrected by grace? Perhaps some of these people will quote the apostle to support their position: *Gentiles, who do not have the law, by nature do the things in the law.* This is my answer: would you find it pleasant to equate your life's dignity with that of the pagans? This is not how the Lord Himself judged, when He rebuked an imperfect life: *do not even the Gentiles do so?* Through this, He let us know that for His follower, for a perfect person, it is far too little to live by nature, as do the pagans. *Romans 2:14* *Matthew 5:37*

To fully define the meaning and worth of living by nature, we must look at the place that such a life has in the dominion of God and Christ. Though this dominion is limitless and immeasurable by us, we can still note certain aspects of its manifestation, and so theologians have, not without justification, noted that in the universal dominion of God and Christ there are three kingdoms: the kingdom of nature, the kingdom of grace, and the kingdom of glory. Entry into the kingdom of nature is opened to man by his natural birth, entry into the kingdom of grace is given through baptism, and the door into the kingdom of glory will be opened by the universal resurrection from the dead and the final judgment. The kingdom of glory is equally extensive as the kingdom of grace, but entry into it is only possible from the kingdom of nature through the kingdom of grace. Consequently, whoever lives only by nature will not pass on the last day, together with the entire kingdom of grace, into the kingdom of glory, but together with *both the earth and the works that are in it will be burned up.* In other words, there will be no place left for a life by nature without grace, except in the abyss. *2 Peter 3:10*

Brothers, you who have received gifts and promises of grace! Let us not be lazy in acquiring God's grace. Let us seek it by knowledge, and by a knowledge of our limitations and sinfulness, through prayer and study of the word of God, through communing of the mysteries of faith, through a sincere desire to live according to the commandments of Christ. Let us accept this grace with faith and a readiness to submit to its suggestions. Let us remain faithful and constant in following its direction. Grace itself will be our secret helper in our labors for her sake, and grace will crown our successes. According to the words of Apostle Paul, *Let us therefore come boldly to the throne of grace, that we may obtain mercy and find grace to help in time of need.* as the prophet promised us, *The Lord will give grace and glory.*

Glory to the Lord God, the Giver of grace, the Father, the Son, and the Holy Spirit, unto the ages of ages, Amen.

13

Obeying the Will of God

Homily on the Annunciation of the Mother of God
(1842)

"Then Mary said, 'Behold the maidservant of the Lord! Let it be to me according to your word." (Luke 1:38)

These are earthly words, but like heavenly ones, they are purer than tested silver, more desirable than gold, more precious than gems. Here is a treasure that the heavens sought on earth for five thousand years, for the revelation of which one of the closest intimates of the heavenly throne itself was sent.

Truly, the Archangel Gabriel not only brought the Virgin Mary a word of divine annunciation, but he sought to hear from her a word of accord as well. When he uttered only the words of greeting: *Rejoice, thou highly-favored one, the Lord is with thee; blessed art thou among women*, the annunciation concerning the Savior of the world was almost complete, because he called her the mother of the Lord. But since the Virgin was distressed, and remained si-

Luke 1:28

lent in thought, the angel continued and strengthened his word of greeting: *You will bring forth a Son…He will be great, and will be called the Son of the Highest… and of His kingdom there will be no end.* Now the annunciation has been completed on the part of the angel, but still he does not consider the work of his embassy done, because he does not yet hear the word that he awaits: "How can this be, since I do not know a man?"

<small>Luke 1:31-33</small>

Finally, he resolves the question: *The Holy Spirit will come upon you.* And then he hears the much-desired answer: *Behold the maidservant of the Lord! Let it be to me according to your word.* Behold, the sought-after treasure is revealed. A joyful annunciation from heaven grants a much-desired good news to earth. The heavenly embassy has completely accomplished its goal. *And the angel departed from her.*

<small>Luke 1:34
Luke 1:38
Luke 1:38</small>

What does this mean? What does it mean that the incarnation of the Son of God is preceded by the good news from heaven, and this annunciation is not only spoken by the almighty will of the Lord, but it also seeks a corresponding answer from His maidservant? Why does heaven so desire these earthly words: *Behold the maidservant of the Lord! Let it be to me according to your word!?* This was necessary both for the dignity of the mother of the Lord and for the accomplishment of the work on the incarnation of God the Word.

<small>Luke 1:38</small>

No one can doubt that to be chosen as mother of the Lord, one had to have the most exalted dignity possible on earth. But what is the nature of this dignity in a reasoning and free creature, if not in the pure and exalted movement of the mind and the free will? It was necessary to give them free rein and space so that the dignity of motherhood for God could be established, founded, and revealed in the Virgin Mary, for the sake of our consolation and our instruction. Her confusion at the exalted nature of the archangel's greeting was the movement of a profoundly humble soul. The reining in of this confusion within a silent contemplation further indicated her wisdom, firmness, and the calm greatness of her spirit. In her question: "How can this be, since I do not know a man?" she revealed her unchanging love for the purity of virginity. Finally, in the firmness of the conviction—"Behold the maidservant of the Lord! Let it be to me according to your word!"—we hear the expression of her obedient faith.

Apostle Paul teaches that *Christ may dwell in your hearts through faith*, having already come close to humanity and tasted of it through incarnation. But how much more perfect and stronger a faith was required of the Virgin Mary to allow for the incarnation of the Son of God within her, since He had not yet come near to humanity, both because of the unreachable heights of His divinity and the wall that had been raised by sin between mankind and God! And such a faith was indeed found in her, making it possible for her to exercise a pure and complete obedience, to answer a call to an inconceivable obedience with no shred of doubt, a call to an infinitely high obedience that would not lead to self-aggrandizement. And this obedience bent her soul under the shadow of the wing of the Holy Spirit; it united her will with the will of God; it opened her heart for the entrance of the power of the Most High. And eternal Light came to illumine her life, a light that was new not only for earth, but for heaven as well, a heavenly light on earth, an eternal light within time, a divine light within man, giving life to all who lived in the land of death. *And the Word became flesh and dwelt among us.* *Ephesians 3:17*

John 1:14

Wondrous are Thy works, O Lord! Wondrous are thy mysteries, O Theotokos! Who hears your quiet words, spoken in the secret room, closed for prayer? Who could predict what wondrous deeds your quiet words would lead to? Does the world even sense this moment, a turning point in its fate, during which the relationship between earth and heaven has been totally transformed? Does Rome even imagine, in its misguided dreams of universal dominion, that in one of its distant provinces, some unknown daughter of kings that calls herself a slave of the Lord has spoken a decree that will establish for the world a new, better, Most High Lord, while declaring for Rome a destruction of its proud and self-willed Lordship? Do the glorious oracles of the pagans even guess that the mouth of an obscure virgin uttered a prophecy that would force them all to fall silent, that would cast down the idols and their houses, that would put an end to blood sacrifices, that would destroy the blood-thirsty priests of the old order? Do the wise of this world have any idea that at the voice of a Hebrew woman Wisdom itself, unknown until then, descended from heaven, this being the Wisdom that will cast down the wisdom of the wise and reject the reason of the knowledgeable, but will reveal mysteries to children, mysteries that the wise cannot understand?

What am I saying? Jerusalem and the tribes of Israel, who from their ancestors knew and preserved God's promise concerning the great Redeemer and Peacemaker, and who *earnestly served God night and day* hoping to attain this promise—did they come to a knowledge of the fact that this day or this night, suddenly, they had reached the limit of the fulfillment of that promise, and that limit was placed in Nazareth? The scribes, who so many times read these words of Isaiah: *Behold, the Virgin shall conceive and bear a Son, and shall call His name Immanuel* (and equally as many times wondered at the content of that cryptic prophecy)—do they think that the one foreseen by the prophet had both come to know the meaning of the prophecy and was ready to fulfill it? In the entire world no one but she alone heard the annunciation of the archangel when it was given. And if someone indeed had heard the simple (it would seem) words of Mary's greeting— *Behold the maidservant of the Lord! Let it be to me according to your word*—who would have understood the entirety of their meaning, who would have sensed the wholeness of their power? For their meaning is lost in the abyss of the reason of God, and encompasses all of time and eternity; their power is united to the power of the Most High, and will transform the earth, and will fill the heavens.

Acts 26:7

Isaiah 7:14

Luke 1:38

Humble yourselves, you inquisitive questioners! Be amazed and rejoice, you humble witnesses! O arrogant mind of man, abandon the fragile instruments of your self-willed so-called wisdom, and come to love the free bondage of faith.

Obedience, by its very name, means to follow the one whom we hear, both in instruction and in command.[1] But in the exalted, essential, spiritual sense of the word, obedience means the subjection of human will, as created and contingent, to the will of God, which is creative and almighty. This meaning immediately reveals to us the responsibilities, benefits, and importance of obedience.

Is it the prerogative of the creature to rise up against its Creator? Is it right for an earthly slave to foment rebellion against the King of Heaven? A mind not yet fully darkened and a heart not yet fully hardened can understand the stupidity of this proposition. The mind and heart together declare the responsibility of human will to obey the will of God.

The will of God is unerring. Consequently, obedience to the will of God must preserve or deliver a person from all sins and delusions.

The will of God is all-good. Consequently, obedience to the will of God must lead a person to all good things.

Without its Creator, a creature is nothing. It is only something by the power of its Creator. And so, of what significance is the will of man if it does not attach itself to the will of God through obedience, if it cuts itself off by disobedience?

A long time ago, the first man was blessed. Why? Because he followed the all-good will of God. He then fell from the height of his blessedness. How? His will fell away from the will of God and plunged into the desires of the flesh. Disobedience, sin, death—these are the links of a single chain; whoever takes hold of the first link will always pull the final link toward himself as well.

---

1 St Philaret here is using a play on words that is untranslatable into English.

And if it were possible for him just to pull that final link to himself alone! But no: *By one man's disobedience many were made sinners. Just as through one man sin entered the world, and death through sin, ... thus death spread to all men, because all sinned.*

Romans 5:19
Romans 5:12

Was it necessary to heal miserable humanity of the universal disease of death? One might guess that an extremely necessary part of that medicine would be a quality the loss of which led to the beginning of the illness, that is, obedience. It was with this exact medicine that the heavenly Physician came to earth. Look at how He, being Himself free from illness, prepared within Himself the poultice for ailing mankind, and how he heals it— by obedience. *He humbled himself and became obedient to the point of death, even the death of the cross. By one man's obedience many will be made righteous. Though He was a Son, yet He learned obedience by the things which He suffered. And having been perfected, He became the author of eternal salvation to all who obey Him.*

Philippians 2:8
Romans 5:19
Hebrews 5:8-9

There is an obedience of love, an obedience of fear, and an obedience of faith. At first mankind lived through the sweet food of obedience to the all-good and all-perfect God in love. But after he poisoned this blessed life by eating of the forbidden fruit, he needed, as medicine, something not without bitterness, to be obedient in fear before God, the righteous Judge. Later, he could be obedient in faith to God and Christ, the Pardoner, Healer, and Savior, so that ultimately, depending on the degree of healing, man might once again eat the sweet and undying food of obedience through love. Therefore, the spiritual life of a person and a Christian depends entirely on obedience; this is why Apostle Peter calls Christians *obedient children.*

1 Peter 1:14

If anyone might think that to live by obedience is only possible for a deluded or hyperbolic imagination, not in actual reality, then call to mind the words of the unerring Teacher, Whose words have no delusion or hyperbole: *I am the vine, you are the branches. He who abides in Me, and I in him, bears much fruit; for without Me you can do nothing.* How can man be in Christ, and Christ

John 15:5

in man, in a union that is as complete as the branch and the vine? This is impossible without the obedience of faith, acquired by the free devotion of the heart and by the silent subjection of man's will to the almighty will of Christ. In this way, the obedience of faith actively pours into a person the power and life of Christ, which is why the actions of such a person are often much more exalted and mightier than what normal human beings are capable of.

He who does not understand this or continues to argue the point might say, "How can one even 'live' by constantly obeying the will of God? Can one possibly not leave any room for one's own will that he received from nature and that is impossible to eradicate? Can one even know the will of God every second of every day? Perhaps there were fortunate chosen ones to whom God sent his messengers, but even for the chosen such events were rare."

Whoever speaks like this does not prove that perfect obedience is impossible, but only that he does not practice it in deed, and so does not know how it works at all.

If you sincerely wish to know the will of God, you have an angel (i.e., messenger) who is close to you and ready to help. This is your conscience. Listen to your conscience; don't drown out its quiet voice by the noise of your passions, and the will of God will begin to reveal itself to you, and you will walk on the path of obedience.

There is a more reliable and more complete knowledge of the will of God, which you can find in the holy books, hear in the Church, see in the examples of the saints. Listen to them, and the will of God will become clearer to you, and obedience will become easier and more assured for you.

Everything in this world occurs by the direction of God's Providence, that, by the will of God and not the will of man. Prosperity comes, and it announces to you the will of God that you thank God. Disaster comes and announces to you God's will: be patient in suffering. And obedience may appear not only in your acting according to the will of God, but also in not acting contrary to the will of God, especially if you suffer by God's will without complaining. Find the courage to answer the messenger of this most exalted lot: "let it be according to thy word." But learn also to say, when you see your cross, *Not as I will, but as You will*, O Heavenly Father!

Matthew 26:39

Though truth and virtue are accessible to all, it is sometimes necessary to follow experienced guides in the doing of God's will through obedience. Thus, if you wish to succeed in spiritual obedience as much as you can, especially if you feel this need within you keenly, choose a special guide who is experienced in this art, who is blessed to this service, whose word is filled with life, illumined with prayer, and protected from delusion by humility. Subject your will to his for the sake of God, and the will of your heavenly God will descend on you from heaven, and your simple earthly obedience will reach the heights, as the God Who gives us pastors and teachers said to His own true and lawful guides (i.e., the apostles): *He who hears you, hears Me.*

Luke 10:16

Yes, it is true that obedience to God through obedience to man from ancient times was the purview not of regular life, but the life of monks in dedicated cloisters, in which they offered and continue to offer fruits for heaven and earth. But does that mean that this art, which is most appropriate in the silence outside the city, should then be considered unnecessary or pointless for the city?

The sons of this age desire greater and greater freedoms for their own will. And to what does this lead? Does it not lead to something that the prophet once predicted: *And it shall be: as with the people, so with the priest; as with the servant, so with his master; as with the maid, so with her mistress; as with the buyer, so with the seller; as with the lender, so with the borrower; as with the creditor, so with the debtor?* But what will occur in this time of limitless freedom for one's own will? The prophet explains: *Behold, the Lord makes the*

Isaiah 24:1

earth empty and makes it waste, distorts its surface and scatters abroad its inhabitants. In other words, God will allow self-will to punish itself with the same disorder that it produces.

And after all temporal punishments, do you know what will feed the fires of hell? Nothing else than self-will with its offspring, that is, sins. Set aside your own will, and hell will not find any food for itself within you. Accept the will of God, and you will accept heaven within yourself, even before heaven accepts you. Wherever the will of God is, there is heaven.

But is it easy to part with the freedom that is natural to man? But who is requiring you to part with your freedom? God gave you freedom so that you could freely make a choice between good and evil, between creation and the Creator, between yourself and God. If you choose yourself, creation, evil, then you will be bound in the prison of self-love. If you choose, and continually choose, good, God, and His will, then you will not lose, but rather establish and expand, your freedom. *Where the Spirit of the Lord is, there is liberty.*   2 Corinthians 3:17

But is it always easy to bend your free will? Sometimes it is difficult, sometimes it is easy, depending on whether you make it easy or hard. When you want to fulfill the will of your beloved father or mother, is it not easy for you to disregard your own will, is it not even pleasant to sacrifice it? Who is preventing you, through faith and love, from becoming a child of God, which would make sweet all obedience to the will of the Heavenly Father?

Our Father, Who art in heaven! Thy will be done in all of us! Amen.   Matthew 6:9-13

14

The Contemplation of Death

Homily on the Dormition of the Mother of God
(1844)

"Remember that death does not delay." (Sirach 14:12)

This is not a festal word for a feast day! This is perhaps what some of you are thinking, hearing me speak. Why do I lessen the brightness of the feast by a dark thought concerning imminent death?

But I do not think in this way, my brothers. Perhaps we are worthy of gloomy sights on bright days, or sad thoughts on feast days, according to our deeds, as the ancient word of God tells us: *I will make the sun go down at noon, and I will darken the earth in broad daylight; I will turn your feasts into mourning, and all your songs into lamentation.*

Amos 8:9-10

However it may be, the God-inspired wise man whose book the apostolic Church passed on to us for our instruction, gives us this counsel: *Remember that death does not delay.* It is unwise to

Sirach 14:12

reject the counsel of the wise man outright. And if you have not yet thought to contemplate your own death today, because this thought seems dark to you, that is, sad or frightening, I think the opposite: this is exactly the reason to contemplate death today, when death does not appear either terrifying or sorrowful, but joyful and triumphant, not the destroyer of life, but the guide to an eternal life, when it breathes on us not with the heavy breath of corruption, but the sweet-smelling savor of incorruption, when the closing of the doors of the tomb leads directly to the opening of the bright door of heaven, when, as we hear in the hymn, "life is betrothed unto death," when death, lest it disturb us even by the sound of its name, is transformed and renamed into "Dormition," that is, calmness similar to peaceful sleep, as well as "translation," that is, an easy passage from one place to another, from a place in the visible world to the state of the invisible world.

And what does it mean that death has become the object of a feast? We triumphantly announce the death of the Lord as salvific and life-giving to all of us. We triumphantly remember the death of the mother of the Lord also, for in the highest degree it is instructive and consoling for us. The Church, having shown us the tomb of Christ with the stone unrolled—empty save for the wrappings—announced that *Christ is risen from the dead, and has become the first fruit of those who have fallen asleep.* It is as though the Church is taking care that our faith and hope do not become exhausted with too long an expectation of the coming resurrection of all the dead, and so it leads us to a different tomb, also opened on the third day after burial, and it is also empty of the body that had been lain there. It is as though the Church is pointing at the tomb, saying, "Look! Here is an active, quick, evident experience of bodily resurrection, of which Christ was the first fruit. By the grace of her Son and God, her life on earth made her so ready for a life in heaven that her body was not containable by the earth

1 Corinthians 15:20

until the time of the general resurrection. Look at her empty tomb, and rejoice in your hope of life after the tomb."

Now the thought of death, darkened usually by fear and sorrow due to our weakness and imperfection, is illumined by the joy of hope in the power and grace of God. And so, we are able to think of our own deaths without distress. This is something we absolutely must do.

To prove that every person needs to think of his own death not too late in life, one can simply resort to rules of common sense. Common sense demands that we try as much as possible to prepare for future events that are especially important or difficult for us, and come up with all the necessary means and tools we can to encounter these events for our benefit, or at least to avoid dangerous outcomes. Before the time of planting, the farmer already thinks of the harvest, and so he makes his plans for the growing season in order to maximize his harvest. In the summer, he thinks of winter and does everything necessary to make sure that the abundance of the growing season will fill the hungry months of winter. That being the case, should not every person think even more of how he might properly plan the summer of his life, preparing everything necessary for the fruitless and severe seasons of death's winter? Should not every person do everything in his power to produce a good and abundant harvest in this temporal life, so that in the fateful time of the resurrection and the judgment, he might "reap," as St John of Damascus says, "the wheat of everlasting life" (Antiphons for tone 3, Octoechos), or, if you will, that he himself might germinate, grow, flower, and become the fruit of good wheat that the angels will then gather into the granaries of heaven?

But we often allow ourselves to be careless in how we follow the dictates of common sense, thinking that some small measure of negligence is not that serious a problem. Therefore, I must prove to you definitively just how necessary remembrance of death is for us, and how dangerous it is to disregard and lose that thought. It is so important that not only the temporal life of earth but the eternal life in heaven simply cannot exist without the thought of death. God created man in perfection, worthy of the all-good Creator; He led him into the garden of delights; He gave him the fruit of the tree of life for incorruption; He warned man against the dangerous tree of the knowledge of good and evil with a commandment not to eat of the fruit of that tree.

But this was not enough. Life in Eden was not without dangers. To preserve man, the thought of death was necessary as a stern protector. *For in the day that you eat of [the tree of the knowledge of good and evil] you shall surely die.* And while man thought of his own death, life in Eden was safe. But as soon as the ageless killer of men cunningly encouraged man's forgetfulness of death— *You will not surely die* - he immediately destroyed life in Eden through sin. Let us wonder, brothers, at the miracles of God's wisdom, and let us lament our own madness. The spirit of evil and envy, having plunged itself into death through departure from God, now plots death for man. But God foresees, and the thought of death, which was intended by the enemy to destroy, becomes, in the consciousness of man, a weapon to protect and to rescue. But man still seeks to avoid this thought of death, given him by God, in order to receive a momentary pleasure of the senses—he succeeds in getting rid of the unpleasant thought of his own death, but by doing so, he dies.

This is the book of the generation of man! What occurred with Adam occurred naturally with us as well, because we are the natural heirs of Adam, if grace and faith have not made us heirs of God and fellow-heirs of Christ. Will a person who has inherited an inclination to sin stand more firmly against temptation than a person who is yet sinless and is tempted for the first time, especially if he sets aside the one thing that could help him? Of course not! And so, if you strengthen and gird yourself with the wise and pious thought of your own death, as a vigilant guard, then without a doubt it will help you guard yourself, not from

Genesis 2:17

Genesis 3:4

Genesis 5:1

death (which by Adam's sin has entered the world and all mankind), but at least from everything that might make death terrifying, calamitous, in the fullest sense of death as annihilation. But if, disdaining and rejecting this remembrance of death, you run away from it to follow pleasures of the senses, earthly prosperity, the dreams of your own imagination, then finally, instead of fear at the thought of death also, which you have always avoided, you will suddenly and inevitably encounter the horrors of actual death, and not physical death alone (which is nothing but a shadow of actual death) but the second death as well, the spiritual, eternal death, where *their worm does not die and the fire is not quenched.*

<small>Mark 9:44</small>

This thought may naturally lead to a question: will remembrance of death, which God Himself placed as a guard against the entry of sin and death into the world, be powerful and beneficial enough when sin and death have already entered the world and rule in it? In answer to this question, the same wise man tells us: *With all your words, remember the time you will die, and you will never sin.* This is quite a saying! But whoever might protest that the elder is exaggerating reveals more about his own ignorance than of any hyperbole of the elder.

<small>Sirach 7:36</small>

If truly you remember your death whenever you speak, that is, if you recall and consider your death, judgment, and eternal fate whenever you think, speak, or act, thereby examining and testing every thought, word, and action in the light of eternity, then will not faith and grace give you more strength to preserve and save yourself than any power your inclination to sin might hold over you? Will not the seductive lure of sinful, sensual pleasure disappear if you counteract it with its opposite—the horror of corruption, the smell of rot, the worms in the grave, and finally the worm of hell that never sleeps? Does not the high-mindedness of the powerful vanish, or will not the hands of the avaricious who hungrily reach right and left to grab everything in sight simply drop to his sides, if he is shown the small square of land that will soon be the limit of his entire property and ownership? What fire of passion or impure desire will not dissipate before the power of the fires of Gehenna that never fade?

And if the thought of death is strong when it is armed with fear against evil, then it must be even more powerful when, illumined by hope, it works for good, for the strengthening of Christian ascetic labors. The salvific death of the God-Man gives a new meaning to the death of those who believe in Him, for now death is imbued with life. Through the wounds of the crucified Christ, the light of immortality streams into this temporal life and even into the region of death, and the sons of light awaken, and with ease they go to the difficulties of the deeds of light to which the Gospel calls them. You must crucify your flesh, and life by the Spirit, commands the Gospel. We obey, they answer, because *he who sows to his flesh will of the flesh reap corruption, but he who sows to the Spirit will of the Spirit reap everlasting life.* Die to the world, and live for God. So be it, for *the world is passing away, and the lust of it; but he who does the will of God abides forever.* Learn to be blessed even in exile for righteousness, in abuse and suffering for the sake of Christ. Even this is possible, for *the sufferings of this present time are not worthy to be compared with the glory which shall be revealed in us.* *Romans 8:18*

It seems to me, brothers, that I have given you cause to see the need, and the profound spiritual utility (and responsibility) to remember your own death. And so, it is perhaps best for me to fall silent now. But since we so often lose or set aside this beneficial remembrance to idly enjoy the goods of this temporal life, it is still necessary for me to show you how dangerous it is to forget the final things, even for the visible good things of this temporal life.

Jerusalem fell. Jeremiah sat over the ruins, lamenting over the reasons for its fall. What reason, do you think, did the prophet reveal for the disaster that befell Jerusalem? Perhaps there were more than one, but he mentioned that the most important was this: Jerusalem did not remember its own death. *She did not consider her destiny.* And so, when the usual flow of earthly, corruptive things does not inspire people to think of death, when they do not pay attention to the ones admonishing them with this short word of salvation, and sin increases, then God, who does not want the eternal death of a sinner, announces human mortality through much louder means for the spiritually deaf: through storms, calamities, and destructive events.

Brothers, fellow communicants in death and immortality, let us not set aside remembrance of death, so that we may not sin, but be saved, both temporally and eternally. Amen.

15

Martha's Earthly Cares

Homily on the Dormition of the Mother of God
(date unknown)

"Now it happened as they went that He entered a certain village; and a certain woman named Martha welcomed Him into her house." (Luke 10:38)

Blessed are you, obscure village with no name, for Christ, the Lord of glory, visits you. Blessed are you, humble home, for Christ, who is rich in mercy, enters under your roof. Zaccheus was perishing from the passion of avarice, but as soon as Christ visited his home, in that same day, *Salvation has come to this house.* Without a doubt, salvation will also come to the house of Martha that received the Savior.

Luke 19:9

Blessed also is every place and home that is found worthy of divine visitation. And how much more blessed is the man who worthily accepts this divine visitation. For if God, Who has no limits, can visit a place, surely He can establish a home inside a man's soul, there to visit him as well.

And what does it mean that the Church so often reads this passage from the Gospel to us? Does she not seek to arouse within us the desire to be visited by the divine? Does it not want to instruct us how best to attract God and how to worthily accept Him?

O great door of divine visitation, living city of the living God, first of Christ's habitations of the soul. Mary, more blessed than the one who chose the good part, for you chose, or rather you were chosen by, the complete and perfect good, you before all others, but for the sake of all others as well, all who sat in the valley of the shadow of death, who were visited by *the Dayspring from on high*, the most high Visitor of souls, Who not only visited, but lived in you, under your roof. As you leave us through the door of the tomb to visit Him and live with Him in His glory, leave the gates of your mercy open behind you, for our sake. Remind Him of the humble village in the crossroads of the world that still belongs to His kingdom. Remind Him of that small house in the valley of shadow that He built for Himself. May not our souls desire His visit in vain, may not the visitation of grace come to our souls in vain, for we are unable to greet it and accept it.

Luke 1:78

I hear what the soul says: O, if only God visited me with His grace-filled visitation! How could I fail to accept Him with reverence, with zeal, as is meet for the Visitor?

And yet, it would be much more accurate to say: O, if only you were capable, disposed, ready to accept worthily this grace-filled visitation! Is it possible that God will not visit you soon? For He, according to Job, *visit[s] him every morning and test[s] him every moment.*

But what prevents us from seeking God successfully and worthily accepting His grace-filled visitation? The Gospel reading concerning Martha who accepted the Lord into her house shows us, for our edification, that what most hinders this visitation is the cares of the world, or attachment to earthly things.

Martha did not desire and seek the visitation of Christ, and yet she received it. She received Him into her house, as the Gospel account tells us. She accepted Him with reverence, for she called him Lord and asked Him to command her sister, though she was in charge in her own home. *Lord, do You not care that my sister has left me to serve alone? Therefore, tell her to help me."* Martha accepted the Lord with zeal, for she assiduously prepared food for Him, just as Abraham did when the Lord visited him. "But Martha was distracted with much serving." Does this not lead us to think that she accepted Christ worthily and properly? But do not hurry with your conviction. Wait for the judgment of Christ. What does the Lord say? He does not accept the way that Martha greeted Him, and He primarily gives a blessing to Mary, who was the subject of Martha's complaining. What is the reason for this? In what way was Martha wrong? She was rooted in the cares of this world. *Martha, Martha, you are worried and troubled about many things.*

Luke 10:40

Luke 10:38-41

If a visitation that had already occurred through grace could have been damaged by the cares of life, or if the fruit of grace could have been more or less stolen by them, then will not these same cares hinder and harm those who have only just started to seek God and His grace?

If we carefully examine the account of the Gospel, we can distinguish several ways that the cares of this life may hinder a person from pleasing God and acquiring His grace, or from preserving grace already acquired. These cares divert and confuse. They cloud the eye of the mind in seeing the light of truth. They weaken the will in the choosing of the best.

Earthly cares divert and confuse. Look at Martha. Christ is in her home. He is the One after Whom many multitudes of people ran from villages into deserts just to see Him, just to hear His word. He is the One Whom *many prophets and kings have desired to see... and have not seen.* He is the One Whose day Abraham, who was acquainted with divine visitations, *rejoiced to see, and [when*

Luke 10:24

John 8:56

he] saw it [from a distance, he] was glad.* He is sought-after, desired by many, an intimate of Martha's, seen and heard by her. And what of her? Does she rejoice in His presence? I doubt it. She has other cares, other thoughts and emotions. She thinks and worries about flower and oil, bread and fish. It's almost as if the divine Teacher of truth, the Giver of grace, is not even there for her: *Martha was distracted with much serving.* Her anger at her sister, who did not share the same worries, finally forces her to turn to the Lord, but she only seeks His help to increase her own worries and diversions, even to lead others into them. *She approached Him and said, 'Lord, do You not care that my sister has left me to serve alone? Therefore, tell her to help me.'*

<small>Luke 10:40</small>

<small>Luke 10:40</small>

Are you aware, O Christian, that Christ the Lord either actively visits the house of your soul or stands at the door and waits for you to accept Him into your house? If this seems not possible, then it is not for me to convince you. Listen instead to His own words: *Behold, I stand at the door and knock. If anyone hears My voice and opens the door, I will come in to him and dine with him, and he with Me.* Will our answer be this: "We do not see you standing here, O Lord; We do not hear your knocking"? This is not an appropriate answer! The Lord does not deceive us; He is *found just when [He] speaks.* How can it be that He stands at the door, and we don't see Him? That He knocks, and we don't hear? Well, this is exactly what happened to Martha.

<small>Revelation 3:20</small>

<small>Psalm 50:4</small>

The cares of this world harry us from thing to thing, from work to work, from care to care, and since our cares for the most part are not as successful as we might want them to be, the failures distress us, the lack of help hurts us, the hindrance of others irritates us, and our desires and passions storm inside us like winds and waves. We rush hither and thither; We worry ourselves to our own detriment and danger. Our soul, attacked from without and within, does not notice the meek presence, does not hear the still, small voice of desired and salvific grace.

Earthly cares cloud the mind, occluding the light of truth and grace. This is the kind of clouding of the mind that the Lord rebukes in Martha when He tells her that *one thing is needed*. How did she not realize this truth by herself before the Lord's rebuke, if not to the full depth of its meaning, then at least on a surface level? Let us assume that she could not immediately rise to an understanding of how God, His word, and His kingdom are the one thing needed: *Man shall not live by bread alone, but by every word that proceeds from the mouth of God.* And again: *Seek first the kingdom of God and His righteousness, and all these things shall be added to you.* But having received Christ into her house, and thus having a certain knowledge of Who He is, how could she still not understand at least that One Who said, *My food is to do the will of Him who sent Me*, One Who fasted forty days and nights, One Who fed many thousands of people with a few breads—Christ did not need great variety of food and drink. How could she not guess that the One Who came into the world to *bear witness to the truth*, He Who called Himself the Bread of life, He Who called to Himself all who thirst, would not be pleased if He were offered an abundance of corruptible food, but would instead be pleased that she accepted from Him a food that does not corrupt, the water of life, a word of truth and salvation? No, she did not understand this, she who worried about many things. She didn't understand *because* she worried about many things, because her habit of worrying about earthly things had made the wings of her mind leaden, not allowing it to rise to spiritual contemplation.

Luke 10:42

Matthew 4:4

Matthew 6:33

John 4:34

John 18:37

Is it not the same with us, O Christians? Even if we sometimes find ourselves under the same roof as Christ, as occurs here in His Church, even though we almost see Him in the mysteries and we hear Him in the Gospels, still we do not know how to benefit ourselves and find pleasure in these good things. The Gospel is not understandable enough for us; the mysteries are obscure; and prayer is tiring. We do not know how to find the divine light within the Gospel, divine power within the sacraments, divine joy, heavenly blessedness within prayer. And why is spiritual knowledge and pure contemplation not given to us? Because earthly cares bind our mind, weighing it down with heavy earthly passions, covering it with the darkness of sensual, vain, impure thoughts. Our mind ceases being an eagle that should be soaring in the pure air, contemplating the sun of spiritual and divine truth, transforming into a mole that digs in the earth, in dust and the corruption of earthly, carnal deeds, abhorrent to the spirit.

Cares of this world weaken the will's ability to choose the good. *Mary has chosen that good part,* said the Lord. And what did she choose? Simply to sit at Jesus' feet and hear His word. How did the other sister not choose the same good part? Did she not want to be close to Jesus? Naturally, for this desire appeared within her even before Mary, when she accepted Jesus into her house. Why then did this seed of desire not equally grow and bring good fruit? Because it grew freely in Mary's heart, while in Martha's heart it was choked by the weeds of earthly cares. *Martha was distracted with much serving.* With the will of her spirit, she strove toward the Lord, and that caused Him to come to her; however, her inclination toward earthly cares distracted her from spiritually pleasing Him, and she did not acquire the intimacy of grace.

In all times and in all places, we can see how the desire for grace and salvation acts differently in human souls, depending on how free, full, and single that desire is, or whether that desire is divided into different actions, hindered, weakened by some desire of earthly nature and the habits of everyday life. We see people who for many years do nothing but continually start the work of their salvation, and do not rise up to perfection. They seek God for a long time, but they do not find Him. They see a certain dawn of grace within themselves, and they cannot wait for the day to start within their heart. Why is this? This is because they begin the work of salvation, but because of a passionate attach-

Luke 10:42

Luke 10:40

ment to the earthly and worldly, they do not completely abandon the works of perdition. They seek God, but they do not want to lose creatures. They seek the consolation of grace, but they do not want to part with the consolations of corrupted nature.

On the contrary, we also see those who later than others begin their service to God, but succeed faster than those who started earlier. The prodigal son takes the place of the elder brother in the grace of the Father. Magdalene rose from the depths of nearly hellish sin (since part of hell actually inhabited within her) to a level of equality with the apostles. Saul the persecutor transformed into Paul the apostle. *Tax collectors and harlots enter the kingdom of God before you,* for they desire to be natural sons of this kingdom. How are such miracles performed? By a firm, determined desire for grace and salvation that defeats and mortifies all earthly desires. *Matthew 21:31*

For this reason, the word of God powerfully rebukes the mixing of earthly cares and desires with those of the spirit. *No one can serve two masters.* And so, if you are a slave of earthly cares, then how can you be a slave of God at the same time? *For where your treasure is, there your heart will be also.* If your treasure, that is, what you desire, love, what you follow with a passion, is found here on earth, then how can it be that your heart will be found in the heavens with God? *No one engaged in warfare entangles himself with the affairs of this life, that he may please him who enlisted him as a soldier.* Thus, if you acknowledge in your heart that your spiritual disposition is still firmly tied to the earthly, how can you flatter yourself with the thought that you are pleasing to the Champion Leader Christ Who has defeated the world? *Matthew 6:24* *Matthew 6:21* *2 Timothy 2:4*

Whoever is attentive to the salvific paths of God's Providence will notice, not without fear, that sometimes God Himself, preparing man for His special visitation or gift of grace, tears apart the bonds that tie him to the earthly and worldly with a mighty hand. What amazing visitations did God make Abraham worthy of! But what horrifying deprivations did he demand of him as well! *Get out of your country, from your family and from your father's house, to a land that I will show you.* Why, it would seem, did God not simply come to Jacob with His visitation and blessing when Isaac blessed Him in his own home? But no, Jacob is taken from the embraces of his pious parents; in danger, without help or guide, he is led to an unknown place, where he bent his exhausted head to a desert rock for comfort, and here is where he found for himself the house of God and the visitation of God and the mighty blessing of God. What path led Joseph to the grace of seeing men's hearts, to the glory of a savior of a nation? The path of Egypt, the path of wandering, slavery, and prison. When and how did God reveal Himself the most to the nation of Israel? When it was taken out forcibly from Egypt and was still tied to the promised land, in a place where the earthly could not attract them with anything passing, but in all things directed their thoughts to heaven.

What are we waiting for when we delay our rejection of earthly passions? Are we waiting for God Himself to pull us toward Him with a mighty hand, as He did with Abraham? But is this not brazen, or even deluded, to have such an expectation? Or perhaps we are waiting for God to lay his *strong hand* on us through the path of unexpected deprivations, troubles, sorrows, defeats, for Him to scatter the glittering chains in which the world and the flesh hold us? But is it necessary to wait for this, or even to be ready for its coming? Is it proper for reasoning and free creatures to wait, like irrational animals, to be *harnessed with bit and bridle, else they will not come near you?*

Let us stop, brothers, delaying and putting off. Let us instead hurry to throw off the burden of passionate attachments, whose weight we perhaps do not even acknowledge, because we have never tried to walk without it. In the daily work of our life, let us set aside excessive worry, busyness, vanity, anything that comes from indiscriminate desires or incomplete assessment of things, from a lack of faith in God and hope in His Providence. As much as we are called primarily to the works of God, to prayer, to instruction in the word of God, to spiritual labors in acquiring the grace of God, "let us lay aside all earthly cares," so that we may accept in our souls and hearts the visitation of the Lord, and in Him come to know and find the "one thing needed," that "good part" that will not be taken away from us either in time or in eternity. Amen.

16

Following the Footsteps of the Mother of God

Homily on the Dormition of the Mother of God
(1845)

> "When Jesus therefore saw His mother, and the disciple whom He loved standing by, He said to His mother, 'Woman, behold your son!' Then He said to the disciple, 'Behold your mother!' And from that hour that disciple took her to his own home." (John 19:26-27)

Today it is not the disciple of the crucified Jesus who takes His orphaned mother into his small home. It is the Lord Jesus Himself, who rules in the heavens, who takes His most blessed mother into His home, into the many mansions of His Father's house, into blessed contemplation and communion with glory that He had with the Father before the world ever was.

Today He does not give her a single disciple as a foster son, that she might be comforted by his filial service, but He gives her all His disciples, all believing Orthodox Christians, as her sons and daughters, so that they might benefit from her maternal care.

As she departs for the heavenly Church, she miraculously gathers to herself all the representatives of the Church scattered about the earth. And by doing so, she gives a sign that her union with the faithful on earth not only is not cut off by her departure, but from this moment becomes even stronger and more active, and that the grace that abides in her, which for so long was concealed by humility, now reveals itself from her tomb to fill the whole Church with her glory, in fulfillment of her early prophecy, which at one point seemed completely unlikely: *All generations shall call me blessed.* Luke 1:48

Such is the fate of the most holy ever-Virgin, in her Dormition to the earthly, temporal life, and in her awakening to the heavenly, eternal life.

What path did she take to reach such heights of blessedness and glory? This question is worthy of examination and study not only for vain curiosity, but for a proper love for salvific teaching. For, although the fate of the most holy Theotokos, in its uniqueness, is without precedent, still, considered generally as the fate of a soul that has acquired perfect blessedness, this fate is the consequence of those powers, dispositions, actions, and labors that lay a universal path to salvation for all humanity.

It would not be easy to look at the entire path of the life of Mary, for it was mostly concealed by her reserve and the silence of the evangelical history. However, we have often pointed out certain events from that life for the attention and emulation of the faithful on other feasts of the Mother of God. Today, let us focus on one exalted moment of this path, which the Gospels do reveal to us, the better to see at least part of this path that opens before us like a view from a hill.

This hill, to which I now direct your gaze, is Golgotha Mount. There, during the hours that saved the entire race of humanity, all creation was terrified. As universal salvation was being accomplished, it was not recognized even by those chosen from the race of man, and universal terror was sensed even by the inanimate stones, when, as the prophet put it, *life hung in doubt before the eyes of men*. People saw nothing but suffering and death at the spectacle, and all, even those who were Christ's enemies, were torn apart by empathy and compassion, *beat[ing] their breasts* as they departed that place. There, at the foot of the cross of the crucified Jesus, stood His most blessed mother.

Deuteronomy 28:66

Luke 23:48

What wondrous light did these dark hours of Golgotha pour into her internal life! Let us remember that during the time of the suffering of Christ, all who were close to Him were in immediate danger of their lives. This is evident from His own words, when He gave Himself into the hands of His enemies: *If you seek Me, let these go their way*. But how could He have demanded amnesty for His disciples from those who refused to spare Him? This is how: by the almighty power of His divine word, which had, immediately before this moment, wondrously revealed itself when it cast to the earth the entire assembled mob with their spears, when He said, *I am He*. When the evangelist described this scene, he added that the Lord had previously predicted this, and this was a fulfillment of His prophecy: *That the saying might be fulfilled which He spoke, 'Of those whom You gave Me I have lost none.'*

John 18:8

John 18:6

John 18:9

This means that the Lord's friends, during His suffering, were not only in extreme danger, but would have perished if He had not prevented this with an act of Providence. Still, *all the disciples forsook Him and fled*" from the danger, from their imminent death. Even Peter, who seemed to have a resurgence of courage when he followed Jesus into the courtyard of the high priests, did not withstand the testing. Even John ran, though his love, it must be said, quickly returned his manliness to him. At that point, he followed His beloved Teacher all the way to the cross. But the mother of the Lord we see neither in fear, nor in flight. We only see her standing *by the cross of Jesus*. And so, do you not see that she stands there in spirit, hovering above the universal fear, above her own personal danger, above the manliness of the apostles?

Matthew 26:56

John 19:25

Whoever would say that it was natural for the most pure Virgin Mother to strive for nearness to Her suffering Son, more than all others, would only show himself to be a weak exegete of her standing on Golgotha. If we were to consider merely maternal, natural love, then how would we expect her heart, her senses, her very life to react at seeing the sufferings of her Son—the sight of which caused even His enemies to beat their breast, the earth itself to shudder, the stones to tear themselves apart, and the sun to hide its gaze? No, natural love does not explain her standing there; on the contrary, it makes it all the more unlikely that she stood at the cross, without being struck down by terror, without abandoning herself to impatient weeping, without casting herself into an unfeeling stupor. And so, what can explain this exalted courage and steadfastness of spirit? Nothing other than her profound trust in the judgments of God, her faith in the divine power of her Son, which she knew better than anyone from the known and secret miracles of her entire life, from her knowledge of Christ's mysteries, which she understood before anyone else and preserved more perfectly than anyone else in her heart. Faith, trust beyond trust, love—not natural love only, but love exalted into spiritual and divine perfection—these fed her internal source of live-giving light, which *the darkness did not comprehend*, which the horrors of Golgotha and death itself did not still. By the guidance of this unwavering light, she walked into the revealed light and joy of the resurrected Christ. *John 1:5*

Come, O Christian soul, look attentively at the footprints of the queen of Heaven, for her footprints are a path to God for you, as it is written, *her companions who follow her, shall be brought to You.* *Psalm 44:14* Do not run away from the thought of Christ's sufferings, neither by inattentiveness, nor by your pride of mind, nor by your weakness in faith, for there is no surer path to salvation than through Golgotha and the cross.

Approach the crucified Lord with faith, hope, and love; place yourself firmly before Him with pious contemplation and prayer.

In this you will find a light for your own path, and strength for your own travels.

Ahead lie dangers, calamities, sorrows, either directly to you or your dear ones. When they undermine your courage and they drain away your patience, remember the mother of the Lord who stood at His cross. By looking at her endless and innocent sorrow, her unconquerable courage and patience, you will arouse within yourself a degree of her own courage and patience, though it only be a small fraction, though your own sorrows are likely not innocent. As you contemplate her sufferings, ask her help from the treasure house of the spiritual fortress of grace, for she herself increased those talents by faithful and blessed activity in her own life.

Let us also look how from the height of Golgotha our eyes can see a certain less exalted, but no less worthy path to emulate, along which the most blessed Mary walked toward eternal glory.

The Gospel tells us that our Savior, seeing His mother and His beloved disciple John at His cross, *said to His mother, 'Woman, behold your son!' Then He said to the disciple, 'Behold your mother!' And from that hour that disciple took her to his own home.* In these words, we see the love of the divine Son for His earthly mother, who He wishes not only to console after the loss of her Son, but as it were to return Himself back to her in a different person, and, in preserving the honor of her virginity, to also reward the virginity of His beloved disciple. And so, he chooses the virginal John to be the foster son of the ever-Virgin Mother. But we would not have guessed what He meant in these words, if the beloved disciple—who doubtless knew better than anyone else the heart and mind of His teacher—did not explain them by fulfillment. What fulfillment? "And from that hour that disciple took her to his own home."

This shows us that the adoption of John as a son called him, among other things, to take care of her housing and the needs of her earthly life, and that, consequently, in this arrangement she had no personal property of her own. It is proper to think that her love and faith in her divine Son inspired her to always be, as much as possible, near to Him in all His wanderings through cities, villages, and deserts. Just as he was *a stranger to [his] brothers*, so she was as well. He *has nowhere to lay His head*, and neither did she.

Psalm 68:9
Matthew 8:20

Thus, the most pure Virgin, walking in her inner life along the path of faith and complete trust in the will of God, walked in her outer life by the path of rejection of earthly attachments, earthly goods and pleasures, a path of simplicity, non-acquisitiveness, willful deprivation, offering all these things in sacrifice to faith and God.

Look, O Christian, at these blessed footprints, and be attentive that the path of your own life might not depart too far from her steps.

And from that hour that disciple took her to his own home. Do you see? The mother of the King of heaven is not in bridal chambers of luxury, not among many servants who await her every command. No, she walks the thoroughfares in the company of a single fisherman, to live in a small house not her own, without glory, without brilliance, in silence, in simplicity, taking advantage only of that comfort and service that might be offered by the pious zeal of a poor and solitary fisherman.

John 19:27

Look at this, and learn not to value riches highly, not to hanker after pleasures, not to rush after glory, not to be deluded by luxury. Instead, learn to love simplicity and quiet ordinariness, not to disdain poverty when you see it in others, and not to fear it if it visits you, nor to be ashamed of poverty if it decides to come live with you.

Nor do I take away from you the earthly goods that Providence has granted you. No, dispose of them with gratitude to God, with generosity to your neighbors, with humility. But be attentive to yourself and to your heart; do not become attached to riches, but seek to relinquish them in any way possible.

If you find yourself on the path to heaven, as you should, then don't burden yourself too heavily with things of this world, lest you lose your strength and fall without completing your journey.

Our Savior revealed to us a wonderful, though terrifying—and without a doubt completely true—law concerning our fate, when He said, *Where your treasure is, there your heart will be also.* This treasure is what captivates our mind, what our inclination strives towards with the strongest force. Therefore, we ourselves determine our own fate. We bear it within ourselves in the inclinations that dominate us. If our treasure, the subject of our dominating inclination, is found, and remains, on this earth, in earthly goods and acquisitions, pleasures and glory, then our hearts will remain here below. And wherever our heart it, there our life is, there our fate is: it will not be found in heaven.

Luke 12:34

Let us choose and prepare for ourselves a better lot. Let us dispose ourselves in such a way that our treasure will not be found on this earth. *Lay up for yourselves treasures in heaven.* Constantly direct your thoughts, your desires, your love to heaven. And then, your heart will be there also, along with your life, your joy, your blessedness, by the grace and abundant mercies of the Father, the Son, and the Holy Spirit unto the ages of ages. Amen.

Matthew 6:20

17

The Seed of the Woman

Homily on the Annunciation of the Mother of God
(1846)

"Then Mary said, 'Behold the maidservant of the Lord! Let it be to me according to your word.'" (Luke 1:38)

How simple these words of the most holy Virgin Mary seem, but how much wisdom they contain! How much do they reveal! What depth of humility do they demonstrate! What height of faith! What bright purity of heart! What power and limitless potential is held in these words!

The work that will occur after the annunciation of the archangel and the answer of Mary is the salvific work of the incarnation of the Son of God. Today, it begins. This work waited for several thousand years (in human terms) until the Virgin's agreement allowed it to begin.

I said in human terms, because in divine terms, this work began before time and continues into eternity. As the Apostle Paul said, *Blessed be the God and Father of our Lord Jesus Christ, who has*   Ephesians 1:3-4 *blessed us with every spiritual blessing in the heavenly places in Christ, just as He chose us in Him before the foundation of the world, that we should be holy and without blame before Him in love.*

But it is not for us to rise to this heavenly height of contemplation. It is enough for us to reach only to the inception of the mysteries of Christ, revealed in earthly Eden.

When the cunning seducer managed to delude the first people and destroy their Edenic blessedness, when death encroached upon man following sin, then the equally merciful and just God, having stopped it, willed to sow in perishing mankind a new seed of life and salvation. In a wondrous manner, even in the word of His condemnation, He partially hid and partially revealed the mystery of His mercy, when he spoke these words to the serpent: *I will put enmity between you and the woman, and between your seed and her Seed; He shall bruise your head.*

Genesis 3:15

In other words: you, the spirit of evil, think that because you deluded the woman, as the weaker vessel of mankind, and through her inclined Adam to sin, that you will have the race of mankind as your slave for all time? You are mistaken. From among those who you defeated, battle will rise against you; it will continue throughout the generations of men; finally, the One, Who before time hid behind the cryptic name "the seed of the woman," "He shall bruise your head," He shall defeat you convincingly; he shall destroy your authority, which is the domain of sin and death, and consequently He will return to man the holiness and life, safe from death, that was stolen from him.

To better understand the mystical meaning of the name "seed of the woman," we can start with the strangeness of the name itself. "Seed," without a doubt, indicates inheritance, or a certain person in that inheritance. But what does "seed of the woman" mean? In the customs of all humanity, the seed always refers to the man, not the woman, and generational naming is taken from the father or forefather, never from a mother or foremother.

And so, what does this strange name, "seed of the woman," even mean? Either it points to something that doesn't exist in nature or it points to a mystery that surpasses nature, a birth that leads nature itself to ask the question: "How can this be, since I do not know a man?", a question which grace shall answer thus: *The Holy Spirit will come upon you, and the power of the Highest will overshadow you.* This is the miraculous birth of the Son of a woman without a man, the birth of Christ, the God-Man, from a Virgin. *Luke 1:34-35*

That Adam himself understood the mystery of the Lord's saying concerning the seed of the woman can be noted from the fact that after this, he gave his wife a new name that would seem to be completely untimely and inappropriate, if it did not refer also this same mystery: *And Adam called his wife's name* Eve (literally, "Life"), *because she was the mother of all living.* Life, the mother of all who live—such names would be appropriate for a foremother in an incorrupt state, since then she certainly would become the mother of all who would subsequently live and would never give birth to anyone mortal, but in the garden, she was not given these names. She was simply called "woman." So why, after the fall into sin, when she would only give birth to mortals, being the source of death for all her progeny, why did Adam call his wife "Life, the mother of all who live"? Was he ridiculing her? No, of course not. It was rather a consolation for her and himself, when Adam saw her through God's prophecy of the coming "seed of the woman," who would destroy the head of the serpent. I will be a father as well, he thought to himself, but I will not be the father of true life. That calling is reserved for a woman without a man, and so I will call her: "Life, the mother of all who live," not by her nature, but because at some future time, from Eve will be born a Virgin, and from that Virgin will be born the One Who is *Truth and Life,* the One Who has the power to raise all who died into eternal life. *Genesis 3:20*

John 14:6

From what I have said here, I hope that you can see, brothers, that the annunciation of the salvific incarnation of the Son of

God was begun not by the archangel in Nazareth, but by God Himself in the garden of Eden, for there God announced His will concerning the victorious "seed of the woman," that is, concerning the birth of Christ the Savior from a Virgin.

But if God's will concerning the incarnation of the Son of God was already established, even announced, in the first days of the world's existence, then why was it not fulfilled for so many centuries? I do not dare to ascribe to myself the ability to give a full answer to this question. *For who has known the mind of the Lord?* However, we may say this without fear, that the reason for the delay was not found in God. *His word shall run swiftly. For He spoke, and they were made; He commanded, and they were created.* For the Eternal One, everything is always ready. For the Almighty, everything is always possible. Creation delays by necessity because it moves within certain limitations of time that cannot be hastened. In free creatures, there is not enough readiness to accept the action of God when in human will there is no correspondence with the will of God. It is especially difficult to prepare such readiness in fallen creatures who must be raised up again and re-created. For this reason, the word of God concerning the Savior of the world flashed over mankind like lightning in the first moments after their darkening by sin, and it continued countless times to shine through subsequent revelations, but the darkness of sin continued to weigh down mankind, and centuries, even millennia, needed to pass before truly *the Word became flesh* and *God was manifested in the flesh.*

During this long interval, the blessing by which God the Father blessed us in the heavens in Christ before the formation of the world rose like a lightning-bearing cloud over the earth, but in the meantime the secret work of Providence sought out and prepared one blessed among women, who might be able through her purity to attract the divine lightning, to accept it, fit it inside her, keep it there, not being burned by the fire of divinity in the process, thereby through herself essentially assimilating the blessing of Christ to the whole of mankind.

Do you perhaps think that it is very easy to accept the blessing of God, even if it comes in the form of a high calling? That is not the case. Look at the experience of Sarah. The Lord said to Abraham concerning her: *I will bless her and also give you a son by her.* Do you see that he prepares her beforehand, in her absence, so that she might prepare herself to the actual acceptance of the gift? And so what? Even after this preparation, when the promised blessing is firmly given in her presence, she, it seems, was found to be not sufficiently capable of accepting it: *Sarah laughed within herself.* No matter how innocent that mirth might be, it still seems to me to be inappropriate before the word of God, before the face of God. And so, the Lord rebuked her, and she then followed her first mistake with a second, as though she might actually hide from the Omniscient One: *But Sarah denied it, saying, 'I did not laugh,' for she was afraid.*

Genesis 17:16

Genesis 18:12

Genesis 18:15

However, let us not demean Sarah, who accepted her blessing as much as she was able, and she became an early image of the one *blessed among woman*, for she gave birth after the withering of her womb (though she did not do it without a man) to an image of Christ, Isaac, who later would show Abraham, in his own sacrifice, the future day of the sacrifice on the cross.

Luke 1:42

But let us offer a just tribute to the reverent and joyful wonder of the one blessed among women, the most pure Virgin Mary, who was found completely prepared for the greatest of Gods' blessings that suddenly appeared to her, and by that readiness helped accomplish the incarnation of the Son of God, which had been prepared and expected for such a long time.

Righteous Sarah responded to the news of her giving a miraculous (but not supernatural) birth to Isaac with bewilderment; a similar announcement concerning the coming birth of the Forerunner of the Lord produced doubt in righteous Zachariah. That being the case, how much greater than the righteous is the most holy Virgin Mary, for she accepted the annunciation of the supernatural, inconceivable, divine birth from her of Christ the Savior with no bewilderment, without any doubt. It is true that before this annunciation, at the beginning of the heavenly visitation, she was disturbed for a few moments, and remained silent in thought. Perhaps this was because she did not immediately recognize the heavenly messenger and, being wise in the spirit, she bowed her head to the rule that applies to us as well: *Test the spirits, whether they are of God.* After all, it was a very unusual greeting. In any case, this confusion was before exalted praise, and as such is no sign of a lack of worthiness. What is far more amazing is that when she heard the incomparably more powerful word of annunciation— *The Holy Spirit will come upon you...You will conceive in your womb and bring forth a son...that Holy One who is to be born will be called the Son of God... of His kingdom there will be no end.*—she no longer shows any confusion at all. This great mystery does not incite her to test the spirit anymore, nor does the unheard-of nature of the mystery stop her from accepting the mystical annunciation.

1 John 4:1

Luke 1:31-35

This incomparably exalted calling does not remove her from the depths of humility. The one called to be the mother of the Lord sees herself, as before, only a handmaid of the Lord. The opposite is also true: her profound humility does not hinder her from believing in the incomparably exalted nature of her calling. We do not see any battle between these apparent contradictions, no vacillation of thoughts or feelings. As pure and quiet water accepts the light of the sun without hindrance and answers with a reflection, so the soul of the most holy Virgin quietly and purely accepts the word of divine revelation, and answers with a word of obedience: *Behold the maidservant of the Lord! Let it be to me according to your word.*

Luke 1:38

This is enough for the attentive. Do not demand any more, O you who are vainly curious. *My sister, my bride, is an enclosed garden; an enclosed garden, a sealed fountain.* This is what the Holy Spir-

Song of Songs 4:12

it said concerning His bride, the first among virginal and pure souls, the divinely-blessed Virgin Mary. We have seen enough with the eye of the mind, as through a trellis gate, into her mystical vineyard. We have seen a few flowers of her virtues; we have smelled the sweet savor of her grace. Now it is necessary to prevent our thoughts from becoming like certain pestilent insects that harmfully buzz around flowers or defile their beauty by their presence. But let us instead emulate the bees that approach the flowers with a humble song, and without defiling with their touch, extract from the flowers their sweet and healthy food.

Reverently penetrating into the mystery of the incarnation of God the Word, let every Christian soul cry out with the Church of Christ: "Let us worthily praise the pure one, O people, the Mother of God who accepted the fire of the divinity into her womb without being consumed." Let us learn from her how to properly respond to God's visitation, how to accept divine mysteries.

If you encounter greetings and praise, especially if they are exalted and spiritual, then be careful lest you indiscriminately accept it and be pleased with the praise, for you will not always be able to easily determine whether the praise is offered by a messenger of truth. It is permissible, in such cases, to be confused by this greeting; however, be careful to restrain your confusion, and in silence to call upon God for help, lest you be deluded by false praise or lest true praise be turned into the poison of self-love and arrogance.

When you hear the annunciation of divine dogmas and grace-filled sacraments, be careful not only of the unbelief of Thomas, but also the lack of faith of Zechariah, and the bewilderment of Sarah. Remember the words of the archangel: *For with God nothing will be impossible.* Do not allow your faith to waver. *Luke 1:37*

If a sign of providence, which is sometimes sent in the clothing of a chance occurrence, announces to you a pleasant, exalted, glorious lot, it should not be difficult for you to say, "Let it be according to your word." But do not forget later to avoid looking at yourself with pleasure as though you were the lord of many things and many people. Instead, look at yourself always with humility, for you are only a slave of the universal Master: "Behold, the servant of the Lord."

Insofar as it is possible that you may receive a sign that is not pleasant, but that threatens with sorrow, deprivation, humiliation, prepare yourself prudently to accept even this with grace. Do not complain against it, and do not cry out impatiently. What virtue is there in eagerly accepting pleasant things? But to accept sorrow calmly, submitting to the will of God—this is a labor, this is a virtue, this is the pledge of a reward to come! Train not merely your lips, but your heart, to freely speak the words of the Savior Who prepared for the cross: *Father...not My will, but Yours, be done.*

Luke 22:42

See and know that this joyful annunciation is the beginning of our salvation, but a bitter cross approaches to complete that salvation, to the eternal glory of the resurrection. May our Lord Jesus Christ make us worthy of that resurrection, by the grace of God the Father and the Holy Spirit. Amen.

18

The Icon of the Dormition

Homily on the Dormition of the Mother of God
(1846)

In the *Exact Exposition of the Orthodox Faith* of St John of Damascus, we find the following discussion of the holy icons: "But seeing that not everyone has a knowledge of letters nor time for reading, the Fathers gave their sanction to depicting these events [which have been accomplished in the incarnation of the Son of God] on images as being acts of great heroism, in order that they should form a concise memorial of them." (Book 4, chapter 16). Accordingly, to look with attentiveness at the holy icons means the same thing as reading Scripture. Thus, it would be correct to assume that one can assimilate knowledge from icons just as well as from books. And though the holy Damascene refers such knowledge to those who are unlettered, we who do know the Scriptures a bit should not puff ourselves up above those who do not, nor should we consider it excessive for us to learn in a way that is beneficial for those. As St Paul said, *Do not set your mind on high things, but associate with the humble.*

Romans 12:16

Those who have zeal to study the mysteries of the most holy Virgin Theotokos from the Holy Scriptures know that they do not speak much about her. And we cannot complain about this, for those holy books keep mostly silent also about the incarnate Son of God, not because of any desire to obscure, but by necessity, as the evangelist who completed the work of the Synoptics himself admitted: *And there are also many other things that Jesus did, which if they were written one by one, I suppose that even the world itself could not contain the books that would be written.*

John 21:25

And so, we consider it to be correct if today, in contrast to other situations when we exercise our strength (or rather our weakness) in examining the Scriptures, we instead read something about the most holy Virgin in the icon of the Dormition. The model for this icon, according to a special providence of God, was brought from Constantinople into Kiev. St. Peter[1], with his holy right hand, copied the version we have here, without a doubt, not for the pleasure of our earthly eyes, but for the sake of our spiritual contemplation.

The first part of the icon, nearest to the viewer, is simple. We see the pure body of the most pure Virgin after her soul departed, lying on a bed. The assembly of the apostles raises this bed and carries it to the place of burial. St. Peter the apostle offers her homage by swinging a censer, though her body in and of itself fills the inner senses of those who approach her with faith with much more sweet-smelling savor. If one could express the sounds of music with paints and brushes, then we would hear the apostolic funeral dirge, in which, as St Dionysius the Areopagite wrote, "the brother of the Lord James and Peter and all the heads of the Churches, who had come together to see the life-giving and God-accepted body, sang of the limitlessly powerful goodness of divine weakness," that is, the goodness of the

---

1 The text does not make it clear who this hierarch Peter is, other than he is a hierarch of some kind and is a canonized saint.

Son of God, Who accepted the weakness of human nature (save sin) in His incarnation. (*On the Divine Names*, chapter 3)

What does this icon remind us of? What does it teach us? It reminds us of the threatening law of death. It teaches us to think in good time of how we will respond to this law.

For dust you are, and to dust you shall return, said the Heavenly Judge to the forefather of the human race. And how inexorable is this judgment! *Death reigned from Adam to Moses, even over those who had not sinned according to the likeness of the transgression of Adam*, as well as over those who sinned in some other way, and even over those who simply did not purify themselves of the sin of the forefather. However, the most blessed Mary, even before she became the Mother of God, according to the text of the sticheron sung on Annunciation, "was purified beforehand by the Spirit," to be a worthy vessel of the incarnation of the Son of God. From the time of the incarnation, since her body and soul both, without a doubt, became the house of God, she became, in her dignity as the Mother of the Lord, more exalted than the Cherubim and Seraphim. And in spite of this exalted dignity, she still bows her head to the law of death, though only in appearance; she descends into the earth, though, it must be said, only for a short time. How could this have been allowed?

Genesis 3:19

Romans 5:14

It was allowed because of her humility, according to which she did not want to remain completely untouched by death, especially when her own divine Son tasted death. Truly, it was allowed by providence for us, the children of corruptible Adam, who do not labor to transform ourselves into the image of the heavenly Adam. It was permitted for us, the children of the sinful, who ourselves are sinners unpurified, so that we, looking at the tomb of the most pure Mother of Life, might come to the firm knowledge that all who are less than she are in danger of perdition, as the apostle said so vividly: *The righteous one is scarcely saved*. It was allowed so that we might profoundly sense the pow-

1 Peter 4:18

er of the subsequent conclusion of St. Peter: *If the righteous one is scarcely saved, where will the ungodly and sinner appear?*

Even in a life renewed by grace, in a life of great holiness and purity, the arrow of death still finds a vulnerable spot in human nature. And so, what will happen to a person who did not labor in the renewal of grace, who lived carelessly in his corrupted nature? What will happen to a soul when, of its own sinful inclination, attracted by the passions, it leads itself into the fires of hell, having cultivated within itself the seeds of spiritual death? What will happen with the body, which, in addition to its natural tendency toward corruption, not only refuses healing by medicine from above, not only fails to be renewed by the grace of life, but also adds to itself new, evil seeds of further corruption and death from a sinful soul, from its destructive passions, from its uninhibited desires, from various forms of intemperance and misuse of the senses?

Let us labor attentively and untiringly, brothers, to correct, purify, and raise up our activity by the commandments of God and the power of faith, striving from the visible, natural life to the mystical life of grace. May our temporary life be the source of eternal life, lest our temporary death become a threshold for us to death eternal. May our tomb be a door to heaven!

Let us once again turn to the examination of this icon. The second part is not so simple as the first. Over the deathbed and the lifeless body of the most pure Virgin, this icon represents Christ the Savior Himself, holding her soul in his hands. The soul has a childlike aspect, which indicates, without a doubt, a birth into a new, heavenly life. The Scriptures do not say that this was visible to the physical eyes of all who witnessed her Dormition. Therefore, we should assume that the iconographer here indicated in visible form something that belongs to the invisible world, uniting that which is visible with that belongs to spiritual contemplation. Having represented the body of the most pure

Virgin, abandoned by her soul, it is as though he is inviting the question: what was happening, during this time, with her soul? And in answer to this question, he visibly represented her soul, borne by the hands of her divine Son.

Here another question, no less important, arises: what power does this representation hold? Is this not simply the product of the imagination? No. To think this way would be incompatible with the dignity of this ancient holy icon. The brazenness to paint icons according to the imagination of the artist is a product of the willfulness of modern times. Ancient iconographers represented only that which they found in genuine Scriptures or tradition. And the painter of this icon, St. Peter, without a doubt was not inclined to depict the product of his own imagination in his icons. We may safely conclude, then, that his icon represents not the fruit of the imagination, but the fruit of contemplation that accords with the essence of the subject.

Should we now, following the ecclesiastical rule of carefulness, show how this tradition accords with Holy Scripture? To do so, we indicate the words of Christ: *So it was that the poor man died, and was carried by the angels to Abraham's bosom.* The fact that these words belong in a parable should not make us doubt the truth of their content, because even parabolic characters are represented in realistic terms. Just as the death and burial of the rich man are parts of natural life, so the angelic bearing of the dead poor man, who had kept his soul in patience, reflects actual reality. And so, let us compare. If the Scripture says that the souls of holy people, as they leave the body, are taken by angels, then is this in complete agreement with the tradition, passed on to us (it must be said) by an icon, that states that the most holy soul of the Mother of God, who was higher than the angels, was accepted by her own divine Son? According to a different tradition, an angel was sent to her before her death to warn her of her imminent death, and later a choir of angels met her with heavenly

Luke 16:22

hymns as she entered heaven. An echo of that singing was heard by some worthy souls during her burial.

Can you see what vast wisdom the God-inspired Fathers imbued into a single image? They represented for us not only the instructive remembrance of visible events from the past, but also the mystical contemplation of the invisible world, belonging to the age to come.

What a sweet, though unapproachably exalted, contemplation this is! How brightly it shines with the love of the divine Son for His mother! What justice here expressed by the Heavenly Judge in rewarding the deeds of her earthly life! Just as the ever-Virgin bore in her arms the Son of God, so the Son of God now bears her soul in His arms, at the inception of her heavenly life.

Whoever you might be, fellow wanderer in this earthly life, hear me now. Sooner or later, both your soul and mine will stand before the invisible domain of the age to come. Have we thought about what we will encounter there? Who will greet us? Will we be found worthy of having our souls borne by the angels to the mansions of light, like the soul of the poor man Lazarus? Or perhaps you do not think of this, and instead imagine that you might manage without this honor? Do not delude yourself. It is true that this is an honor for those who are worthy, but is it not also an aid for those in need? If we need the protection and guidance of angels in this visible life, will we not need them all the more when we step into the unknown and limitless invisible world? Now the physical world stands before us like a wall that separates us from the bright kingdom of heaven, but it also protects us from the dark kingdom of hell. But now, more or less, the influence of the abyss comes through to reach us, and so we need the helping influence from the kingdom of light all the more! What will happen when our souls, separated from our bodies, step beyond the threshold of the physical world and enter into direct contact with the spiritual world? Will we not then be threatened by an open attack from the dark powers, at the moment when we will not be able to say, as the Sinless One said, *The ruler of this world is coming, and he has nothing in Me?*   *John 14:30*

Blessed is he, who, when looking at his own tomb, has enough presence of spirit to say with David, *If I go into the valley of the shadow of death, I will fear no evil, for You are with me,* You, Who are the light of the world, the Harrower of hell, Who illumines the shadow of hell with the shining of Your cross, Who tasted of death for the sake of all, so that death would be swallowed by life, Who commanded the angels to preserve those who live under the shelter of Your wings in all the paths of their visible and invisible life, both in time and beyond its limits! But in order to have such presence of spirit, it is necessary for Christ to truly be with us, in our faith, in our love, in our activity according to His will and commandments.   *Psalm 22:4*

Prophet Isaiah said, *Blessed is he who has a seed in Zion and kindred in Jerusalem.* If these words refer to earthly Jerusalem and the nation of Israel, then all the more so do they refer also to the spiritual Israel and the heavenly Jerusalem. If a Jew cannot stay at a relative's house in Jerusalem, he can always find himself an inn and receive, through money, what he could not receive from familial connection. But in the heavenly Jerusalem, there are no inns, no money, no markets, no sale. Either you come there as a member of the tribe and a relative or you will not be admitted. But can we become related to the inhabitants of heaven, most of whom we don't even know? We can, and not only of the inhabitants of heaven, but even their King. Read in the Gospel this long-prepared declaration for us concerning our exalted familial relationship: *My mother and My brothers are these who hear the word of God and do it.*   *Isaiah 32:1*

   Luke 8:21

And so, brothers, be diligent to hear the word of God, especially when it is read in Church. Be active and faithful in doing Christ's commandments, and you will enter into a heavenly relationship with Christ. You will have "kindred in [heavenly] Jerusalem" and

Ephesians 2:19 "seed in [uncreated] Zion." Even on this earth, you will be *fellow citizens with the saints and members of the household of God.* Finally, they will accept us into the eternal mansions of heaven, into the communion of blessedness, into the contemplation of the glory of the Father and Son and Holy Spirit. Amen.

19

The Beauty of the Heavenly Queen is Within

Homily on the Dormition of the Mother of God
(1847)

"The queen stood at Your right hand...All her glory as the King's daughter is within." (Psalm 44:10, 14)

Whom does the Prophet describe in such unusual words, in one of the most exalted and mystical psalms, sometimes called "the song of the beloved"? Even if we had no other source than this verse to find the person here described among all the children of men, we would not labor long in finding these qualities, so well described by the prophet, in the incomparably bright light shining from the face of the most holy mother of God, Mary. She is the daughter of the King; truly, for she descended from David and his sons who ruled in Jerusalem. She has "all the glory" that is possible to be attained by a created being, for she is the mother of the King of glory, the mother of God the Son, and for this unequaled honor she is called more honorable than the Cherubim and more glorious than the Seraphim. But all her glory is "within," for it is not found in external luxuries or majesty, but in internal perfections and virtues, for truly the most pure Virgin, in her entire life on this earth, humbly contained her glory within her own heart and kept it from being manifest.

Just as quickly as we recognized the most pure Virgin Mary in the prophetic description of the King's daughter, we must recognize her equally quickly in the same prophetic hymn in the representation of the "queen [who] stood at the right hand" of the King whose throne is "forever and ever," Who, being God, was anointed by God *with the oil of gladness more than Your companions.* Here the prophet speaks of the incarnate God-Man, our Lord Jesus Christ.

Psalm 44:8

When and how did she stand at His right hand so triumphantly? Without a doubt, she did so after completing her earthly journeying, in the heavens, where He has with His Father *the glory which I had ... before the world was.*

John 17:5

She stands at His right hand, but she stands in a manner that slaves stand before their Lord, because she is His handmaiden by her created essence, but she also stands as a queen, because she shares in His glory, because she has motherly boldness before Him.

And should we think that she stands before the King of glory in vain and without effect? While He still lived on earth, in the time of His hiddenness as well as His glory, she stood at His right hand with a request for help in our needs, even seemingly insignificant ones, such as the time when she asked for wine for innocent joy at a wedding feast, though it was not yet the time for His glory to be manifest. How much more, then, does she now actively intercede for us, when her love for her fellow men and her boldness before her Son and God have been freed from the limitations of the earth, now that she stands in the heavens with Him! She asks for grace-filled help in our needs, troubles, and sorrows; she begs for the peace of the whole world, for the

John 2:1-9

salvation of every soul that sincerely desires salvation. And as a queen (for in the heavens there are no names without meaning, power, and action), she herself has the authority to intercede, preserve, and give gifts of mercy to those who run to her powerful protection.

Do you see that in the words of the prophet we have found that which we already have in the tradition of the Church, which is often not found in written words, but in the faces of the holy icons that today we honor in triumphant glory? We have found the most holy Virgin Mother of God, having ascended into heaven after her Dormition on earth, as a queen standing in the glory of the King of glory and interceding for us in a grace-filled and salvific manner.

Rejoice, you virgins! Virginity has been enthroned in the heavens, and it protects you in a kingly manner from above. And yet, do not despair, you who give birth! For the mother of the Lord, though she never felt the pain of childbirth in her sinless birth giving, still profoundly knows the experience of the sorrow of maternal love and care. For this reason, like her divine Son (for she herself also suffered), she wishes, and in her mercy is able, *to aid those who are tempted.* Rejoice, all who are born of women, for if the Son of God, by His incarnation, *is not ashamed to call [us] brethren,* then, of course, His most pure mother is not ashamed to call all of us children, and to have mercy on us in her motherly heart.

Hebrews 2:18

Hebrews 2:11

But this is not enough, that we give hope and consolation to you through the patronage of the queen, who stands at the right hand of the King of glory in the heavens. We must also lead you up, and you must also yourselves rise up, though not to the same height as she, but at least to some degree of closeness to her. The prophet announces that this must happen by necessity: *The virgins behind her shall be brought to the King.* What virgins are these? Without a doubt, these are not simply virgins in the flesh, since *flesh and blood cannot inherit the kingdom of God.* These are virgins in spirit, especially souls that have been purified and exalted by the

Psalm 44:15

1 Corinthians 15:50

grace of natural virginity, as well as souls in general that have preserved and increased their spiritual virginity, which is the state of rebirth in the Spirit from the laver of baptism. These virgins also include those who have corrected their damaged natures by complete repentance and by a repentant way of life.

O Christian souls! Can it be that you will not strive with zeal to join that host of wise virgins who follow the ever-Virgin queen? Can it be that any of you will willingly choose the path of the foolish virgins? Can it be that your hearts will not thirst to approach the heavenly Bridegroom, Whom the Father in heaven has repeatedly called "His beloved," not because He had any need to express His love for Him, but to inspire our love for Him?

Or are you weakened by the faithless thought that it is impossible to reach such a height? But there is no place for doubt in the possibility of something that the unerring word of the prophet has predicted and promised as inevitable: "The virgins behind her *shall* be brought to the King!"

Or perhaps a sense of unworthiness presses you down and hinders this divine desire from being uncovered? Separate this sense of unworthiness (which is just) from an oppressive lack of hope (which is false). Did the Son of God come to earth for those that are worthy? *I did not come to call the righteous, but sinners, to repentance. For the Son of Man has come to save that which was lost.* If He came not only for the unworthy and the sinful, but also for those who are lost, then that means that not only the unworthy and the sinful, but also those who are lost have hope to approach their Savior. They must only desire it, move toward that desire, labor to prepare themselves for this approach, not with their own power, but by His own grace-filled aid.

Mark 2:17
Matthew 18:11

Souls that desire to be brought behind the queen, who stands at the right hand of the King of glory, must prepare themselves for this by decorating themselves in the same way as she is: "All her glory as the King's daughter is within." What does it mean for glory to be within? St Basil the Great tells us: "He who decorates himself for the Father Who sees in secret, and prays, and does everything in such a way that it not appear before other people, but only before God—such a person has his glory within, like the daughter of the King."

And so, Christians, this is our direction for you today, on the way to the kingdom, following the queen who ascends into heaven. This is today's lesson in the school of Christ: Have your dignity and your glory within you, have your piety and virtues in your heart, in the depths of your heart, before the eyes of the One Who sees all, and not only for show in our words and actions, before the eyes of other people. This lesson is always beneficial and salvific, but it seems to be to be especially worthy of attentive study in our time, during which people live so much on the surface, not looking inward enough.

How many things absorb our attention! How much time is lost, how much money spent on a passionate desire for luxuries and pleasant things in the external life, in our homes, in our clothing, in food and drink and diversions! And many people still think, or even say, "What is the harm if we seek our own comfort?" But what a pathetic justification for a reasonable, normal person to contend that there is no harm! Such a justification does not answer the rebuke that such a life has no good, no benefit, no dignity. But if you require the threat of imminent danger to change your behavior for the better, then look: The more you seek after excess, the more the lower classes sink into degrading and filthy poverty. And just as a passion for shiny things, passing from the rich to the poor, produces an inability to discern how best to use one's money and destroys personal and social morality, causing danger to the social fabric, so also the habit to find comfort in the pleasures of an external life seeps into the spiritual life, damaging the moral sense. In such cases, when a person does a good deed, he remains unhappy until it is broadcast and publicly praised. Whoever helps another person will not be calm in the knowledge of his virtue, but is instead tormented by a desire for external validation.

Let us be very careful not to sin in giving more value to the external than the internal, lest we trade away our gold for brass or our silver for lead, lest, having focused too much on the external, we become mired in busyness. The inner does not exist for the sake of the outer, but the other way around. External good things are for the body, the body is for the soul, the soul is for God and the kingdom of God, and the kingdom of God, as the Lord Himself said, *is within you*, but only if you have not worked exclusively for the external and have become lost there.

Luke 17:21

By all means, take care for your external needs and benefit from them, but with moderation. Do not always rush to turn to external needs.

Say to your well-furnished house: You are not the dwelling place of the Bridegroom. His bridal chamber is a pure heart. He only dwells *in your hearts through faith*.

Ephesians 3:17

Say to your fancy clothing: Not one of you is worthy of being *a wedding garment*, appropriate for entry into the King's bridal feast, and without which you will be cast out into outer darkness. That garment will not be woven on a loom, nor brought from an exotic land. It is given, in part, from above, and in part is made by the personal labors of each, as it is written, *But put on the Lord Jesus Christ, put on tender mercies, kindness, humility, meekness, longsuffering.*

Matthew 22:12

Romans 13:14; Colossians 3:12

Say to your luxurious dinner: The heavenly Guest will not come here, even though he promised to come and feast with anyone who will open the door to Him. He has other food: *Man shall not live by bread alone, but by every word that proceeds from the mouth of God.* He must open the doors of the heart, and they are opened by prayer, love, and the fulfillment of these words: *If anyone loves Me, he will keep My word, and My Father will love him, and We will come to him and make Our home with him.*

Revelation 3:20

Matthew 4:4

Say to your vain and avaricious thoughts when they approach your good deeds: *Depart from here, you 'foxes, the little ones that spoil the vineyard.'* We want to preserve the fruit of the Master's vineyard whole."

With the help of these and similar spiritual thoughts and exercises, may the heavenly Father "grant you," my brothers, *according to the riches of His glory, to be strengthened with might through His Spirit in the inner man* that, having your glory within you, you may appear worthy of being led into eternal glory. Amen.

20

The Humility of the Virgin

Homily on the Annunciation of the Mother of God
(1848)

"He has regarded the lowly state of His maidservant." (Luke 1:48)

Today we return with our triumphant remembrance to the depth of the past, when a wondrous event occurred, and in what silence it occurred!

One of those closest to the throne of the Almighty, Archangel Gabriel, "having accepted mystically the command in his reason," (as the Church tells us today, for it knows the heavenly language and customs) flies through all nine ranks of angels from the highest to the lowest heaven, and strives toward the earth. The inhabitants of heaven look and do not understand what is happening. The *angels desire to look into* this mystery. Where is he going? Is he going to Sinai, to the Law-giver Moses, with a new revelation? But Sinai no longer flashes with lightning or booms with divine thunder. Moses is no longer there. He

1 Peter 1:12

completed his great work, when he said and wrote, *The Lord you God will raise up for you a Prophet like me from your midst, from your brethren. Him you shall hear.* *Deuteronomy 18:15*

Is he going to Jerusalem, to the temple there, to the place where the miraculous cloud descends, together with heavenly fire, onto the ark of the covenant? But the ark is no longer there, and Gabriel goes to begin the work of a new, animate ark to the hypostatic Word of God. Where is the archangel going? To little-known Nazareth, into a small house, to a poor virgin, known only to a few people because of her unusual love for God and virginity. She alone hears the words of the archangel. She alone knows what happened after their conversation. Even her faithful custodian, the righteous Joseph, does not know what happened.

But what did happen? The pre-eternal determination of God concerning the salvation of the fallen race of man has been brought into action. *The fellowship of the mystery, which from the beginning of the ages has been in hidden in God*, a mystery inconceivable even for the angels, has been revealed to a daughter of man, of course, not for her comprehension, but neither only for her faith, but for her action through her fulfilling the mystery. And her faith helped encompass that which is un-circumscribable even for angelic minds. The "seed of [this] woman" will bruise the head of the serpent of hell, which had dealt a fatal blow to mankind in Eden. Or, to put it another way, the seed of Abraham, which all generations would bless, now comes to fruition in the womb of the Virgin, ushering in the divine life into mankind, utterly destroying the poison of death within human nature. The prophet that Moses, as well as all the other prophets, promised is approaching, and in Him alone the Law and old covenant would reach the *end of the law for righteousness to everyone who believes*. This Prophet is hidden behind the veil of the uncreated temple, His mother. The Holy Spirit descended on the most blessed Mary, and the power of the Most High illumined her. The Son of God, *Ephesians 3:9*

Genesis 3:19

Romans 10:4

Luke 1:35

co-eternal with His Father in divinity, did not abandon His seat on the divine throne, but was conceived on earth, in humanity, as a child. *And the Word became flesh and dwelt among us.* And from this day He becomes—if it is possible to say this, not in a spirit of exaltation, but in the wonder of this unutterable condescension—closer to us than to the angels, because the angelic nature only approaches Him, but human nature now is united in His hypostasis with the divinity. *For indeed He does not give aid to angels, but He does give aid to the seed of Abraham.*

John 1:14

Hebrews 2:16

Why is such a wondrous and great action of God, as the incarnation of the Logos, accomplished in a way that is hidden both from heaven and earth? Hidden from heaven, perhaps, because this mystery was not prepared or necessary for the heavenly inhabitant; hidden from earth, likely, because the divine light of this mystery would not have been borne by weak human eyes if they suddenly saw it. These weak eyes had to be prepared for the revelation gradually. In general, this hiddenness accorded to the fact that the mystery is essentially inconceivable for created minds.

It must be said that in order for the salvific work of God not to remain too long concealed, the key to this ark of God, to the heart of the Theotokos, was given to the righteous Elizabeth by the Holy Spirit. And she, as soon as she saw the most pure Virgin after the angelic annunciation, immediately opened the treasure house of the mystery, when she exclaimed, *Why is this granted to me, that the mother of my Lord should come to me?* In this way, she proclaimed the incarnation of the Son of God as already accomplished.

Together with the righteous Elizabeth, we can also say with joy: Why is this granted to us? What is this undeserved and unexpected gift, that the mother of the Lord is related to us by nature, that the Lord Himself wondrously approaches us, having truly communed with our nature, our weaknesses, and our sicknesses (save for sin), even our death, so that, having assumed all these, in return He might give us life and the ability for our faith to seek Him and find His grace, through the intercession of His mother, the mother of light, love, and mercy?

But if someone would think to ask how this occurred, how the One without beginning had a beginning, how the Logos assumed flesh, how two completely divergent natures were united in the person of the God-Man, let us cover our ears, mind, and heart from this spirit of inquisitiveness. Let us instead honor the divine mystery, which the *angels desire to look into* with silent reverence. For the angels desire to look into the mystery not because they have brazen inquisitiveness, but because they love the wisdom of God, because they revere God's unapproachability. *Do not seek things too difficult for you, nor examine what is beyond your strength.* This is the teaching of the wise man. There is no small wisdom in the person who calmly remains in his ignorance of the mystical because of piety and humility. *1 Peter 1:12* *Sirach 3:20*

If you want to philosophize, then at least do not construct elaborate (but still useless) lattice-works of conclusions regarding that which cannot be conceived. Do not be curious about questions such as how the endlessly exalted divinity could have approached mankind through a limitless mercy, and united with him. Philosophize instead about things that are not so obscure, things that are beneficial for your wisdom, such as: how can man approach God, or not remain distant from him when God desires to approach him? Without any danger, you can ask the following question: "How did the mother of God become worthy of her highly exalted calling? How did she prepare herself for such miraculous communion with God? What were her labors? What were her virtues? For she does not hide the answers to these mysteries, because she desires to show you the path of approach to God, though no path can equal hers, only approximate it to a limited degree.

She explains the essence of her great labor in a single small sentence: *He has regarded the lowly state of His maidservant.* Saying *Luke 1:48* this, the most holy Virgin, without a doubt, thought only to exalt God's condescension, not to ascribe anything to herself. However, the Holy Spirit, Who inspired her words of praise, arranged her words in such a way as to reveal the face of a virtue, which, more than any others, makes us close to God. Prayer, fasting, chastity, faith, love for God, in a word, all the virtues surrounded the soul of the most pure Virgin; but they were all crowned, perfected, exalted before God's very eyes by the queen of virtues: humility. *He has regarded the lowly state of His maidservant.*

Luke 1:48

According to the tradition of the saints, it seems that we know of a specific event in which the humility of the most pure Virgin attracted God's grace to her. She loved both to speak to God through prayer, as well as to listen to Him speaking to her through the Holy Scriptures. One time she read in the book of Isaiah the prophecy concerning Christ and His mother: *Behold, the Virgin shall conceive and bear a Son, and shall call His name Immanuel.* Faith illumined her at that reading, and love lit up her soul. However, in her humility, she did not dare to pray that she would come anywhere near Immanuel Himself, the God-Man. She limited her prayer to this petition: that she be given the gift of seeing His mother, to come close to her, to be no more than her personal slave. Thus, through humility of heart, she prepared for herself a path for Jesus, Who is meek and humble in heart. Even before He said these words, they came true over her: *He who humbles himself will be exalted.* She then extended her prayer to the unknown future mother of God, seen through the mirror of prophecy, that she might be found worthy to be her slave; and through this, in actual fact, she herself became the mother of God. *He has regarded the lowly state of His maidservant.*

Isaiah 7:14

Luke 18:14

Luke 1:48

Brothers, let us learn this teaching of humility from the grace-filled Teacher of grace, for she shared this humility with Christ. For He said, *Learn from me, for I am gentle and lowly in heart*, and for this He promised both the fruit and reward of humility: *And you will find rest for your souls.*

Matthew 11:29

Matthew 11:29

If it still seems strange to someone that humility, which is not an impressive virtue, is held in such high esteem by God, that *God gives grace to the humble*, let such a person think of the relationship between humility and the other virtues, as well as its opposite vices.

1 Peter 5:5

If there is nothing more abhorrent to God as pride (because it hides within itself the desire for self-deification), then humility must be the most pleasing virtue to God, for, since it sees itself as nothing, it ascribes all good, honor, and glory to God. Pride does not attract grace because it is full of itself; humility accepts grace in abundance, because it is emptied not only of itself, but of all creation. If the pride of the angels in heaven cast them to the depths of hell, then, by contrast, we must conclude that humility may be able to raise one up from hell itself (i.e., the depths of sin) all the way to heaven. If the greatest of virtues is "love," according to the Apostle, for it *suffers long and is kind...does not envy... does not parade itself...is not provoked...never fails*, then this is only true because love is supported and aided by humility.

1 Corinthians 13:4-8

Humility is the salt of all virtues. Just as salt gives food flavor, so humility gives virtues perfection. Without salt, food easily spoils, so also without humility virtues are quickly corrupted by pride, vanity, impatience.

There is humility that a person can attain through his own efforts by knowing his own weakness, unworthiness, nothingness, secretly rebuking himself for his sins and limitations, never allowing himself to condemn his neighbors, mortifying himself with hard work and obedience, choosing in all things simplicity and lack of sophistication. There is also humility that leads people to God through His judgments by allowing them to endure insults, rebukes, humiliation, and deprivation.

Actively seek to humble yourself with hope, and arouse yourself with the words of Apostle James: *Humble yourselves in the sight of the Lord, and He will lift you up*. With trust, let us commit ourselves to the God that humbles us, attending to the words of

James 4:10

1 Peter 5:6   Apostle Peter: *Therefore humble yourselves under the mighty hand of God, that He may exalt you in due time.*

Psalm 33:19   The Lord will visit with His grace every soul that humbles itself, and He will give us experiential knowledge that *the Lord is near those who are brokenhearted, and He will save the humble in spirit.* Amen.

21

The Translation of the Virgin

Homily on the Dormition of the Mother of God
(1848)

"The assembly of disciples and divine apostles gathered to bury the God-pleasing body of the one and only Mother of God."

(From the first hymn at the Aposticha, small vespers of Dormition)

With this hymn, the holy Church catechizes us even before the beginning of the feast itself. The Church speaks as though it sees this even happening before it, and so it tells us all of it. It seems to me the Church does this so that all of us would not merely remember the event, but would, as it were, see and participate in the Dormition and burial of the mother of God.

Can we participate in this intention of the Church? It is not difficult to understand that this would not be the work of our physical eyes. We require two eyes: The eye of the purified mind and the eye of the faithful and loving heart. We admit the imperfection of our eyes. But can we not at least see with the eyes of the saints, who were able to contemplate these mysteries, and who desire to help our own contemplation? Let us try to see the death of the mother of God through the eyes of the saints: Dionysius the Areopagite, Juvenal of Jerusalem, Andrew of Crete, and John of Damascus.

Yes, even St. Andrew encounters a certain difficulty. In his homily on today's feast, he speaks of the confusion of inquisitive minds: "Why did none of the evangelists describe the Dormition of the Theotokos?" However, he does answer this confusion, saying, "This could be because her God-pleasing Dormition occurred many years after the ascension of the Lord, for, as they say, she departed this life in deep old age. Another reason could be that events of that time did not allow for such things to be written down."

Later, in the same homily, St. Andrew does what we do today. He looks at the Dormition of the Mother of God through the eyes of a contemporary of these events, St. Dionysius the Areopagite, offering this citation from his book on the divine names:

> We, as you know, and yourself, and many of our holy brethren, were gathered together to the depositing of the Life-springing and God-receptive body, and when there were present also James, the brother of God, and Peter, the foremost and most honored pinnacle of the Theologians, when it was determined after the depositing, that every one of the hierarchs should celebrate, as each was capable, the Omnipotent Goodness of the supremely Divine Weakness.[1]

In other words, as St. Maximus explains, they celebrated the willing condescension of the Son of God, Who had accepted into Himself the weak body of man (save for sin).

Seeing this event as described by St. Dionysius, I cannot stop myself from exclaiming: here is a truly great Cathedral of the

---

1 Book 3, section 2: https://www.tertullian.org/fathers/areopagite_03_divine_names.htm

Dormition, the source and model of our own temple in which we serve today, and all temples of the Dormition. O, if only our own cathedral, in emulation of the apostolic gathering of hierarchs singing abundant hymns, if only our own temple would not lag too far behind its model, both in the sincerity of our prayer, and in the spirit of grace, and in the zeal of glorifying the incarnate Word of God and His most pure mother, beyond all words and hymns, in our very actions and lives!

But St. Dionysius only revealed to us a part of the spiritual vision, as we see from his own words: "But [I] pass over the mystical things there, both as forbidden to the multitude and as known to thee."[2] Let us then humble ourselves if we belong to the afore-mentioned multitude for whom seeing the mysteries is forbidden, but that which was known to St. Dionysius's reader, St. Timothy, became known also to other worthy saints, and from their knowledge some more details have come down to us as well.

One of these mysteries likely includes the manner in which many apostles gathered to the burial of the most pure Virgin, when they were scattered all over the world, preaching the Gospel. This mystery is somewhat elucidated by St. Andrew, when he writes, "It is not strange that the Spirit, Who had once raised Elias in a heavenly chariot of fire, gathered them all suddenly, bringing them on the clouds in the spirit. For God everything is possible, as we know from the examples of Habakkuk and Daniel." As for St. John of Damascus, in his homily on today's feast, he explains more definitively that for the sake of the Dormition of the mother of God, the apostles were carried "by God's command, as in a net, into Jerusalem, and from the ends of the earth, like eagles, they all flew to a single place, gathered together."

The holy Damascene contemplates another mystery in the Dormition of the mother of God, and reveals it to us, more specifically, "the coming of the King Himself to His birth-giver, that

---

2   Ibid

He might accept with His divine hands her holy, pure, and incorrupt soul."

Finally, St. John calls to his aid St. Juvenal, Archbishop of Jerusalem, to help elucidate the mysteries of the Dormition, by excerpting the following account from certain historical books. During the reign of Marcian, Empress Pulcheria built and decorated a temple in honor of the mother of God in Blachernae. Desiring to acquire a relic worthy of such a temple, and having heard that near Jerusalem, in Gethsemane, there was a temple on the place of the most holy Virgin's tomb, the emperor and empress write to the Archbishop of Jerusalem with their request to have the Virgin's relics translated to the newly-built Church, for the protection of the imperial city.

In his answer, St. Juvenal cited an ancient and true tradition that told of a miraculous gathering of the apostles who were suddenly carried from many different countries to the deathbed of the most holy Virgin as she was committing her soul into the hands of God. He then told of how the apostles processed with her body to the singing of angels and placed it in a tomb in Gethsemane. Then he wrote:

> The angelic dancing and singing continued without pause in that place for three days. But after three days. the song of the angels ceased; the Apostles were there, and since one of them, Thomas, had not been present (for her burial and came at the end of three days) and wished to reverence that body which had housed God, they opened the coffin. And they could not find her body, which had been the object of such praise; all that they found were her burial wrappings. And being overcome by the ineffable fragrance that came out of the wrappings, they closed the coffin again. Amazed by this miraculous discovery, they could only draw a single conclusion: the One Who had deigned to become flesh in her own person, and to take His humanity

from her, the One Who willed to be born in human flesh as God the Word, the Lord of glory, and Who had preserved her virginity intact even after childbirth, now chose, after her departure from this world, to honor her immaculate and pure body with the gift of incorruptibility, and with a change of state even before the common, universal resurrection.[1]

St. Juvenal further adds the witness of St. Dionysius, which we have already cited. As for St. John of Damascus, he finishes his account with a report that an ark with the clothing of the Mother of God was instead brought into the Church at Blachernae from Gethsemane.

Do you see the mysteries and miracles of the Dormition of the Mother of God? Do you see the earthly triumph, which is also a heavenly one? Do you see the light, short-lived cloud of death, through which the light of eternal light shines brightly and majestically? Do you see the tomb, transformed into a window opening into the invisible world, facing the light that knows no evening?

But be attentive to how you regard these mysteries. Do you look at them with inquisitiveness? That is not a trustworthy way of seeing! Curiosity is more capable of stealing the forbidden fruit of dangerous and delusory knowledge than of revealing the life-giving fruit of truth. Do you look at them with wonder? That is merely the natural way of looking at the miraculous, but it is not enough. The God of wonders reveals miracles not only to make us wonder, but so that through the wonder He might arouse our attention, through this aroused attention might make evident His invisible hand, and by this hand guide mankind to the path of truth and righteousness.

Do you look at these mysteries with faith? That is the properly Christian way of looking at holy and divine things. All the

---

1 https://stgregoryofnyssa.net/2019/08/12/the-dormition-of-the-theotokos/

same, the gaze of faith must be not only content in the pleasure of what is contemplated, but it must be active, because faith is not our ultimate goal, but rather a means to attaining the Christian life. Do we desire to emulate the holy and to strive toward the heavenly? This is what should be the primary fruit of every spiritual contemplation, including what we see today.

We see a wondrous death, which is miraculously decorated with the presence of the apostles, angels, and the Lord Himself. And we know that this is a consequence of the most pure and most holy life of Mary, fulfilled according to the highest degree of the law of divine righteousness, according to which *precious in the sight of the Lord is the death of his saints*. Let us come to love all things that lead to a death that is precious in the sight not only of people, but before the Lord first of all. Let us come to love purity and holiness of life. Let us come to abhor sin. Let us cast aside the impurity of our actions and thoughts. Let us purify ourselves through a strong desire of the heart, and let us not stop purifying ourselves through daily struggle, *cleans[ing] ourselves from all filthiness of the flesh and spirit, perfecting holiness in the fear of God*.

Psalm 135:6

2 Corinthians 7:1

We see an unusually quick awakening after the wondrous Dormition, an immediate immortality after death, in the fullness of its power. We see the soul of the most holy Virgin in the hands of the Lord, and consequently on the highest step of blessedness, because nearness to the Lord is the height of blessedness. We see her ever-virginal body, not subject to the law of corruption, not awaiting the coming day of resurrection for all mankind, but instead growing from a seed into heaven and bearing fruit at the exact moment of the sowing. Let us look at the immortality, which for us to a certain degree is already familiar; let us remember and cease to forget that it is the intention of the Creator and the gift of the Savior to give us *citizenship... in heaven*. And what is better for us to care about: our earthly acquisitions and pleasures that often run away from those who seek them, or do not satisfy those who achieve them, or delude those who take

Philippians 3:20

pleasure in them, or enslave those who own them, or disappear from those who had them, and do not follow those who leave this life? Let us limit our earthly desires. Let us not allow ourselves to treasure dust and corruption. Let us not allow our immortal soul to dig itself into the mud of passionate inclination, where even our body is not fated to remain forever. Let us find ourselves "treasure in heaven." As the Lord Himself said, *where your treasure is, there your heart will be also.* In this way, our heart will pull us to the heavens, for wherever the heart of man is, there the whole of man is, his entire fate!

Matthew 6:21

Amen.

22

The Holy Seed of God

Homily on the Annunciation of the Mother of God
(1849)

"That which shall stand therein shall be a holy seed." (Isaiah 6:13)[1]

Glory and thanks to the Creator of ages, who created the day that we renew today in our remembrance and our triumph: the day of the incarnation of the Son of God! This is one of only several days that stand as a foundation for all other days on earth, without which all days would simply collapse into a single, endless night of hell. This is because the incarnation of the Son of God is an event that upholds the standing and prosperity of the human race, as well as all other creatures, which were created to serve mankind and whose fates are subject to our own. This, I think, is the substance of the thought given to Prophet Isaiah, when he heard the divine word: "That which shall stand therein shall be a holy seed."

---

1 Only the Douay-Reims translation fits the Slavonic with any sort of sense, at least in the way that St. Philaret means this sentence.

Let us see if this small sentence about the "holy seed" will grow into fruitful thoughts of the mind, for the nourishment of our souls.

In order to fully understand this thought about the "holy seed," we must first examine the context from the prophet's own life that gave rise to this prophecy.

In Jerusalem, either in the Temple or above the Temple, Isaiah had a vision of the Lord seated on an exalted throne, filling the Temple with His glory, surrounded and proclaimed by Seraphim with such power that the lintel of the Temple moved, and the Temple was filled with smoke. The prophet was terrified, because he thought he was about to die, for he saw the King, the Lord of Hosts, and he had, according to his own admission, impure lips. But the Lord immediately revealed Himself as one who raises the humble. For a Seraphim took a fiery coal from the altar of incense, and having touched the lips of Isaiah, announced that his sins were purified. The mystical fire pierced the soul of the prophet, and it inspired him with courage and zeal. *Whom shall I send*, the Lord asked, *and who will go for Us?* That is, who will go to the chosen nation, whom the prophet himself had declared to be *a people of unclean lips* and impure life? Isaiah, aroused with divine fire, no longer feared to answer: *Here am I! Send me.* The Lord, answering, told him to go and tell the people that though they listen, they hear nothing, though they look, they see nothing, for their hearts have become corrupt, their ears hard of hearing, their eyes willfully closed, and so they would not hear or listen and would not turn back to the Lord until God healed them. The prophet felt sorry for his people, and asked, *Lord, how long?* How long will they continue to refuse to turn back to You to be healed by You? *until the cities are laid waste and without inhabitant, the houses are without a man, the land is utterly desolate.* But the nation of Israel will be like a terebinth tree or an oak that grows anew from a bit of root or an acorn. *That which shall stand therein shall be a holy*

Isaiah 6:5

Isaiah 6:5
Isaiah 6:8

Isaiah 6:11

Isaiah 6:11

Isaiah 6:13

seed. The holy seed will give the nation firmness to survive the difficulties ahead.

If these prophetic words are then connected with historical reality, their meaning can be explained in the following manner. The Jews lived in their sins, and they continued in their sinful ways. They did not listen to the prophets who rebuked them and called them to repentance, faith, and salvation. For this reason, they were punished with the Babylonian captivity. From that captivity they returned, but only a smaller group than was taken into captivity, and once again they would be subject to difficult days in the times of the Maccabees. But for all that, the chosen nation would not be destroyed. Why? Because it preserved the holy seed, and for preserving that seed, Providence preserved them. "That which shall stand therein shall be a holy seed."

Here a question naturally presents itself: what is this holy seed that preserves the sinful and unfortunate nation? Let us remember David's words: *I was conceived in iniquity and in sins did my mother bear me*. If we further apply the reasoning that there is no particular reason to limit David's admission exclusively to him and his mother, and that this sentence must therefore refer to all the sons of Adam, then we can deduce that the holy seed cannot exist among those born by the natural law of human nature. What was the holy seed that God then indicated to the prophet? It was the same one that He promised Adam when He said this following to the serpent: *[the seed of the woman] will bruise your head*. This is the same seed that God blessed Abraham with, when He said, *in your seed all the nations of the earth shall be blessed, because you have obeyed My voice*. This is the seed that God revealed to David anew in the person of the eternal King and Son of God: *I will set up your seed after you...I will establish the throne of His kingdom forever. I will be His Father.* In short, only one person in the entire race of man can be the holy seed, for He was conceived of the Holy Spirit and born of the holy Virgin—our Lord Jesus Christ.

God, Who knows all His works from eternity, and Whose all-seeing eyes *saw me when I was unformed,* saw, before the ages, all the generations of the sons of fallen Adam, and He foresaw, and chose one race among them. This people, though not worthy in all its representatives, at least in some preserved the greatest remains of the primal-created goodness. This people had given way the least to the infection of sin, and was the most inclined to accepting and faithfully preserving God's grace. Finally, this nation was able to produce, after long and gradual cleansing through grace, a pure virgin who was capable of being the vessel of incarnate divinity, a light that could only find communion with purity, a fire that would consume all impurity. Therefore, it was necessary to preserve this people until it would produce the most beautiful flower and the most perfect fruit of mankind— the Virgin Mary, the mother of the God-Man. Since this particular generation of men was found in the nation of Israel, then the whole people had to be protected. That is the reason why prophets were sent primarily to this people, filling it with grace-filled light, lest they lose the treasures of faith and perish from their sins and delusions. And lest this people be destroyed by enemies or natural calamities, often God used miraculous powers and actions, such as leading them across the sea as on dry land, feeding the entire nation in the desert for forty years with manna, sending an angel to defeat the 185,000-strong army of Assyrians when King Hezekiah was not strong enough to protect his own people.

Acts 15:18
Psalm 138:16

Thus, the holy seed was the foundation and the preservation of the nation of Israel, until, finally, *There shall come forth a Rod from the stem of Jesse, and a Branch shall grow out of his roots.* The Son of God was born of a daughter of Jesse. Appearing on earth, He lived, taught, performed miracles, suffered, died, rose from the dead, ascended into heaven, sent down the Holy Spirit, and confirmed the salvation of men in the midst of the earth. The goal of Providence has been achieved. There was no longer any

Isaiah 11:1

need to keep preserving the Jews as they were before. Moreover, they themselves rejected the holy seed, having committed Christ to death. And therefore, they, though in latter days have been quite numerous and strong, have spent most of modern history without a homeland, scattered throughout all the world, and if they did not disappear completely, it is solely for this reason: that they might be a sorrowful and instructive reminder of the holy seed that was preserved within them, but was not acknowledged by them, as well as for the hope that the same holy seed might someday bring them back to the fold.

What do the children of all nations not chosen by God now think? Do they perhaps have an envious thought: How fortunate the nation that was given the gift of preserving the holy seed, and of being preserved by it in turn! But do not envy; rather, thank God. He chose only one nation to be the protector of the holy seed, that is, the people of the generation of Christ. But He did this so that salvation could be effected in all nations and all peoples, both in the time to come and to a certain degree in this temporal life.

If they to whom the secret holy seed—the coming Christ, hidden in promises—were fortunate, then how much should we feel fortunate, for we have been given the revealed holy seed—Christ, Who has come to those who accept Him by faith? Have we not been *born again*, as Apostle Peter said, *not of corruptible seed but incorruptible, through the word of God which lives and abides forever?* Or, as Apostle Paul said, *Do you not know yourselves, that Jesus Christ is in you? Unless indeed you are disqualified. Christ in you, the hope of glory.* In Christ, *godliness is profitable for all things, having the promise of the life that now is and of that which is to come.* From Christ Himself, the true Church received a promise that the *gates of hell shall not prevail against it.* Thus, is it not natural that the quality of unconquerability should to a certain degree transmit also to the protector of the true Church, if true and pure, since this guardianship is formed in an Orthodox nation, in a pious kingdom, under the aegis of a God-chosen Tsar, Who, of course, is given the name and station of "anointed one of God" from Christ Himself by the word of God? Thus, for the new Israel, like the old, this prophetic word has its own proper meaning: *That which shall stand therein shall be a holy seed.* Isaiah 6:13

And so, all you who are members of the new chosen nation, the grace-filled people of God, do not stop upholding within yourself this holy seed, and it will never cease to protect you in turn. The seed of the word of God in the mind, the seed of faith in Christ and love for Him in the heart—these are fed by prayer and are cultivated by asceticism. The seed will reveal its power in your life through your good deeds, and by inculcating faith in Christ in your heart, establishing His Church in each and in all. This seed will be for you the foundation of an unshakable standing, a wall of safety, a light of peace within you, and your victorious weapon against any external attack of visible or invisible enemies. This is true, by the grace of the Lord. And if anyone still doubts, this is only because you have a lack of that necessary grace: *Unless indeed you are disqualified.* For this reason, the Apostle warns us to "examine yourselves as to whether you are in the faith." 2 Corinthians 13:5

If we think that the Apostle warned the Christians of the early, bright days of the Church, whose faith grew not only through visible signs but through the cultivation of spiritual gifts, healings, gifts of tongues, prophecy, and still he found it necessary to ask them the brazen question of "whether you are in the faith," then how much more should we, steeped in the leaven of modernity, test ourselves to see whether we are in the faith! We should be terrified to end up untested in our faith; we must labor to acquire the art of faith, not only appearing on our lips or in our minds for a short time, but profoundly, through the heart, by a constant, living, loving life animated by the commandments of God, purified of incorrect thoughts and of incorrect actions, ready to sacrifice ourselves for the sake of truth and righteous-

1 John 5:4 ness. This is *the victory that has overcome the world—our faith*. A faith that must still overcome the world and continue to do so until the entire Church militant in time passes to the Church triumphant in eternity. Amen.

23

The Virgin's Unblinking Gaze into Eternity

Homily on the Dormition of the Mother of God
(1849)

"For this we groan, earnestly desiring to be clothed with our habitation which is from heaven." (2 Corinthians 5:2)

Wondrous is the death on the cross of our Lord Jesus Christ. Wondrous is His three-day resurrection. But it is no wonder that they appear so wondrous to us, because an inconceivable mystery of God's unthinkable wisdom is hidden in these events. They miraculously answered a question that could not be answered by natural means: How is the fallen race of man to be saved?

How is it even possible that the Son of God suffered and died? It is only possible because that is the will of His Father, as well as His own will, for which nothing is impossible. By the cup of His willing, innocent sufferings, the God-Man drank to the fill and emptied the cup of the eternal, just sufferings of mankind, condemned for sin. By His death, He pierced through into the closed-off domain of mankind's universal mortality, so that He might dispel its darkness by the light of His divinity, so that He might break death's chains by the power of His Godhead.

He resurrected no later than the third day after his death, because He was to be the first fruits of the dead who are to resurrect, and no earlier than the third day, so that the work of our salvation might be sealed by the sign of the most holy Trinity, to Whom He completely belongs.

Evidently, the death of the most holy Virgin Theotokos, and her resurrection, are not as wondrous as the death and resurrection of Christ. Yet they are still wondrous. For how is it possible that the one who is more honorable than the Cherubim and beyond compare more glorious than the Seraphim died? The Cherubim and Seraphim are lower than she, and consequently they must be less blessed than she, but they do not know death. How can it be that the tabernacle of the incarnate Son of God, Who of course never stopped being the habitation of divinity, died? Was it necessary for her who accepted within herself the fire of the Godhead to give way to the power of earthly mortality? Truly, one may assume that the most holy Virgin, in the words of Apostle Paul, could have not been *unclothed, but further clothed, that mortality may be swallowed up by life.* In other words, she could easily have forborne to take off herself the clothing of the earthly body through death, but instead, in the blinking of an eye, been clothed by transfiguration into a glorified body. So why did this not happen?

We must assume that her constant humility and desire to emulate the humiliation of her divine Son led to her not having this desire to avoid the lowly path of temporal death. And providence, which arranges all things, did not hinder this deepening of hers into humility, which would lead to an even greater future glory and would further allow the death of the mother of Life to remind us that the death present in human nature still has no small power over us, even after the life-giving death of Christ. If the most pure mother of Life did not avoid death, though it was quiet and short-lived, then we who are far from perfect purity, who are plunged into the impurity of our own thought, passions, actions, life—we are in great danger of a fierce and eternal death!

The glory of the eternal life began to shine through even the death of the most pure Virgin. Three days before her death, a heavenly messenger appeared to call her to eternity, and he brought her a sign of the paradise that awaited her. Miraculously, the assembly of the apostles gathered to honor her passing and burial. Those worthy among them saw her own divine Son, surrounded by the heavenly powers, come to accept her soul into His own hands. Her body, though it had no breath, still performed miracles. On the third day after her death, like Christ's, her complete resurrection was made evident. Her earthly body no longer remained in the tomb. And to the assembly of the apostles, she appeared in heavenly glory.

This is the event that the synaxis of the Church remembers today in triumph, though we still call the day by a humble moniker: The Dormition of the mother of God. We emphasize rather a softened vision of death than a spectacle of triumph and glory. What is the thought of Mother-Church in doing so? What does the Church desire? Naturally, she does not think to augment the most exalted glory of heaven with our worthless earthly glory. No, our mother Church wants to place us into a state of contemplation, as though in tension between life and death, earth and heaven, time and eternity. She wants to tell every one of her children: Look beyond the limits of the grave; Think of heavenly things while still on earth; Remember eternity within time; Be instructed in all this from the books of life and the Dormition of the mother of God.

Truly, in the book of her earthly life, since this book is now open to us, we can find everywhere a single dominating theme: The striving toward heaven, eternity, God. When her childish mind and childish feet were not strong enough yet to carry her to heaven, that striving was expressed in her coming into the earthly heaven—the tabernacle of God, and here she stayed to live. This unusual early striving led to an equally unusual early spiritual progress: In her youth, she was already so close to heaven that an angel used to visit her and feed her with heavenly food. And for what reason did she assume the pledge of virginity—so unusual for that time—if not to strive all the quicker to heaven, not being tied down by any earthly bonds? When she, after the incarnation of the Son of God within her, became a second heaven, we cannot even dare to think than anything earthly attracted her gaze any longer. Being the living throne of the incarnate Son of God, Whom she bore in her womb and in her arms, like the living thrones in the angelic hosts, of course she lived only in Him Whom she bore. She placed into her heart all the words of His mysteries and judgments; before all others she revealed His divine power when she asked Him to perform His first miracle in Cana of Galilee. Before the apostles she understood that whoever sees Him sees His Father. She followed Him not only along the difficult paths of His wanderings while preaching the Gospel, but also along the terrifying path of his cross, death, and burial, drawing up unfading courage from her limitless love. Finally, when her only treasure returned to heaven after the resurrection and ascension, her heart abode constantly there, where her treasure was, not only because of her maternal love, but much more because of the grace poured out on her. The rest of her life was a single unblinking gaze from time into eternity, a single long sigh, reaching toward the heavenly life with Christ in God.

This is how the life of the most holy Virgin reached such a level that *death is swallowed up in [the] victory* of resurrection and glory, so quickly and so majestically.

You may think that perhaps I demand too much of you, since I am indicating a path for your own life in emulation of the life of the most holy Virgin. Mary, according to the witness of heaven itself, was *highly favored* and *blessed among women*. Can normal people, especially those burdened with sins, possibly follow her? According to the contemplation of the Church, she is higher than the Seraphim. How far then is our baseness from a path that follows her footsteps? *Luke 1:28*

We must not let such doubts lead to sloth; truth easily dissipates them. The mother of God is called blessed because of her primacy, but there is a degree of grace available for all, depending on our faith and our needs. We have access to grace that is enough for our salvation: *The grace of God that brings salvation has appeared to all men.* The mother of God was blessed among women in a way that has no comparison in the race of mankind; however, Apostle Paul said that God blessed all of us *with every spiritual blessing in the heavenly places in Christ.* Can we follow the footsteps of the mother of God? Not only is this possible, but it is necessary, according to the words of David: *The virgins, her companions who follow her, shall be brought to You.* A person can even emulate the God-Man, for He calls us to do exactly that, and even gives us hope of achieving this exalted goal: *If anyone serves Me, let him follow Me; and where I am, there My servant will be also.* Emulation does not require equality, or even anything close to equality. A lesser man can emulate a great man in that which is accessible to him. Not everyone is capable of acquiring the wondrous and miraculous, just by wishing it, but the true and the good are accessible to all, though to each in a particular measure and degree, depending on one's faith, the purity one's desires, and the zeal of one's ascetic labors. *Titus 2:11* *Ephesians 1:3* *Psalm 44:15* *John 12:26*

In fact, I do *not* tell you to do everything as the most holy Virgin did. I don't tell you to speak with the angels or to rise up higher than the Seraphim. I only point to what it achievable by all: Aroused by the remembrance of her life and Dormition, look beyond the limits of the grave; Think of the heavenly while on earth; And remember eternity within time. This is so natural for Christians that the apostle Paul speaks of this not as something that is necessary and required, but rather essential and typical: *For this we groan, earnestly desiring to be clothed with our habitation which is from heaven.* [2 Corinthians 5:2]

Many of us look at heaven and eternity without any great eagerness, partially because we see that between us and them lies death and the grave, and partially because our vision is too occupied with earthly matters.

Would you not ridicule a person who sees a danger coming, and instead of taking the necessary measures to learn what exactly is the nature of the danger and how to avoid it, he closes his eyes not to see it! But isn't this exactly what you are doing? Death is approaching you, and will come without a doubt. But you, instead of examining it without delay to see what dangers it might hold and what measure you might take to make it safe for you, shut your eyes tightly, lest the gloomy spectacle of death disturb you! You say that you fear death, but think logically: What is more frightening? Death, which will become safe, even blessed, for those who prepare for it during this life, or an unprepared life, which will make death a fearsome thing?

What would you think of a son, who, living far away from his father, was so occupied with the works and pleasures of a foreign land, that he didn't even think of returning to his father, and took no opportunities to find out how he was doing? Without a doubt, you would say that this son does not love his father. What then must we think of a person who is so occupied with earthly cares and pleasures that he thinks nothing of his return to his heavenly Father in his heavenly home, who never thinks of heaven and eternity? We must say this: Evidently, this person does not love God, or at the very least, he loves the world more than he loves God.

True is the apostolic word: *If anyone loves the world, the love of the Father is not in him.* [1 John 2:15] Not only does he "not love" God, but he also *does not know God.* [1 John 4:8] What is left for such a person? What dignity in the present? What hope for the future? O mother of life! By the light of your life-bearing Dormition, awaken us from the death-bearing sleep of negligence concerning our eternal salvation.

Unto You I lift up my eyes, O You who dwell in the heavens. Give us "the first fruits of the Spirit," that, having disregarded both the joys and sorrows of this earth, we may *ourselves grown within ourselves, eagerly waiting* to be adopted by You, *desiring to be clothed with our habitation which is from heaven. Turn away my eyes that I may not see vanity; give me life in Your way.* Amen.

Psalm 122:1
Romans 8:23
2 Corinthians 5:2
Psalm 118:37

24

The Exalted Faith of the Virgin

Homily on the Annunciation of the Mother of God
(1850)

"And He will reign over the house of Jacob forever, and of His kingdom there will be no end." (Luke 1:33)

I**n today's Gospel reading, we heard the wondrous conversation between the archangel and the most pure Virgin, a conversation that spoke aloud, as much as this is possible, a great mystery of heaven and earth. Through this conversation, we can see an event that is incomprehensible for earthly and heavenly minds alike. When the archangel said to the Virgin: *Behold, you will conceive in your womb and bring forth a Son...the Holy Spirit will come upon you...*, and when the Virgin answered, *Behold the maidservant of the Lord! Let it be to me according to your word*, at this moment, through the mediation of their words, the earth was betrothed with heaven, mankind with God. As a direct consequence of this conversation, the One without beginning was conceived; *The Word became flesh*; the Son of God became the

Luke 1:31-38

John 1:14

Son of man, without ceasing to be the Son of God; A virgin became heaven and the throne of God; And the active principle of our salvation and blessedness (not merely the promise of it) was placed inside her.

How can this be? asked the most holy Virgin at first, not because of a lack of faith, not because of curiosity, but because of a sense of pious wonder, as well as a care for the preservation of her virginity, dedicated to God, when it was declared that she would be a mother. Do not dare, O inquisitive mind, to continue asking the same question after the event occurred. The angel will not come to resolve your inappropriate question. That the salvific incarnation of the Son of God occurred, you yourself can see by the miraculous and salvific results. Do not test what cannot be measured. Humble yourself before infinite wisdom. Be reverent before its mystery. Wonder at the profound condescension of the Almighty. Glorify and thank him for this undeserved, priceless gift. Embrace with faith the salvation offered to you, and do not test the Savior-God with the judgments of human reasoning. *Luke 1:34*

However, the Lord Himself did say, *Search [i.e., "test"] the Scriptures.* So we will allow ourselves this small examination, for it will be accessible and instructive for us. *John 5:39*

After the first, exalted, but still obscure greeting, the angels saw that she was terrified. *Do not be afraid, Mary,* he said. So why, at the same moment that he is trying to assuage her fear, is he telling her something that is even more wondrous and terrifying, when it seems that his message could have been delayed somewhat? Why did he not only tell her that she would give birth to a Son, while still remaining a virgin (for this was the point of his embassy), but wait until later to add that this Son would be Great, the Son of the Most High, the Savior, the King, and of such a kingdom that would have no end? This was necessary according to the law of faith, which is known to us from the following words of Christ: *If you can believe, all things are possible to him who* *Luke 1:30*

Mark 9:23

believes. For this reason, the most blessed Mary was capable of accepting as much as she believed. Thus, to make it possible for her to give birth to the God-Man, the Savior, the King of an eternal kingdom, it was necessary that she *first* hear and come to believe that she was to give birth to the God-Man, the Savior, the King of an eternal kingdom.

Let us then be amazed, brothers, at this exalted, unprecedented faith of the most holy Virgin, before which the faith of the father of faith, Abraham himself, at the prophecy of the birth of Isaac from barren old age, pales in comparison, like a mustard seed before the Cedar of Lebanon. With piety and joy, let us thank the most blessed Mary for having the power of such a faith, without which we would not have Christ the Savior, the King Who promised us a heavenly and eternal kingdom.

At the same time, let us instruct ourselves, brothers, about the power of faith. Faith was capable of fitting the limitless God in the person of the most holy Virgin, not only in a spiritual sense, but bodily. And I say to you again that faith fit God bodily within her; and I only wonder at this the more when I consider that compared to the spirit, the body seems completely foreign in nature to God the Spirit, both by its physicality and its limitation in space and its corruptibility. How could our faith every fail to satisfy us, when our requirements are so much less expansive that what was required of the faith of the Virgin? But how often among us is faith manifested in ways that are palpably above nature, clearly sealed by the presence of grace? For this reason, do we not need to pray, together with the apostles, in these words: *Increase our faith?* But the Lord, not rejecting the prayer, instead offers us the requirements of faith: *If you have faith as a mustard seed, you can say to this mulberry tree, 'Be pulled up by the roots and be planted in the sea,' and it would obey you.* In other words, if only you had the first fruits of faith from the sincere disposition of your heart! Then truly you would receive great power from grace. So, it is up to you, not to God. Cultivate a disposition of heart to believe, for this depends on you, and God will not delay to multiply strong faith in you, which is the gift of his grace.

Let us not also leave without attention the detail that it was required of the faith of the most holy Virgin Theotokos that she first accept the Son prophesied to her, not only in His capacity as Son of God and Savior of man, but in his role as King, for this was absolutely necessary for the mystery of the incarnation: *And He will reign over the house of Jacob forever, and of His kingdom there will be no end.* Thus we must conclude that it is essentially necessary for our salvific faith that we also accept—in the person of Jesus, the Son of God, the God-Man, our Savior—Him as our King. *Luke 1:33*

Truly, it is evident that such a faith is necessary, especially when we consider that the Lord Jesus, though usually avoiding human glory (and even once hurrying to conceal himself from a crowd that wanted to forcibly make Him king, did not deny His own kingship during His triumphant entry into Jerusalem. When the Pharisees insisted that He stop the people from exclaiming "blessed is the coming King," not only would He not do so, but He even confirmed that if all the people were to fall silent, the stones themselves would proclaim Him King: *I tell you that if these should keep silent, the stones would immediately cry out.* Similarly, when His title of kingship threatened death at the hands of the Romans, He only corrected an incorrect understanding about His kingdom, saying to Pilate: "My Kingdom is not of this world." But when Pilate asked Him, "Are you a king then?" He did not deny it, saying, *You say rightly that I am a king.* Finally, after His resurrection, He declared His kingly authority openly: *All authority has been given to Me in heaven and on earth.* He also called Himself a king during His prophecy of the final judgment over the whole cosmos: *Then the King will say to those on His right hand...* *John 6:15* *Luke 19:40* *John 18:36-37* *Matthew 28:18* *Matthew 25:34*

Christ rules over all the whole cosmos as its Creator and Provider, especially in the heavens as the King of glory. But He does also rule on earth in the Church's kingdom of grace. He rules as King here through His Word, as the law of the kingdom, and through His Spirit, as the power of kingship. His kingdom reaches all the way to the depths of the soul through the grace that He gives, as well as through our faith and love, as He said, *The kingdom of God is within you.* This is why we pray, *Thy kingdom come.* From the kingdom that is not of this world, He extends His kingly power both on the kingdoms and the peoples of this world, blessing, providing for, and giving grace to authorities and nations that live according to His spiritual kingdom. Those who rebel against Him, especially those who betray Him after first being loyal, will be subject to the threatening conviction of God the Father, Who gave Him the authority: *He shall break them with a rod of iron, He shall dash them to pieces like a potter's vessel.* Finally, on the last day of the world, Christ will appear as the Kingly Judge of the world to render to each according to his deeds, so that the temporal and transitional kingdom of nature and grace will be transformed into a single, eternal kingdom of glory.

Luke 17:21
Matthew 6:10

Psalm 2:9

Christians! It is pleasant for us to look at Christ as our Savior Who will forgive us our sins, Who reconciles us with eternal justice, Who frees us from eternal condemnation, Who makes us sons of God from sons of wrath, with the right of inheriting the heavenly. But let us be fair and appreciative. Let us not fail to remember to see Him as our King as well, Who has mastery over us in order to arrange our spiritual life, to preserve and protect us from enemy powers, to make of us worthy citizens of the kingdom of heaven, capable of accepting eternal blessedness, and Who, for this reason, requires of us complete submission to His majesty.

One is the Son of God, Jesus Christ, both Savior and King. He does not divide these qualities that He ascribed to Himself in His incarnation. If you do not want to have Him as your king, then you cannot have Him as your Savior.

Has your godfather never told you that gave an oath of fidelity to Christ the King? Truly, you did, when the lips of your godfather confessed several times that you reject Satan and all his works, and that you unite yourself and offer worship to Christ as King and God. And so, be constantly attentive that you are not deluded, lest you become an oath breaker and traitor. If you do not preserve your fidelity to Christ the King in your heart and life, in your words and deeds, and if you cannot repair the damage done by any infidelity through weakness or carelessness, then you will lose your right to Christ the King's patronage and Christ the Savior's mercy both. By your own deeds, you will add yourself to those raging nations and vainly plotting people who will be broken with a rod of iron.

Be faithful to Christ the King through your Orthodox faith, through obedience to His holy Church. Be faithful with love that has no taint of hypocrisy, a love that destroys all earthly passionate attachments. Be faithful by living according to the laws and teaching of the Gospel. Be faithful by hurrying to sincerely admit your falls into sin and restore the purity of your conscience, lest death itself hurries to shut the doors of your repentance. Listen to the words of Christ Himself, who commands and promises: *Be faithful until death, and I will give you the crown of life.* Revelation 2:10

Amen.

25

A Good Encounter with Death

Homily on the Dormition of the Mother of God
(1850)

"For to me, to live is Christ, and to die is gain." (Philippians 1:21)

It seems to me that today we are at a funeral, and yet, we are not at all sorrowful! How could two such opposites have met and reconciled?

The holy icon that has been placed here to instruct us about the meaning of this day and the subject of this assembly offers our gaze a deathbed, and on it we see the holy and life-bearing, but already life-less body. Around it we see the assembly of those bearing her body to its burial place in Gethsemane. Truly, this is a funeral. However, our own assembly, joining the assembly depicted in the icon, rejoices and celebrates. How have these opposites met and reconciled? And why have they been so united by nothing less than the imprimatur of the Church?

Here we see the power of grace-filled holiness. It transforms death into life, and then it transforms sorrow into joy. The most holy Virgin had a much greater right to say these words than Paul: "For to me, to live is Christ, and to die is gain." The mother of Life was not required to be subject to death, though she did need to pass through its domain. The Church thus looks at the tomb of the mother as a ladder to heaven where she goes, as the prophet foresaw, as a queen to stand at the right hand of Christ, *Psalm 44:10* the King of Heaven, not only so that she herself might be blessed in the kingdom, but, through the action of her prayerful intercession might also send down on us the rain of her blessings. Why should we not rejoice at this? How can we fail to celebrate?

And the Church, for all its joy, did not conceal the sad aspect of the funeral, naturally because simple truth requires that we remember the event. But also, because the Church, our mother, wishes for us to raise our gaze in contemplation of immortality and heaven, but also finds it necessary to offer a spectacle of death and the tomb for our attention and contemplation.

As we pass this earthly life, we never truly know what we will encounter: riches or poverty, honor or humiliation, love or hatred, joy or sorrow. Despite this indeterminacy, we still take care, more or less, to make sure that the pleasant encounters don't pass us by and that we might somehow avoid the unpleasant ones. But there is one meeting that we will never be able to avoid: This is our encounter with death. Should we not think of it? Having encountered the unpleasant things in life, such as poverty, you may continue your path with that unpleasant fellow traveler, still hoping for a better encounter in future, but having encountered death, you will fall into its hands, and they say that death is not gentle with everyone. *Precious in the sight of the Lord is* *Psalm 115:5* *the death of His holy ones. The death of sinners is evil.* And so, does not *Psalm 33:22* right reason simply demand that we take care—in good time, without delay—about how we can best prepare ourselves for a good encounter with death? Without delay, I say, because death never promised us to take its time until we are ready to greet it.

Should I speak of those who think not merely to avoid the question of preparation for death, but to destroy it completely by imagining there is no life after death? I know from the words of the rebuking wise man, that *they said among themselves, as they reasoned incorrectly: ...we were born by chance, and after this we shall be as though we never existed...our body will turn to ashes, and our breath will disperse like empty air.* It would have been difficult to believe that there are people who think like this, except that it is well known that evil requires falsehood and madness for its existence. It is interesting that the Wise Man here says, "they reasoned incorrectly," for these people do not say the things they do because they are convinced of them, but because their thoughts have turned aside form righteousness and virtue. They strain to express their false thoughts in a seductive manner, because that way they can justify their sinful way of life: *Let our might be our law of righteousness... let us lie in ambush for the righteous man, because he.... accuses us of sins against our upbringing. He has become to us a refutation of our purposes.* I don't want to speak of these people anymore. It is a shame for humanity that there are people who imagine that they are wiser than others, but who are more foolish than the silkworm, which prepares itself for death by weaving a silk coffin, not to dissolve in it, but to resurrect into the aerial life of a butterfly.

Wisdom of Solomon 2:1-3

Wisdom of Solomon 2:11-14

Some, though not brazen or mad enough to deflect thoughts of death by unbelief, still think very little, or not at all, about death, because they are so occupied with other objects. There are very many such people; It is not difficult to find them. They are the world. Passionately attached to sensual pleasures, they either seek these pleasures or plunge themselves into them or rest from them in exhaustion or once again seek them passionately. This is the substance of their days and nights. Such a person has no time to think that his soul is not properly aligned to converse with the unsmiling thought of death. If the thought does occur to him, he hurries to dispel it, not thinking that if it is difficult to bear the accidental presence of a thought of death, then how much more difficult will it be to bear the sudden appearance of death itself, which he will not be able to send away!

A person who is constantly busy working or hunting or in service or in need of food or in love with money lives for this state of busyness. It dominates his time, abilities, powers, thoughts, and desires. If he does extend his gaze to the future, it is only to see what future work awaits him or what future success he may attain. Together with the parabolic rich man, he builds new granaries in the future, assembling new plans of earthly prosperity, and he has no time to think that maybe, without any warning (a warning the rich man in the Gospel did receive), *this night [his] soul will be required of [him]*? A slave of his habits and vain rituals, even when he approaches death in his old age, he doesn't want to notice death's approach, though it is almost before him already. Food and clothing, visits and parties, habitual pleasures occupy him, as do his service and duty; These childish games are his daily lessons of wisdom. At leisure from these active forms of leisure, he wanders in his thought into imaginative remembrances of the past, lest he might touch the unimaginative future with his thoughts, and there encounter death.

_{Luke 12:20}

What else will this inattentiveness to death lead to, except to difficulties at death and even after death? If it was not told to us that there is a hellish abyss and fire on the other side, yawning to swallow all those who did not built a ladder for themselves to heaven during this life, we would still, by the very qualities of our soul and the experience of our earthly life, be able to realize how dangerous will be the passage into the world of the spirits without any spiritual preparation, with only our habits and passionate attachments to the earthly and sensual. The soul finds pleasure in the things that surround it, in the things to which the mind and will attach themselves. If the soul is deprived of these things, it will feel hunger, sorrow, suffering, and death. But tearing away the mind and will from a single object and attaching it to another occurs slowly because of the way of nature. Therefore, any soul that passes through death into the world of the spirits with only its habits and passionate earthly attachments, without spiritual preparation, will naturally encounter something like what occurred with the rich man in the parable of the rich man and Lazarus.

This man occupied himself before death primarily with food and drink that sweetened his tongue. Therefore, after death he found no better thought or desire than finding something that would cool his tongue, but he could not find the drop of water he desired. The soul, upon arriving in the unfamiliar spiritual world, dreams of its typical earthly cares, thirsting for its habitual sensual pleasures, but they do not exist there. On the contrary, there we have more exalted objects of contemplation, more pure sources of joy and blessedness, but they are foreign to the soul's mind and will. And so, what is left for the soul? Its inner emptiness, hunger, sorrow, suffering—its eternal death.

Therefore, it is obvious that we must prepare and dispose ourselves for a successful passage beyond the grave while still on this side of the grave. How? We must, as much as possible, reject ourselves and free ourselves from attachments and passions to earthly, carnal, sensual things, because *flesh and blood cannot inherit the kingdom of God.* Since *we look for new heavens and a new earth in which righteousness dwells,* we must seek for righteousness to dwell in us, so that we might live in the kingdom of God after death together with righteousness. We must be inspired by love for good; We must do good deeds.

Perhaps some people might think: How can good deeds done in our earthly life be beneficial to us beyond the grave? Will they not remain on earth, like everything else that we have and do here? No, brothers. This is not the thought of those who know the mysteries and judgments of God. They believe that good deeds

1 Corinthians 15:50
2 Peter 3:13

pass together with us beyond the grave. The voice from heaven that spoke to the seer John called those who die in the Lord "blessed," and it promised them "rest," and it gave this as a reason for their blessed rest: *Their works follow them.* If the essence of some good deeds, such as almsgiving, for example, does belong to this earth and remains here, still, the spirit of these virtues belongs to the soul, the heart, the will, and the conscience. Therefore, these deeds will be carried on into eternity, revealed by the world of the conscience, by the holy power of the will, by the joy of the heart, and by the blessedness of the soul. *Revelation 14:13*

Moreover, we will fool ourselves if we say: We will begin to do good deeds, and this is enough to prepare ourselves for death and eternal blessedness. The Word of God says concerning the law of God and the good deeds of the Law: *The man who does them shall live by them.* But He also says, *Whoever shall keep the whole law, and yet stumble in one point, he is guilty of all.* Who of us has not sinned in some "one point," and much more than in "one point"? Consequently, who has not damaged, more or less, any good deeds that he may have accomplished? Who has not become guilty before the eternal justice of God? And guilt does not lead to eternal rest and blessedness, but to judgment and punishment. Thus, in order to properly prepare ourselves for our future, we must also take great care to purify our good deeds from being intermixed with sin, to free ourselves from guilt. But if our good deeds do not help us enough, requiring us to work even to purify them, then where will be find the necessary help? Can heaven and earth, or the very angels in heaven make a guilty person righteous, or a sinner a saint? Naturally, they cannot. So, what will become of us? Must we then admit that, because of the sinful corruption of our nature, we are fallen creatures? Truly, we are fallen, but let this admission be made without despair, and not without hope, and here we can begin to see the true path to salvation. *Galatians 3:12* *James 2:10*

For the Son of Man has come to save that which was lost. The incarnate Son of God frees us from guilt before eternal justice, for He *Matthew 18:11* is *the Lamb of God who takes away the sin of the world.* He gives our good deeds power, purity, and perfection, for *what the law could not do in that it was weak through the flesh, God did by sending His own Son in the likeness of sinful flesh, ... that the righteous requirement of the law might be fulfilled in us who do not walk according to the flesh but according to the Spirit.* He speaks to us, and His words are *spirit, and they are life.* He commands, and with this command He unites blessedness and the kingdom of heaven: *Blessed are the poor in spirit, for theirs is the kingdom of heaven.* He commands that we believe, and He promises, *where I am, there My servant will be also.* He suffers on the cross, and He gives us the image and the power to *crucify the flesh with its passions and desires.* He dies and rises again; by doing so, He blazed a trail through the domain of death to life eternal.

Do you now see, O Christian, what is most needful for a proper preparation for death and the eternal life? Believe in the Lord Jesus, and call upon Him. Follow His teaching and example; attach yourself to Him in thought, mind, and heart; and you will be able, without error, to say together with Apostle Paul, "For to me, to live is Christ, and to die is gain." Amen.

26

The Consent of the Virgin

Homily on the Annunciation of the Mother of God
(1851)

"Then Mary said, 'Behold the maidservant of the Lord! Let it be to me according to your word.' And the angel departed from her."
(Luke 1:38)

Every major feast of the Church calls us to contemplate one of the mysteries of faith, which comprises the subject, soul, holiness, and glory of that feast, so that we might benefit our souls from this contemplation. This is certainly true of today's feast. For the feasts of the Church were established not only for rejoicing, as civil feasts are, but for consolation and instruction that might aid the salvation of our souls. On earthly feast days, that which was gathered during days of work is habitually wasted. However, on the feast days of the Church, we can and must gather spiritual treasures of contemplative and active wisdom just as abundantly, or even more abundantly, than in non-festal days.

The mystery of this present feast is usually expressed in the name "annunciation," that is, the announcement from God and the bringing of the good news by Archangel Gabriel to the most holy Virgin Mary that in her would be accomplished the incarnation of the Son of God. She would give birth to the Christ.

But if all that was required was to bring news, then it would have been enough for the archangel to say a few words only: "You will give birth to Christ." But this is not what happened.

The archangel approaches the most holy Virgin with a greeting: *Rejoice, highly favored one, the Lord is with you. Blessed are you among women.* This greeting is triumphant, but vague. It disposes the hearer to expect a miracle, but it is unclear what sort of a miracle will come. The most holy Virgin, who knew the Scriptures well, could perhaps have remembered that when the angel approached Gideon with a greeting: *The Lord is with you*, he was preparing him to deliver Israel from its enemies in miraculous fashion. She *was troubled at his saying*, the evangelist tells us, though she was not troubled by doubt or unbelief, but rather this was the confusion of her humble-mindedness before an exalted and unexpected visitation. The bright spirit of the archangel saw this emotion and hurried to return peace and quiet to the soul of the most pure Virgin, because those were necessary for her to accept the most exalted spiritual light: *Do not be afraid, Mary, for you have found favor with God.* Then, he pours divine light in its fullness, as into a specially prepared and open vessel: *Behold, you will conceive in your womb and bring forth a Son...He will be great, and will be called the Son of the Highest...And He will reign over the house of Jacob forever, and of His kingdom there will be no end.*

In this way, the great will of the heavenly Father was announced. The mystery of the incarnation of the Son of God was revealed. However, this was not the end of the annunciation. A question arose in the soul of the most pure Virgin, and the angel did not dare depart until he answered it, because the question did not arise from unbelief or inquisitiveness, but from a dominating love for the purity of virginity. And he answered her also because this dominating love for complete purity was the worthy vessel for the mystery of the incarnation of God the Word. This love for perfect purity spoke aloud in Mary's question: "How can this be, since I do not know a man?" This question attracted yet a new stream of divine light and power in the words of the archangel: *The Holy Spirit will come upon you, and the power of the Highest will overshadow you.* *Luke 1:34-35*

What can be stronger than this word? However, having uttered it, the archangel still does not consider his embassy at an end. He awaits still another word from Mary. Evidently, it was not enough for her to silently accept the heavenly news. It was necessary for a word of agreement to betroth itself with the word of divine annunciation. To achieve this, the archangel points to an event that, though much lower in significance, still was only possible through a miracle of God. He indicated that the righteous Elizabeth, who was infertile and past the age of childbearing, had conceived a son. He also pointed to the wondrous omnipotence of God in general: *For with God nothing will be impossible.* *Luke 1:37* And so, finally, the humble will of Mary was aroused to meet the almighty will of God: *Then Mary said, 'Behold the maidservant of the* *Luke 1:37-38* *Lord! Let it be to me according to your word.'* Now, it seems, Gabriel was satisfied that the work of the pre-eternal counsel, given to him, was fully accomplished: *And the angel departed from her.*

And still, some might think that we might hear the annunciation of the mystery of the incarnation, we might see the acceptance of this good news, but where is the mystery itself? It is not merely the gift of God, but God Himself Who fills the most pure Virgin. so how do we not see this actual appearance of the divine, neither in a reflection of God's light in Mary's face, nor in an expression of joy from the archangel? *And the angel departed* *Luke 1:38* *from her.* That is all.

It is easy not only for philosophy but also for foolishness to ask questions that no wisdom can ever answer. *For who has known* *1 Corinthians 2:15 the mind of the Lord that he may instruct Him?* If you wish to plumb the depths of the mystery of the incarnation of the Son of God, or bring down the mystery of this supernatural action to you in a form you can understand, then you wish to be greater than the angels. This is doubtless an inappropriate pretension! For, as Apostle Peter said, even the angels only *desire to look into* the mysteries of God, that is, they desire to see the full depth of their meaning, but cannot understand it. They desire to do so by their love for God, but they cannot understand, because of the unapproachable nature of the Divine, because they have limited vision, being limited beings looking at a subject of infinite vastness.

1 Peter 1:12

"She who encompassed the uncircumscribable God," without a doubt, sensed internally the light, the glory, and the blessedness of this unique union with God. It is also likely that the gaze of the archangel wondrously sensed the dawn of the divine Light and was joyful at it, but the inconceivable must remain unknown, a *mystery…hidden from ages and from generations*. The time had not yet arrived to reveal this mystery to many, and it was only proper for the mother of God to cover the descent of the divine light by the cloud of her humility, and for the archangel to honor her who is "more honorable than the Cherubim and beyond compare more glorious than the Seraphim" with a silent reverence.

Colossians 1:26

Examining this conversation between the heavenly messenger and the most holy Virgin, we may be led to another kind of question, more appropriate for our instruction. Why did the archangel not find it sufficient to merely speak the words of greeting, but instead used, one might say, insistent means to acquire her words of consent? Can it be that without this word of Mary, the incarnation of the Son of God would not have occurred? Can it be possible that the almighty will of God needed the consent of the will of a woman? These are apparently difficult questions, but they can be easily answered.

We find these answers in the Gospels. Archangel Gabriel, without a doubt, did exactly what God's commanding word told him to do. But the archangel, not limiting himself to the words of annunciation, did not stop conversing with the most holy Virgin, until he heard from her the words of consent: *Let it be according to your word.* Consequently, this was God's will. Consequently, that is how it had to be. Consequently, this consent was required by God's wisdom and judgment. *Luke 1:38*

If we wish to understand why the almighty will of God acts in cooperation with human wills in the working out of His Providence, we must turn to the principle and essential qualities of human nature. Man was created in God's image. An important quality of this image was placed into his will: This is the reasoning freedom that separates man form the lower orders of God's creation, none of whom have God's image. Therefore, God always preserves the free will of man inviolate, preserving this aspect of His own image in man. Therefore, even when He acts in His limitless omnipotence, He always considers the free will of man whenever Providence's actions affect the inner, spiritual state of man. Man, for his part, is only capable of closer communion and union with God because of the power of God's image within him, because the best that exists in created beings, all that is worthy of God's approval and good will, all that can aid man's approach to God and a blessed union with him, is of course the image of God. Therefore, to acquire communion and blessed union with God, man must turn toward God with the qualities that are stamped with the qualities of His image, i.e., man must strive toward Him with his mind, will, heart, and especially to unite his will with God's will by the movement of his own free choice, through the aid of faith and love.

When David foretold the exalted communion of God with the most blessed Virgin Mary through the incarnation, within her, of the Son of God, he added the following: *The virgins behind her shall be brought to the King.* These "virgins" symbolize the souls that have not been corrupted by love for the flesh and the world, or those souls that have been purified of this disordered love. If you wish, these, O Christians, are your souls, since they preserve their spiritual virginity, in which they were reborn in the laver of baptism, or into which they return after repentance. They must also be *brought to the King,* God, though not next to the queen of heaven, who is ahead of everyone else, for she is higher than everyone else. Still, *behind her* means that we must follow, to a certain degree, her own example, that is, our souls must be brought to a certain degree of communion with God. Do not be slothful in using this advantage that is offered you and is almost ensured by the prophecy. Examine carefully the path laid by the queen of heaven, and then actively follow it. You will then also have a certain kind of annunciation, proper to your own level: You will hear a personal proclamation of *His salvation from day to day.* Accept this word of salvation as the parched earth absorbs the falling rain.

The One Who descended into the Virgin with His hypostasis still continues to descend, *that Christ may dwell in your hearts through faith.* Do not remain inactive: *Behold, the bridegroom is coming; go out to meet him!* Meet the approach of God's grace with your own heart's desire. The One Who created you without your will has determined to save you not without your own will, and by doing so He indicated the exaltedness of your nature, even in its fallen state. His will, always salvific, awaits our will, which must accept salvation. Do not delay, do not vacillate, make a firm decision to subordinate your will to the majestic will of God in fearful obedience. Commit your will to the all-good will of God through faith in the hope of finally uniting them with the bonds of love: *The bond of perfection.*

The blissful light of God can only shine in an atmosphere where the darkness of willful, passionate, sensual, earthly desires has been cleared. Only a will dedicated wholly to God can rule with God in the heavens. And, on the contrary, if anything in our present life causes the fire of hell to come alight in our hearts, this will become the food of hell for eternity. This is a will disobedient before God.

Amen.

27

Death Rendered Into Sleep

Homily on the Dormition of the Mother of God
(1851)

"After that He said to them, 'Our friend Lazarus sleeps.'"
(John 11:11)

Today we remember the Dormition of the most holy mother of God piously and festively. What does "Dormition" mean? The literal meaning is "falling asleep." That is, the end of the earthly life of the mother of God. It is interesting that the Church wanted to avoid using the word "death," when speaking of the mother of Life. But where did they find this word, "Dormition," to substitute for "death"? We must assume that it came directly from the lips of Christ the Savior. *Our friend Lazarus sleeps*, the Lord said to the apostles, telling them of Lazarus' recent death, though he was far away from the place where it happened.[1] Clearly, this was a new kind of language for

---

[1] Unfortunately, this central point that St Philaret makes is untranslatable. In the Slavonic, the word used for Lazarus's "sleep" is the verb form of "dormition." So the

the apostles, because they didn't understand him, and so the Lord found it necessary to translate his original phrase to their quotidian language: *Lazarus is dead.* *John 11:14*

What is this new language? Why did Christ and the Church call death a kind of sleep? What sort of contemplation do they hope to arouse in our hearts by doing so? Today is a good time to answer these questions.

Why the death of Lazarus is called "sleep" is not difficult to understand. After all, his death had one unique quality shared with sleep—imminent awakening, that is, a return to previous life. In the word, "he fell to Dormition," Christ simultaneously told them of Lazarus's death and prophesied that he would rise again in four days.

A similar reason can be extrapolated for why the death of the mother of God is called "Dormition." Her death had the same unique quality shared with sleep—imminent awakening—that is, she was soon to resurrect fully to the eternal life. In the word "Dormition" we have a cryptic reference to the ecclesiastical tradition that the mother of God, three days after her death, appeared to the apostles in heavenly glory. This was not merely her spirit, but it was her glorified body and soul reunited, for later they could not find her body in her tomb.

Moreover, in the writings of the apostles, we see the established custom to generally call death by the name of "sleep." Thus, for examples, Apostle Paul wrote concerning the witnesses of the resurrected Lord: *He was seen by over five hundred brethren at once, of whom the greater part remain to the present, but some have fallen asleep.* He also wrote concerning the resurrection of the dead: *We shall not all sleep, but we shall all be changed.* That is, not all of us will die, because the last day of the world will find some people still living on earth; But all will be changed, because those whom the final day finds living will have no time to die and be buried. *1 Corinthians 15:6*   *1 Corinthians 15:51*

---

technical translation would be "Our friend Lazarus has fallen to dormition."

Their bodies, without undergoing death, will transform from their corruptible to their incorrupt forms, the same bodies as those who are resurrected from the dead.

This change in the name of death to sleep was doubtless intended to inspire in Christians the need to look at death as the *ignorant...concerning those who have fallen asleep, lest you sorrow as others who have no hope,* who think that death is a complete end of life and a dissolution of personality and being. Instead, Christians can hope that just as one who has fallen asleep at night wakes up the next morning with a renewed strength to live, so also he who falls asleep in death will awaken on the morning of the universal salvation into a new, eternal life. Therefore, if we are attentive, then as we say the word "Dormition," we are actually reminding ourselves of the teaching concerning the immortality of the soul and we are confirming ourselves in the hope of the resurrection of the body.

1 Thessalonians 4:13

Let us now turn from the New Testament writings to the Old. We note that in the Old Covenant, there is no such consoling care to cover the thought of death with bright clothing. Even the death of the righteous and the saints is never called a falling asleep, but simply death. In the book of Genesis, Adam's death is treated thus: *Adam lived... and he died.* The father of the faithful is treated thus: *Abraham breathed his last and died.* The same was said of Samuel: *Samuel died.* The Patriarch Jacob spoke of his death in even more stark terms: *For I shall go down into the grave to my son in mourning.* Why do even the saints of the Old Testament have such a joyless view of death, even though they, without a doubt, believed in the resurrection of the dead, as we do, and the life of the age to come?

Genesis 5:5
Genesis 25:8
1 Kingdoms 25:1
Genesis 37:35

The answer is this: *Death reigned,* for it was not yet vanquished by the life-creating death of Christ. Another answer is this: *The way into the Holiest of All was not yet made manifest.* In other words, the way to heaven was not yet opened, *where the forerunner had entered for us, even Jesus.* The Old Testament patriarchs, prophets,

Romans 5:14
Hebrews 9:8
Hebrews 6:20

and righteous ones *all died in faith, not having received the [fulfillment of the] promises, but having seen them afar off were assured of them, embracing them.* Therefore, the near darkness of death left more of an impression on them than the distant light of the resurrection. *Hebrews 11:13*

The opposite state of mankind in the Old and New Covenants reveals a new reason for why we cease to look at death as death, but only as a kind of sleep. If we, condemned to death in our first parents and daily confirming our own personal condemnation by willful sins, were not redeemed from this condemnation by the suffering and death of Christ, then our temporal death would accompany us into eternal death, with no hope of being reawakened to life. This would have been complete death. But when *Christ died for us,* when we *were reconciled to God through the death of His Son,* when *God, who is rich in mercy, because of His great love with which He loved us, even when we were dead din trespasses, made us alive together with Christ,* when *in Christ all shall be made alive,* even after death, coming back to an eternal and blessed life (which no life in Christ can fail to be), then death truly ceased being death and became a kind of sleep. This is a short-lived sleep compared to the eternal life that is to follow it, a calm sleep, a rest from labors, a consolation from sorrows, a comfort for those who have been pacified by Christ in their consciences. This will not be a sleep without consciousness—for the body sleeps, but not the soul—but a consciously sweet one, like a foretaste of future blessedness. *Romans 5:8, 10* *Ephesians 2:4-5* *1 Corinthians 15:22*

Moreover, we must not forget that the advantage of the grace-filled state of mankind in the New Covenant, though open and accessible to all, does not automatically belong to each of us merely because we live in the time of the New Testament. There were people living in the distant times of the Old Testament that had a New Testament spirit. One of these was Abraham, who *rejoiced to see* the day of God and *was glad,* and, of course, he enjoyed *John 8:56* all the benefits that Christ revealed to mankind. The opposite is also true: There are in these grace-filled times of the New Testament also people who do not belong to the grace-filled Covenant of God by their inner disposition, even if they carry the name of Christian superficially. The door of grace is opened to all in Christ, Who said, *I am the door. If anyone enters by Me, he will be saved.* But you must still enter that door, and you can only enter with faith, and not just any faith, but living and active faith. *I live by faith in the Son of God*, said the Apostle Paul. Whoever inflamed this life within him and preserved it, in the tomb he will not *sleep unto death*. Instead, he will rise from his bed of corruption into incorruption, into life, into heaven, into blessedness, into glory.

John 10:9

Galatians 2:20

Psalm 12:4

But whoever does not strive to enter the exalted, blessed life of the spirit and continues to live the life of the old Adam, a life of carnality, sensuality, sin, driven by thoughts of passions and lusts, though appearing to be alive, he plunges into actual inner death, because *sin, when it is full-grown, brings forth death*. Later, if he will not turn and repent, he will die the visible death of a sinner, which is evil, because by that death he finally passes into eternal death. No matter how much he would like to transform it into a deep sleep to forget its tortures, he will not be able to, because he will be constantly awoken by the fire that does not fade, the worm that does not die, the boiling brimstone. This awakening will not be to life, but always to renewed death.

James 1:15

Psalm 33:22

Oh, my mortal brother! May your life be as long as possible; however, our deathbed is not far, and as often happens, it is likely nearer than we think. Think, then, in good time, what you would desire to find on that bed: A peaceful sleep or an evil death? Truly, you will find what you yourself have chosen and prepared. *Whatever a man sows, that he will also reap.* Let us stop sowing death and suffering for ourselves through our sins. Let us instead sow life and rest for ourselves through repentance, faith, and virtue. Amen.

Galatians 6:7

28

Cultivating Pious Contemplation

Homily on the Annunciation of the Mother of God
(1852)

"She...considered what manner of greeting this was." (Luke 1:29)

Look at how the most holy Virgin stands in thought. It seems to me that she teaches us how to contemplate. I will explain. When the archangel Gabriel, sent to announce to her the incarnation of the Son of God within her womb, began his annunciation with a greeting, *Rejoice, highly favored one, the Lord is with you; Blessed are you among women*, she, as St Luke tells us, *was troubled at his saying*, and as the archangel himself saw, grew afraid. For he, as a spirit, saw through her silence to the disturbance in her soul, and said, *Do not be afraid, Mary*. [Luke 1:28-30]

What happens to us when we are terrified or distressed? We shake, cry out, try to run away, and sometimes get so thrown off balance that we can't control our thoughts, words, or movements. This is due to our imperfections, our lack of courage, our weakness. This is not how it was in the grace-filled Virgin. After the external stimulus that led to her unwilling confusion and fear, she immediately contained her confusion and calmed her fear. How? By contemplation. *She considered.*

For fear is nothing but the betrayal of the assistance that comes from reasoning. The most wise Virgin was not long abandoned by this assistance, but immediately took advantage of it. "She considered."

Both the reason for her confusion and fear, as well as the subject of her contemplation, was the unusual greeting of the Archangel. *She was troubled at his saying and considered what manner of greeting this was.* The archangel called the Virgin Mary a *highly favored one*, that is, one who is filled with the exalted gifts of God, surpassing natural goodness, and one *blessed among women*, meaning more blessed than all women at all times in the entire human race. Therefore, it is not surprising that she was confused and terrified, like a person who has suddenly been raised to a mountain peak. So how did she seek the "assistance that comes from reasoning" and find it? The gaze of the archangel could plumb the depth of that mystery, but we can only guess at it.

Likely, her thoughts went something like this: "What am I to do? Will I accept this unusual greeting? I fear, lest it be to my pride. Will I reject it? I fear, lest I offend with my unbelief not only God's messenger, but God Himself. I will wait in silence and see what God will reveal further."

And so, she did not accept the exalted greeting, and by doing so preserved her humility, but neither did she reject it, and so preserved her faith. By preserving both her humility and faith, she kept that pure disposition of spirit that had made her capable of accepting this most exalted of divine revelations. As for the divine annunciation that she would give birth to Christ God, that the Holy Spirit would descend upon her, only the most complete humility could answer in a worthy fashion: "Behold, the maidservant of the Lord," and only perfect faith could have said

Luke 1:29
Wisdom of Solomon 17:11

Luke 1:29
Luke 1:28
Luke 1:42

to the angel, with unconfused boldness, *Let it be to me according to your word.* ⟵ *Luke 1:38*

Do you see, brothers, that the mother of God, in one of the most difficult moments of her spiritual life, sought her aid in pious and humble contemplation? And truly, she found her deliverance there. And if the Spirit of God showed us this quality of her spiritual life in the evangelical account—and *whatever things were written...were written for our learning,*—then we must admit that the Spirit of God instructs us to emulate her pious reasoning. ⟵ *Romans 15:4*

The fact that we see the mother of God run to the aid of pious contemplation in one of the most difficult moments of her life does not mean that she only used her pious reasoning in similarly difficult moments. We know from experience that whoever has not trained himself to use calm reasoning will not be able to use it in difficult or sudden situations. Thus, if the mother of God did run to the aid of pious reasoning during a sudden or difficult moment, that meant that she had earlier trained herself to think in this way, and had acquired a habit of it. And so, the teaching offered to us in her example becomes more detailed, and we must now conclude that pious reasoning must be a constant companion for a person in the spiritual life.

Just as a tree with all of its fruits grows from a seed hidden underground, so a person's moral life, with its deeds, grows from thoughts that are concealed in the soul. The kind of seed that is fed by the soil will determine the kind of tree and fruit; The manner of thoughts fed by the heart will determine the kind of life and deeds. Whoever permits distracted, inconstant thoughts, unguided by pious reasoning, will naturally give rise to a life of distraction, inconstancy, and disorder. Thus, labor to sow pious and good thoughts in your mind and heart, so that you might give fruit to a pious and virtuous life. Moreover, don't throw the seeds superficially, accidentally, wherever they might fall, but as a skilled and careful sower, with discernment and order, in moderation. Sow them into the deep furrow of the mind and constantly nourish them with the sensations of the heart; And as the soil allows the roots of the seed to push deep into it, thereby allowing the plant to grow tall and broad, so also should you allow your thoughts and contemplations, like the roots of a tree, to deepen all that is good and holy within you, so that your active life may rise high in labors and broaden in the number of good deeds.

In our time, when people *have sought out many schemes* more than in the past, when from the earliest years people try to arouse and strengthen the activity of the mind, when people seek so-called education, refinement, pleasure, gain, glory in a variety of thoughts, when the soul, as a result, is so easily sowed with tare-like thoughts—we must especially call people to the foundational kind of reasoning, which is pure, exalted, and pious.

Ecclesiastes 7:29

But we see in the Holy Scriptures that in the times of ancient simplicity God Himself taught people pious reasoning. Moses said, commanded by God, "Hear, O Israel: The Lord our God, the Lord is one! You shall love the Lord your God with all your heart, with all your soul, and with all your strength." In order to root these most important truths of piety in the chosen nation, Moses added, *And these words which I command you today shall be in your heart. You shall teach them diligently to your children, and shall talk of them when you sit in your house, when you walk by the way, when you lie down, and when you rise up.* From the last two—lying down and rising up—it becomes clear that talking of these truths is not limited to conversation with others, but with yourself as well, that is, in contemplation.

Deuteronomy 6:4-7

King David declared that blessed is the man who roots his will in the law of the Lord and who instructs himself in the Law day and night. How can one instruct oneself in the Law both day and night? In David's time, the world was not so filled with teachers and books as today, and still, even in our present abundance of teachers and books we still cannot spend both day and night with them. However, it was not some dreamer, but a prophet, who promised blessedness and gave a specific means toward that blessedness in the study of the Law both day and night. How is this possible?

It is possible through the aid of pious reasoning and the prayer of the heart, because these are things that a person can occupy himself with, as Moses said, "when you sit in your house, when you walk by the way, when you lie down, and when you rise up." For what reason do you allow your thoughts to run around without direction or without a goal, like untrained and untamed horses? Train yourselves to *squeeze their jaws with bit and bridle*, with a firm will and a confirmed reasoning. Depending on need, either lead them to rest or direct them to the right path, to a beneficial goal, primarily to the most important goal of your existence: God, Christ, heaven, eternity. Psalm 31:9

Will you perhaps say that the objects of this world unwillingly defeat your senses and distract your thoughts? It is true that they unwillingly defeat your senses, but they have no power to distract your thoughts if you do not abandon yourself to this inclination. You can, especially with God's help, *turn away [your] eyes that [you] may not see vanity*. Or, gazing at your physical eyes with your spiritual eyes, you can, like St. Tikhon, "gather a spiritual treasure from the world." As St. Makarius the Great said, "Everything that is subject to our gaze is a shadow and an image of things that refer to our soul." And so, as he also teaches, "when you look at the sun, seek the true Sun, for you are blind. When you look at the light, turn from there with your eyes to your soul, and see if you have any true and good light there, that is, the Lord." (Homily 33) Psalm 118:37

How much more natural is it for a Christian to diligently extend the thoughts of our heart to the One Whose name you bear, to remember the life of Christ the Lord, the better to follow Him, to attend to His teaching and commandments, the better to fulfill them, to piously contemplate His suffering and crucifixion, for the sake of the purification of our sins, and His glorious resurrection, for the sake of our blessed resurrection. If we feed and strengthen our faith, love, and hope in this way, Christ God will live within man while he is still on this earth, and later, man will live in God in the heavens for all eternity. Amen.

29

The Inheritance that the Virgin Bequeathes

*Homily on the Dormition of the Mother of God
and Her Appearance to the Apostles on the Third Day
(1852)*

After someone dies, there is usually a time of sorrow, then a time of consolation for the sorrowful. After both comes a time during which the deceased's children and dear ones take advantage of the righteous inheritance of those who have fallen asleep.

The Dormition of the most holy mother of God should be accompanied by a similar inheritance that is natural, since we are related to her by nature, and that is abundant, since she has been given abundant grace.

The apostles wept when the life of the mother of the Light, as a quiet dawn after the shining of the divine Sun, Christ, for the Church, went out before their eyes. They wept bitter tears of natural grief, but at the same time they wept sweet tears of grace-filled compunction, because their faith in the undying grace of the mother of the Lord and their sense of reverent love for her ruled over their feelings of loss.

Naturally, they received a complete and perfect consolation when, three days after her Dormition, they opened her tomb for the always-dilatory Thomas and did not find her body there. Immediately after this, they saw her in the glory of the resurrection, and heard from her own lips these words of consolation: "Rejoice, for I am with you for all times."

If the joy given by the resurrected mother of God has as its source the presence of the mother of God with us at all times, then it is obvious that this joy, as the stream pouring from such a source, should pour out into all times until it falls into the sea of eternal blessedness. And this is the wondrous and unexpected inheritance that the mother of God, after her death, not only bequeathed to us, but also definitively appointed and offered to those who are her children and near ones by grace. "Rejoice, for I am with you for all times."

The Church of Christ accepted this inheritance from the mother of God and preserves it from day to day, from year to year, from age to age, never ceasing to distribute it. For what other reason than this has the Church today gathered this assembly, so that each individually might accept a portion of this holy and beneficial joy from the grace-filled treasure-box of the Queen of Heaven?

Truly, she did not promise this joy to all without distinction, but primarily to the apostles; However, since she promised to continue this joy, together with her presence, in the Church for all times, she extended this promise to all of us who lived after the apostolic age, as long as we become her children and dear ones, through our faith in her undying grace and our reverent love for her own person.

And so, rejoice, O souls who labor in the faith, in emulation of Peter, who confessed Christ to be the Son of God more quickly than all others, and, believing in Him, found the courage to walk on water! The mother of the Master and Completer of our faith is with you, and she will aid you through all temptations and dangers to achieve blessedness.

Rejoice, O souls who strive toward the perfection of love, like the beloved apostle, who contemplated God primarily in His quality of love, with the eye of love, and contained his entire teaching of life within love! His adopted mother is with you, and she will not reject you as her adopted children, so that she might direct your spiritual formation from slavish fear to *perfect love [that] casts out fear.*   *1 John 4:18*

Rejoice, zealots of the word of truth! The mother of the eternal Logos is with you and constantly intercedes on your behalf before Him, that He will give you *a mouth and wisdom which all your adversaries will not be able to contradict or resist.*   *Luke 21:15*

Rejoice, keepers of chastity and virginity! The ever-Virgin is with you, and just as virginity brought John closer to her, so it will also bring her closer to you. Those who live in seclusion from the world, wisely remaining chaste in spirit and body, know this very well from their own experience, and some of these have shared their knowledge with the world, including Anthony of the Kiev Caves and Sergius of Radonezh.

Rejoice also those of you who are in the blessed state of marriage! The betrothed Virgin and unwedded mother—who not only found it right to visit a bride and groom in Cana of Galilee, but even to request the first open miracle of her divine Son for their sake—does not turn away from you either. She loves virginity, but she does not demean marriage, nor does she deprive you who pray to her of her grace-filled aid, if you consider your marriage state as a union not only of body, but of spirit, being an exalted mystical image of the union of Christ and the Church.

Rejoice, you pious parents who raise your children in godliness! The daughter of the prayers of the righteous Joachim and Anna, who was raised in the house of God, the mother of the Son, from Whom all sonship in heaven and earth has its principle, calls you her own dear ones and children in spirit, and she extends her grace-filled protection over you, from the heavenly house of God to the earthly.

Rejoice, even through your tears, you who are tested by various sorrows, but who hold firm in patience and hope in God! She who was tested with sorrows more than anyone else on earth (save her only-begotten Son alone), she whose soul was pierced by a sword, knows from her own experience what you are feeling, and she suffers with you, and she wishes and is able to lessen your sufferings, which is why she is called the Joy of All Who Sorrow.

Luke 2:35

But we cannot fail to notice that many do not enter into the promised inheritance of the Queen of Heaven. What remains for such people? What can they expect, who do not labor in the faith, who do not strive to the perfection of divine love, who do not have zeal for truth and righteousness, who do not honor virginity or sanctify marriage, childbearing, and child-rearing, who do not bless God in their happiness, and who curse God in their misfortune? We must say the truth: It was not to them that the mother of God uttered her immortal "Rejoice!" It was not to them that she promised her grace-filled presence. However, did she perhaps leave something also for these, similar to charitable testators who not only leave good things for their worthy heirs, but also leave something for their unworthy heirs, in the abundance of their mercy?

In the book of Solomon, there is a proverb about the kind of inheritance that a righteous man leaves behind him after his death. It is natural that she who is greatest among all righteous leave the same inheritance as all righteous men do. And what is this inheritance? Repentance: "When a righteous man dies, he leaves repentance." Those who do not come near to the mother of God through the labor of faith, the sincerity of love, who do not emulate the example of her virtuous, and so have not acquired the right to inherit her grace-filled joy, have been left as an inheritance, as a final blessing, repentance. This inheritance may be bitter at first, but it is salvific afterward, if it directed toward the correction of life.

If we did not have the ability or, to speak more plainly, if we did not labor to acquire, in emulation of the most holy Virgin, the joy of spirit in God the Savior, then let us hurry to take up "godly sorrow" which *produces repentance leading to salvation*. Through repentance, we may be able to find the joy of salvation in the end. Amen.

see Luke 1:47

2 Corinthians 7:10

30

Secret Interiority: The Primary Law of the Virgin's Life

Homily on the Dormition of the Mother of God
(1854)

"All her glory as the King's daughter is within." (Psalm 44:14)

T he spirit of prophecy in the forty-fourth Psalm describes the King: "I tell my works to the King." But in this depiction, the psalmist also includes such qualities as might refer to human perfection, such as: "You are more beautiful than the sons of men," as well as qualities that could never refer to any earthly king, and that are incomparably higher than any human perfection, such as this: *Your throne, O God, is forever and ever.* No matter how much you might search in the history books for the model of this prophetic image, you will only find it in the person of Jesus Christ, Who, as a man, "is more beautiful than the world of men," for in Him alone is human nature sinless, and

Psalm 44:2, 3, 7

Who, as God, rules in eternity, and as the God-Man *reigns...over... His kingdom [which] will [have] no end.*   *Luke 1:33*

In that same psalm, the spirit of prophecy depicts a queen, the daughter of the King, who approaches the King already described above, and stands at His right hand: *The queen stood at Your right hand.* In this depiction of the queen, there is also an unusual quality: *All her glory as the King's daughter is within.* Where can we find a person such as this? That which is hidden within is usually secret or mystical; Glory is usually called something that is open and obvious to everyone. But in contrast to this, the spirit of prophecy commands us to seek someone who has all her glory within her, and this quality leads us to recognize the *daughter of the King* whom the King glorifies.   *Psalm 44:10*   *Psalm 44:14*   *Psalm 45:13*

But will we find the explanation of this prophecy in the subject of today's reverent remembrance? For today we must gaze with the eye of the spirit at the most blessed Virgin Mary, the *daughter of the king,* for she comes from the line of King David, and the daughter of the heavenly King, for she was overshadowed by the holy Spirit. She is both queen and daughter of a King together, for she is both mother and virgin. Today, she rises to heaven to stand at the right hand of Christ the King, and, in accordance with the dignity of being His mother, to accept the glory of becoming the Queen of Heaven.   *Psalm 45:13*

If anyone ever had her entire glory within her, completely distancing herself from any external glory, it is certainly she. What can be greater or more complete that her inner glory—her incomparable purity, her spiritual perfection, her holiness? But all this, during her entire life on earth, was covered by a nearly impenetrable veil—her profound humility. Everything that might have glorified her before people she either hid or distanced from herself. The glorious annunciation of the archangel concerning the incarnation within her of the Son of God—this she hid from everyone so completely that even her protector Joseph had to be informed of it by an angel. She hid it also from righteous Elizabeth, though they were of the same mind, so that the Holy Spirit had to reveal it to her. The wondrous miracles that surrounded the birth of Jesus Christ, as the evangelist wrote of it many years later, she *kept...and pondered...in her heart,* instead of speaking of them in the hearing of others. For this reason, naturally, the Jews only knew of His coming from Nazareth, and did not even know that He was born in Bethlehem!

Luke 2:19

When Jesus, Who did *not receive honor from men,* was nonetheless glorified by His miracles and His divine teaching, then His mother, if she did appear near Him, it was to share in His sufferings, as she did on Golgotha at the foot of His cross. But wherever a bright ray of His reflected glory might fall on her, such as during His triumphant entry into Jerusalem, there we do not see her. After He saw her suffering at His cross and consoled her, can it be that He would not console her far more than anyone else with His appearance after the resurrection? However, this appearance is not written of in the Gospel, while appearances to Magdalene and others are, and our own ecclesiastical traditions concerning such appearances to His mother are incomplete. This is, of course, a result of her humble secrecy, which Mary held as the primary law of her life.

John 5:41

Being unquestioningly the first daughter of the nearly-revealed Church of Christ, and the mother of all the faithful whom her divine Son called His *brothers,* she still continued to live in her secrecy, turning away from any glory and honor. In the book of Acts, the history of the early Church of Christ, we only once see the name of *Mary the mother of Jesus.* And even this reference comes after the names of all the other apostles. Finally, the mother of Christ the King, the mother and queen of the faithful, passes from this earthly life into the heavenly, and what remains after her? Did she leave behind kingly mansions, glorious regal attire, precious adornments and treasures? Nothing of the sort. All that she left were two items of clothing, and such items as would only be worth giving to destitute widows. Truly *all her glo-*

John 20:17

Acts 1:14

Psalm 44:14

ry as the King's daughter is within. Be amazed, you who understand, at the fullness of her inner glory, which required no addition from the outer.

Rejoice, all you who love simplicity, non-acquisitiveness, and the silence of obscurity. Rejoice all you who labor in secrecy, hiding your virtues, for the path of the Queen of Heaven is proof that you are on a kingly path.

Be warned, all you who love honor and ambition. Can you hold external brilliance and human glory in high esteem when she who is more honorable than the Cherubim and beyond compare more glorious than the Seraphim had neither? Should we forcibly rush after perishable glory before mortals, when it comes and goes like the wind, when it only clouds those who are besotted with it, then fades like smoke? Would it not be better to seek a glory within, a true glory of piety and virtue, a glory that internally proclaims the law of God, a glory that is heard by the blameless conscience, that does not depend on the inconstancy of human opinions, that is not damaged by slander, that is held in high esteem by the inhabitants of heaven, that is blessed by God Himself?

Be warned, all you who love money, for riches often reach toward external glory. Is it worth the effort to exhaust yourself in constant striving for money that is beyond what you need to live, just so you could boast in the brilliance of dust, just before it is dispersed by the wind of unexpected calamities or until the moment comes for the boaster himself to turn into dust and ashes? Would it not be better to *sell everything*, that is, to lay aside any attachment or passion for earthly things, the better to acquire *one pearl of great price*—Christ's life in your heart? Would it not be better to use these earthly riches to acquire the priceless, incorruptible treasure of heaven? *Matthew 19:21* *Matthew 13:46*

Be warned, all you who like luxury and vanity, who also imagine glory for themselves, but, as the Apostle Paul so astutely noted, *whose glory is in their shame*. In truth, is not this glory shameful when it merely highlights one's subtle refinery, one's limitless ability to waste money for gluttony, for lack of self-control, for passionate attachments to seductive spectacles and sensual songs, for an advantage in some useless game that might even be harmful? I am ashamed to speak of the more profound shame that results in their unrestrained luxury and sensuality. How far from true, inner glory are these people, whose external glory is their shame, to the abasement of the intellectual and moral dignity proper to mankind!

All of us Christians must insistently admonish ourselves concerning the glory within. For the Spirit of God calls our souls to walk the path of internal glory, following the footsteps of the queen who entered heavenly glory: *The virgins behind her shall be brought to the King*. The virgins here can indeed represent those who live a life of bodily and spiritual chastity, because of a special love for purity and because of an oath of chastity. But they can also represent every Christian soul who has betrothed herself to Christ in faith and love, for Apostle Paul said this of all Christians: *For I have betrothed you to one husband, that I may present you as a chaste virgin to Christ.*

And so, if we are called to heavenly glory by following the queenly path of the glory within, how will we find the way? Here is an instruction of St. Basil the Great: *Whoever adorns himself for the Father who sees 'in secret,'* and prays and does everything to avoid the gaze of men, but only to appear before God alone, such a one has all his glory within like the daughter of the King."

If anyone remembers and notices that this word of St. Basil the Great was already spoken by me on this same day, in this same place, several years ago, then I will answer him thus: If only the word of truth and spiritual benefit spoken here once would not be forgotten and abandoned without fulfillment! I would joyfully force myself to abstain from repetition, but neither should you complain when I repeat instructions that, upon repetition, should be turned to your own glory, not my rebuke. Amen.

31

Lessons in War and Peace

Homily on the Annunciation of the Mother of God, before the Thanksgiving Molieben after the End of the War
(1856)

Isaiah 9:6

On this day, when heaven gives good news to earth—secret at first, glorious later—of the coming of the divine *Prince of peace*, our own pious Tsar triumphantly announces peace to this ruling city, ending a difficult war. What do you think of today, faithful sons of Russia? What do your hearts feel? Do they feel an inner peace? Or is wrath still not put out within you, or does anger still boil within you against the unrighteousness that pushed us to war, and that has made that war so terrible?

Psalm 119:6

Let us remember the law and let us fulfill the will of the divine Prince of peace: To not remember evils, to forgive offences, to be peaceable even with those that hate pace. So how much more should we do the same to those who have offered to end hostilities and who extend the hand of peace? Let wrath subside. Let anger cease. Let peace reign not only over weapons and cities and villages; Let peace extend to the thoughts of our heart, the deeps of our souls.

Let us thank God, Who has sent down help to us in this war. Let us thank God Who gave us this peace. Let us incite ourselves to take advantage of this peace.

We cannot remember with indifference what difficulties our Russian army had to overcome, what hardships our people had to endure, what deprivations and sufferings our fellow Russians were subjected to merely for being near the theater of war. But these sorrowful thoughts unite with consoling and triumphant ones as well. Our navy, having begun its work by destroying the Turkish fleet, not only did not retreat before the superior navies of several enemy countries, but made of their own ships an underwater fortification to protect the shoreline and its cities. Then, members of the navy and land army united to fight off numerous armies of four different countries, armed with the most devastating new military technology, for eleven months in Sebastopol. Finally, though the enemy was allowed to take the ruins we abandoned to make yet more ruins, there is still a Russian army in Sebastopol. In the far East, a small fortification with a tiny group of soldiers repulsed attacks from land and sea of enemies that were far stronger than they, and this was done, according to witnesses, more because of prayer than military power.

In the West, two of the most powerful navies wasted their strength against a single fortification, while they could only look at a second from a distance. In the North, we had a strange battle: From one side, we were attacked by warships and artillery, and on the other side we see priests and monks walking along the walls of a monastery with holy objects and prayer, protected by a few people with weak and imprecise weaponry, and the monastery remained undefeated, and the holy objects were not defiled. Four powers fought against Russia, among them were the strongest powers of the world. From among the peaceful powers, some remained completely at peace, and several, with their unclear position, negatively affected our own ability to act, and this also aided our enemies. And, in spite of it all, we were not defeated in Europe, and in Asia, we were the victors. Glory to the Russian army! Blessed is the memory of those who labored for their country, who offered it their courage, their artistry, and their life as sacrifice. But greater than all this, let Russia speak with the prophet's voice: *Blessed is the Lord my God, Who trains my hands for battle, my fingers for war; He is my mercy and refuge, my helper and my deliverer, my protector.*

> Psalm 143:1-2

I bless God, *who trains our hands for battle*, seeing how peasants and peaceful citizens suddenly transformed into the warriors of defense, fighting equally with trained soldiers.

> Psalms 144:1

I bless God, our protector, hearing how our sailors in the east, on a few boats, sailed through far superior naval powers of the enemy without being destroyed, back to the peaceful shores of the fatherland.

Let us bless God, Who is our mercy," Who inspires in our hearts compassion for the labors and the laborers, a desire to help their labors, to lessen their burdens. How eagerly and abundantly did everyone offer their aid for the war and the soldiers! The talents of the rich and the mites of the destitute poured into the war coffers and collections for aid for the wounded and sick and their families. Especially in the house of the Tsar these sources of mercy poured forth abundantly, and they poured, and continue to pour with merciful streams.

Let us bless the God of mercy also that He revealed in us not only righteousness, but mercy for our enemies. Not only do they have no reason to rebuke us for cruelty or unnecessary destruction that is not demanded by the expediency of war, but they cannot fail to admit that we have been merciful to their prisoners of war. Entering this time of peace, we have no desire to rekindle even a war of words. Let us only allow ourselves to remember that in the time of ceasefire, when it was no longer possible to battle against our soldiers, some of our enemies continued to battle against the stones of our peaceful settlements. For this reason, even the stones were angered at them and struck them down, burying in their rubble one of the enemy's wise men of destruction. We dare, not praising ourselves, but thanking the God of mercy, to say that there is a bloodless victory on our side: A moral victory.

It must be said, however, that is the war does offer our side some consolations, this should not incline us to a desire to continue it. Glory to God that Orthodox Christian Russia was not the cause of the war; And not having declared it, accepted the declaration from others. We had to protect ourselves lest there be even the smallest guilt on our side of prolonging the war unnecessarily. I thank the righteous Tsar Emperor who protected us from this, who honorably spared the blood of his and others, who preferred a meek, Christian peace to vengeful demands. Blessed be God, Who aids him in this.

God spoke through the mouth of the prophet: *I form the light and create darkness, I make peace and create calamity; I, the Lord, do all these things.* How wonderful and strange! God is good, is goodness itself, Who witnesses concerning Himself that He *created darkness* and *creates calamity*. But whoever looks deeply into the works of Providence will not be disturbed by this. For example, it was necessary for God to darken the eyes of the Syrian soldiers, lest Elisha be killed by them, for at that time he was almost the last prophet and protector of faith in the living God. It was necessary for the corrupt tribe of the first world to perish in the flood, so that the small leftovers of the good tribe would not be infected, and the earth itself be turned into hell.

If the Providence of God guides the forces that punish mankind, then it is clear that He guides the beneficial forces. If God allows war to happen, then all the more will He *make peace*. Is today's world order only established by the powers and means of human beings? It is true that those who fought against us bore a great burden both of war and the calamities sent by God,

Isaiah 45:7

Isaiah 45:7

Isaiah 45:7

but they continued to lean on their numbers, and their further preparations for continuing the war, done on the eve of peace, showed both their power and their readiness to continue fighting. However, peace has been offered to us, and the noise and wailing of the enemies of war cannot drown out the quiet voice of peace. Who calmed the hearts, then, of those who were roaring to continue the war? Let us not be nearsighted in our minds and hearts. Let us look at the active work of the mystical will of the invisible Creator of the world. Let war pass, for it is God's punishment over the nations. Let us accept peace with gratitude as the gift of God Who "makes peace."

The sooner we admit that peace is the gift of God, the sooner we must admit and internally sense our responsibility not only accept it worthily, but use this gift of God actively. Every gift of God is a talent that must be put into circulation for our benefit, according to the intention of the Giver. The evangelical parable teaches that those who used the talents given them wisely will receive an increase of gifts from above, while those who did not use them well will lose even what they had before.

What can I tell you about the proper use of peace? Will I recommend that you use peace to restore the material well-being lost during the war? But do I really need to counsel this? Our own need and benefit will counsel this, and not much more need be done to begin this work, since doing otherwise would be not only the lack of spiritual wisdom but human reason, if we use the time given to us by peace to idle about and do nothing, to go to parties and waste our money, instead of using our wealth to do good.

Let us labor primarily and most zealously to acquire and preserve spiritual wealth—God's grace, faith, righteousness, and virtue. These will build and preserve our inner peace, and they will exalt and make firm our earthly peace as well.

Isaiah 48:17-18 *Thus says the Lord, your Redeemer, the Holy One of Israel...Oh that you had heeded my commandments! Then your peace would have been like a river, and your righteousness like the waves of the sea.* Hear the commandments of the Lord now at least, if you had not listened to them before. And then your peace will be like a river. Amen.

32

The Incarnation of the Son of God

Homily on the Annunciation of the Mother of God
(1857)

Today the subject of our contemplation and our conversation, our reverence and joy, must be the incarnation of the Son of God.

What is this incarnation? By the will and providence of God the Father, the Son of God, one in essence with the Father, descended to earth without leaving heaven. Under the aegis of the Holy Spirit, Who is one in essence with the Father and the Son, He entered the womb of the Virgin who was pre-purified by the Spirit (see the Stichera for Annunciation). He accepted a human body and soul, and He united within Himself a single person—the God-Man Jesus Christ—preserving the qualities and energies of divinity and humanity unchanged in this union, thereby being born into our human life, to be able to walk through its stages and states and even through death itself. Everything human that was fallen because of sin and was being dragged to hell, but that could attract itself to the Incarnate One by common nature and faith, He raised on the shoulders of divine power, carrying it higher than the state from which it fell—into the eternal, heavenly kingdom of God.

What an exalted and wondrous dispensation of God! What a profound and incomprehensible mystery! Truly it is right to say, together with the apostle: *Great is the mystery of godliness: God was manifested in the flesh.* My thought loses its wings at the immeasurable height and depth of the mystery. My contemplation loses its strength before the power of the invisible light, like the physical eye before the visible sun. My word falls dumb before the immensity of the contemplation. *(1 Timothy 3:16)*

What mind can pierce the "pre-eternal counsel," within the holy of holies of the tri-hypostatic divinity, unknowable to creation?

What hearing can discern, in answer to the will of God the Father, the equally willing word of God the Word, which did touch the hearing of one of the prophets: *I willed to do Your will, O my God?* *(Psalm 39:9)*

How did the heavens not quake and collapse at the coming down to earth of the One Who lives above the heavens, whom the heavens themselves cannot encompass?

How did the earth, *cursed... in toil* by the first man, and further defiled by the sins of the human race over the course of many centuries, not go up in flames at the arrival of God, Who is a fire consuming impurity? *(Genesis 3:17)* *(Hebrews 12:29)*

How was the womb of the Virgin not immolated when she accepted the fire of the divine?

How and when did the Holy Spirit "pre-purify" her for this calling, leading her up to a height worthy of unmediated contact with the purity of God?

How, beyond all the laws of nature, did she give birth to the New Adam, who is the Lord from heaven, and how did the Lord from heaven not disdain to put on the aspect of the slave, to put

Genesis 3:19 on the natural form of the old Adam, who was the dust of the earth that returns to the dust?

Let us constrain the movement of our inquisitive thoughts by the words of the wise man: *Do not seek things too difficult for you, nor examine what is beyond your strength. Think about what is commanded you.*

Sirach 3:20-21

Can you scoop out the entire sea with the palm of your hand? And even if you could (for the sea does have its limits of breadth and depth), it would still be impossible for the small vessel of human reason to entirely scoop out the abyss of God's wisdom, which has no limits of breadth or depth. Therefore, wisely and righteously is it forbidden us to be brazen in testing the mysteries of God. Rather, it is commanded that we reverence them and attach ourselves to them by faith, and in this faith is laid the hope for our blessedness: *Blessed are those who have not seen and yet have believed.*

John 20:29

And so, let us embrace with simple faith this salvific mystery of the incarnation of the Son of God.

Humbly let us bow down before the incomprehensibility of the wisdom of God and the paths of that wisdom.

With grateful joy let us wonder at the love God showed to man, a love that sows miracles with a generous hand even when our own means and powers fade to nothing, the better to cultivate the first of salvation for sinful man, accursed and perishing.

Psalm 8:2, 5

O Lord, our Lord, how wondrous is Your name in all the earth! What is man that You remember him, or the son of man that You visit him? Help us remember constantly this, Your mercy to us, and as much as we are able, to answer it with our own love for You, our mercy to our neighbors, our active fulfillment of Your holy will, that we may, finally be eternal communicants of Your eternal goodness in Your kingdom of heaven. Amen.

33

Vigilant Watchfulness

Homily on the Annunciation of the Mother of God
(1858)

"Take heed how you hear." (Luke 8:18)

Carefully, prudently, attentively examine yourself: how do you listen to the things that reach your ears, how do you accept it, and how should you accept that which you hear? This is the instruction of Christ the Savior to His disciples. His most pure mother, the most blessed Virgin Mary, perfectly fulfilled this teaching even before it was spoken.

Christians! This teaching of Christ the Savior refers to us because we are Christians, that is, the disciples and followers of Christ. The example of His most pure mother can lead us to better understand this teaching.

Our foremother Eve did not have this as her rule: "Take heed how you hear," when she began to speak with the serpent-tempter, though the very unusual nature of this appearance should have inspired carefulness. In her ears, opened by inquisitiveness, the verbal poison of the serpent reached even her heart and poisoned her soul with sin, even before the taste of the forbidden fruit poisoned her body. Neither did our forefather Adam protect his hearing from the sinful word of his wife, and through an inattentive ear, he allowed death to enter the entire human race.

It was not so with the most pure Virgin Mary. As one foreordained for service to the mystery of the healing of the human race from the death-dealing infection of sin, she, at the moment of her stepping into this calling, corrected the original sin of her forefathers. She hears the greeting of the angel, who was already more or less known to her from her time in the temple of Jerusalem, and in spite of that familiarity, she "took heed how she heard." She didn't immediately allow the exalted greeting to enter her humble heart; She did not answer the greeting; She stopped in careful contemplation. *She was troubled at his saying, and considered what manner of greeting this was.*

Luke 1:29

What was this word that produced distress in a pure and peaceful soul? It was this word of the angel: *Rejoice, highly favored one, the Lord is with you; blessed are you among women!* But what is so distressing about these words? The reason for confusion is usually a sorrowful or strict or humiliating or insulting or threatening word. Nothing of the sort is found in the words of the angel. Instead, we see: The joy and reverence of the angel, her worthiness, God's blessing on her. But delve into this matter with spiritual knowledge. That which cannot bear a sorrowful, strict, humiliating, insulting, or threatening word is our pride and our lack of patience. These qualities were lacking in the most pure Virgin, which is why even such heavy words would not have brought her any distress. But instead, profound humility abode within her, and so she could not accept a word that exalted her. Humility does not love loud praises; It turns away from them; It fears lest they might harm it; And so, when she hears the words of praise, she internally asks the question with instinctive atten-

Luke 1:28

tiveness: Are you truly an angel of light? This is the meaning of her confusion.

But a sinless confusion is still not a natural state. Once a soul feels itself in such a state, it immediately seeks a way out of it. What path did the most holy Virgin find for her own soul? The path of silent contemplation. "She considered what manner of greeting this was."

Listen carefully to the silence of the most holy Virgin before the annunciation of the angel. You will find that this silence is as wise as words. If Mary had hurried to answer this praise-filled annunciation of the angel without rejecting the praise she heard, this would have been a confirmation and acceptance of the praise, and this would have been difficult for the Virgin's humility. If she had answered with a contrary word, this might have offended the messenger of heaven. Both paths she avoided, having hidden her words in silence and having used contemplation instead.

She considered what manner of greeting this was. What does this unusual greeting mean? How should she act with this greeting that is difficult and frightening to accept, but equally difficult and frightening to reject? If this word comes from God, then will He not reveal some sign that will cease her confusion and fear, and would instead resolve her dilemma? The sign did come. The angel answered her profound silence as though she had spoken aloud: *Do not be afraid, Mary.* This made it clear to her that God had revealed her inner disposition to the angel and had sent her a word of comfort. She now knew that it was necessary to listen with calm and faith to the further annunciation of the angel. This is how she prepared and was prepared to accept the annunciation of the incarnation of the Son of God, the Savior of the world, within her. And she was able to utter, from the bottomless depth of her humility, a word of immeasurably great faith: *Behold the maidservant of the Lord! Let it be to me according to your word.* *Luke 1:38*

Luke 1:29

Luke 1:30

Can you see, Christian soul, at least in part, the soul of the most holy Virgin, her inner disposition, her attentiveness while standing guard over her moral self-preservation? Learn her wisdom in secret; Emulate her vigilant carefulness in conversation. "Take heed how you hear." Do not be put off by the height of her path and by the fact that your own path is much lower than hers. If you are lazy and will not find the zeal to follow her, at least from a distance, on the ascendant path, then easily you will be diverted to the path of Eve that leads down to perdition. It can easily happen that you might be approached by some garrulous serpent, *more cunning than any beast of the field,* but who is far from even simple human wisdom, much less heavenly wisdom that is seen only by the inhabitants of heaven and is invisible to the inhabitants of hell, whose *words are smoother than oil, and yet they are darts,* who in his delusive and seductive words will deify you, while in actual fact will infect you with slander and blasphemy against God, who will offer you a beautiful and sweet fruit, but you will taste it in nothing but sin and death.

Genesis 3:1

Psalm 54:22

The example of the most holy Virgin shows us that we must be careful even when listening to an angelic word. And if such carefulness was needed even for her, then how much more is it needed for us! For, as Apostle Paul warns us, *For Satan himself transforms himself into an angel of light.* Therefore, a careless person might be fooled to accept shining brass instead of gold, or a word of flattery and falsehood for a word of truth. If your inner or outer ears hear an unusual word, contemplate on it in silence, test whether it agrees with the trustworthy word of God and the teaching of Christ. Protect yourself with humility, prayer, as well a triple prayer, as the wise in God teach us. Then, as much as possible, seek the counsel of those who are spiritually experienced. The truth will not be offended at your carefulness, and falsehood and delusion will not have the time to charm you.

2 Corinthians 11:14

If we must even be careful of the words of an angel, then what is there to be said about human conversation? How many false and blasphemous thoughts are found in men, how many passions, how many sins! They all can become contagious, more or less powerfully or visibly passing to us through word and conversation. Many obvious and hidden dangers lie here: We need a great deal of wisdom and care.

Do you hear a word of praise? Be careful. Praise often conceals flattery, or it can make you a flatterer to yourself if you are captured by it. It can destroy humility within you and settle self-trust in its place, making you careless about your continued work on perfecting your works and your self. Having heard some word of praise, think of how you actually are and remember your shortcomings. Try to cultivate properly praiseworthy thoughts, intentions, and deeds, instead of catching the fading echo of someone else's praise.

Do you hear a word that insults or humiliates you? Be careful lest you become aflame with wrath that *does not produce the righteousness of God*. Instead, tell yourself: Here is a chance to practice patience and humility. Then, answer the one insulting or humiliating you either with silence or, if necessary, with a shot word of righteousness. *James 1:20*

Do you hear a word that censures and condemns others? Be careful, lest your hearing take part in the sin of another's tongue. Do not apply your heart to these words, which are more harmful for the judge than for the condemned.

Do you hear a word that is filled with sorrow at some present or future calamity? Be careful lest your sorrow become more powerful than your reason or your will. *Sorrow has destroyed many, and there is no profit in it.* Dissolve your sorrow in prayer and give yourself inner peace through faithfulness to the will of God and hope in His mercy. *Sirach 30:23*

What if you hear or see in your reading an indiscreet, doubting, or faithless word? Hurry to stop your ears and close your eyes against this ill wind. Do not delude yourself that you can listen or read this word from mere curiosity or as a passing fancy. Do not touch smoldering ashes. Do not play with fire. Do not desire to know the taste of poison. *Do not be deceived: Evil company corrupts good habits.*

1 Corinthians 15:33

Perhaps someone might say: Shouldn't we also be careful when listening to words of spiritual and moral instruction? Truly, you must be attentive, you must take care lest you be "hearers of the word only," like a person who looks at himself in the mirror, walked away, and forgot what he looked like. For it is not this forgetful listener, but *a doer of the word, this one will be blessed in what he does.* Amen.

James 1:22-25

34

The Second Man

Homily on the Annunciation of the Mother of God
(1859)

"The first man was of the earth, made of dust; The second Man is the Lord from heaven." (1 Corinthians 15:47)

I offer for your contemplation the utterance of the holy Apostle Paul concerning the first and second man, and the reason I do so today will be clear from the contemplation itself.

The first man was of the earth, made of dust; The second Man is the Lord from heaven. Who is the first man? Naturally, our forefather Adam. His body was formed by the hand of God from the earth, and even though he was spiritual as well, for God breathed into him the breath of life from His own lips, later his spirituality was darkened and weakened by sin, constrained, put down and closed off by the flesh. Later, he lost the right to call himself spiritual at all, and in fairness was subject to the humiliating term *made of dust*.

1 Corinthians 15:47

1 Corinthians 15:47

Who is the second man? In terms of sequence of creation, the second person was Eve; However, it is evident that the apostle is not speaking of her. She is not from heaven, but from Adam's rib. She is created not for lordship, but to be a helpmeet and to serve Adam. And since she once lorded it over him for a moment, leading him to sin, she was given to him to command.

Do you want to seek the second man in the natural order of human progeny from the first man? Many centuries and millennia will pass; You will examine thousands, millions of people; You will study the great and chosen from among them; And still, you will not find this second man that the apostle desires to show us. There is not one among them who is "the Lord from heaven." It might have seemed to David that he found such people, but he soon found out that this was but a phantom: *I said, you are gods, and you are all sons of the Most High. But you die like men.* What are the thousands and millions of Adam's sons? They are all the outgrowth of the first man; Consequently, they share his nature. All of them, like he, are of the dust; All are infected with the wound of sin; They must all, like he, pay *the wages of sin*, which is the temporal death of the body and the death of the spirit which can become eternal.

Psalm 81:6-7

Romans 6:23

Here we encounter a terrifying question: What can possibly follow the first man, who is of the dust in all his progeny, to whom we all belong? Can man, can the human race heal itself from the death-bearing infection of sin that has imbued itself into our very nature? No, it cannot. You can chop a tree at the root; It might wither and die, but then you can no longer make it green, flowering, fruit-bearing. For this, you need the power of creation. The tree of the human race is like this. It is chopped down at the root by sin; It can no longer bear flowers or the fruits of a true, spiritual life. For this, we need the power of creation. This is why one of the best of Adam's sons cried out to God: *Create in me a clean heart, O God, and renew a right spirit within me.* In other words: I acknowledge the impurity of my heart; But I do not have

Psalm 50:12

SERMON 34: THE SECOND MAN, 1859

enough strength to make it pure. It requires not merely correction, but re-creation. You must *create in me a clean heart*, O God! I admit myself to be guilty of sin, and I find in myself no means of renewing my lost righteousness. You, limitless in righteousness and mercy, You must "Renew a right spirit" in my inner life. *Psalm 51:10*

The prayer of King David concerning the recreation of his heart and the inner renewal of his spirit must be the universal prayer of all sons of the Adam of dust, since they only know themselves and the profound damage of their nature superficially. But none of them, without a special revelation of God, could have possible known how that prayer would be answered, how a grace-filled life and holiness might be renewed within a nature not only infected and defiled, but killed by sin. They could not have imagined how one who was condemned for the ages by eternal justice might be redeemed from this condemnation without doing offense to eternal justice, how man, after an infusion of creative power, would become a *new creation*, while retaining still the same personhood. This, as the apostle said, *is the ... mystery, which from the beginning of the ages has been hidden in God, the mystery which has been hidden from ages and from generations.* *2 Corinthians 5:17* *Ephesians 3:9* *Colossians 1:26*

But Apostle Paul also announces the revelation of this mystery hidden from generations within God. Today, he says, it *has been revealed to His saints*. And this day the Church, appropriating the words of the apostle, triumphantly declared, "Today is the beginning of our salvation, and the revelation of the mystery hidden from the ages: The Son of God becomes the Son of the Virgin." (troparion to the feast) *Colossians 1:26*

And here is "the second Man...the Lord from heaven," Who is compared to the first man of the dust, Who fulfills and resolves the first man's fate, and Who transforms his calamity into blessedness. Jesus Christ is this Man in his humanity, which He received from the most holy Virgin, who was pre-purified by the Holy Spirit. He is also the Lord from heaven by His divine nature, for He is the only-begotten Son of God, one in essence with the

Father and enthroned together with Him in heaven, Who came down to earth as the God-Man, and to reveal Himself as the living mediator between God and mankind. He is the second Man, skipping over millions of other people, who unlike the first man were coming downward on the natural ladder, born in slavery to sin. He is the second Man without progeny, for He alone in the human race is comparable to the first man, having come from God directly, wondrously, without being touched by sin, revealing in Himself a new source of grace-filled birth for the human race.

The Lord from heaven, having become a man, leads mankind through grace-filled faith into a divine life of the spirit, light, purity, holiness, before which the dark, carnal life of sin weakens and dies. Having assumed everything that belonged to the first man except for sin, He accepted man's guilt and his condemnation to death, and by the three days of his death—which, because of the presence of the divine nature, are not less than eternity—He satisfied divine justice on behalf of the guilty one. By His cross, He turned aside the fiery sword that prevented man's entry into paradise. Sin—though it had profoundly damaged the nature of man, having made him old, corruptible, even death—could not destroy either man's existence or his personhood. So, the Lord from heaven poured into this existence and personhood His own creative power and Spirit, like the water of the first creation hovering over the water of baptism, giving the old man a second birth into a new creation, the image of God. From carnal, He makes man spiritual; From earthly, He makes him capable of becoming heavenly.

Examining the qualities of the first man of the dust and the second man, the Lord from heaven, in this way, we cannot fail to see how calamitous the fate of the first would have been if the second man had not come to his aid. Let us remember, brothers, that we are all natural outgrowths of the first man, made of dust; Consequently, his calamitous fate is our own inevitable fate if we do not run and commit ourselves completely to the Lord from heaven, who came to earth to save us, if we do not attach ourselves to Him in faith, love, and emulation of His teaching and example, if we do not fulfill His commandments.

Let us not be deluded by the brilliant illusions of Adam's carnal, sensual, passionate life. Illusions disappear quickly; The disillusionment of the deluded will be bitter, and if we do not come to our senses in good time, we will fall, not from Eden to earth for a time, but from earth to the pit of hell for eternity.

Let us love the truth of Christ; Let us seek the life in Christ. If it is not without its sorrows in the beginning, it will be joyful and blessed eternally.

And as we have borne the image of the man of dust, we shall also bear the image of the heavenly man. Amen.   1 Corinthians 15:49

35

The Half-Night Vigil

Homily on the Annunciation of the Mother of God (spoken by Hieromonk Philaret, Bachelor of Theology, at the Lavra of St Alexander Nevsky) (1810)

"The Lord God will give Him the throne of the His father David. And He will reign over the house of Jacob forever." (Luke 1:32-33)

In the name of the Father, the Son, and the Holy Spirit. Amen.

1 John 5:19

Come, rule over us, O King of blessedness and glory! Without You, *the whole world lies under the sway of the evil one.* The darkness of Egypt is spreading and threatening the entire earth! Your enemies are roaring like lions or simply falling asleep pointlessly on the corpses of their prey. The remaining drops of oil are burning out, it seems to me, in the oil lamps of Your vigilant servants. With that dim light, they illumine what is otherwise midnight everywhere else. Hurry, O Bridegroom of pure souls! Arise, Sun of righteousness! Take your throne, King of blessedness and glory!

SERMON 35: THE HALF-NIGHT VIGIL

For a long time now, human catastrophes have called for the Redeemer. Finally, the long-awaited day has arrived. The broken scepter of Judah, the completion of the seven days of Daniel, the rumors of the coming kingdom, predetermined by fate, that must begin in Judea, have even spread among the pagans who tell of its imminent coming. The angel brings a direct promise of the coming and prophesied Seed. The blessed Virgin prepares to be His mother; Those who await the redemption of Jerusalem are filled with impatience.

But what follows this expectation? The great heir of David will be born in the poor family of a carpenter; He will be raised in poverty; He will lead His entire miraculous life in worries and dangers; One moment, He will be acclaimed as king, and the next, instead of a throne, He will be raised on a cross. It seems that He almost refuses the crown of David His father: *My kingdom is not of this world.* John 18:36

Seeing this, sin once again raises its head; Those who are weak in faith falter; Faith and virtue raise their hands to heaven and call upon consolation.

O gentle light of the holy glory! Send your ray to disperse the darkness of our disturbed thoughts, that we who sit in the valley of the shadow may at least see the dawn of hope.

My dear listeners, truth should not terrify lovers of truth, for *perfect love casts out fear.* Let us listen to love, and then love's terrible voice will be sweet to our hearts. *My Kingdom,* Truth says, *is not of this world.* I do not reject the kingdom that belongs to me indelibly; But it is not this world. It is in the world, but it is not of the world. I have a small flock, but it is dispersed from the East to the West, from the South to the North. I have the most expansive kingdom, but its heart is greater than all the capitals of the world. In the temple, in the palace, in the hut I find those who are faithful to Me. In the hut, in the palace, and even in the temple I see my enemies as well. 1 John 4:18
John 18:36

The prince of darkness encompasses the greater part of the earth under his authority: *But I was established as King by Him over His holy hill of Zion, declaring the Lord's decree.* The Lord's decree, the word of God, is My scepter. Those who hear and preserve this word are the servants of My kingdom. Until the time appointed by the Father in His authority, the word of this kingdom is hidden, and it is not separated by fortified borders. The world, as the kingdom of darkness, does not see it, but always opposes it as the kingdom of light. *My Kingdom is not of this world.*

Psalm 2:6-7

John 18:36

Do you hear how a single word terrifies and yet encourages, defeats and yet fortifies? Or rather, at first it encourages and fortifies, then terrifies and defeats. *My Kingdom*— this is an encouraging hope! *Is not of this world*—this is a terrifying defeat. What prophetic care concerning our weakness! What a wise primer in courage! Before he reveals the reason for distress, He already points to the source of consolation. He already offers us a completed victory, and only then arms us for war. He gives us a shield, and only then strikes us. Why do we wait?

John 18:36

Let us overcome the temptation with the power He has given to us; Let us banish fear with love. Christ rules: What can be more desirable than this? *The Lord reigns; Let the earth greatly rejoice.* There is no longer need for *clouds and darkness [to] surround Him*, or for His kingdom to be limited in physical majesty. There is no need for it to appear as though it is sometimes swallowed up by the kingdom of darkness. It is time: *The Lord reigns; let the peoples be angry* as much as they like. Let impatience fume, impiety mock, and wrath be furious. Let the world rage, for this is its misfortune: It is not satisfied with having such a great and good Master. Why should Christians be distressed? *All things work together for good to those who love God.*

Psalm 96:1
Psalm 96:2

Psalm 98:1

Romans 8:28

And so, Christians, this temporary opposition to the kingdom of Christ, and His, as it were, exile from the world (sometimes obvious and forceful, sometimes subtle and cunning) are events that the man-loving God predestined for the benefit of those people who love him. He tests them like gold in a crucible, so that finally He might accept them like a whole burnt offering. The world is that crucible in which the fire of temptation, which gradually destroys the flesh, purifies the spiritual treasure and raises its value before the eyes of heaven. If the heavenly King requires that we freely serve Him from the heart, if He is building a kingdom of children and brothers, then is it strange that He does not buy our submission with visible advantages, that He does not enslave us with the fear of imminent loss, that He conceals His reward from our gaze, or even sometimes places some unpleasantness in our way, so that we might the more freely and more unselfishly choose Him as the Master of our heart? If grace and eternal hope is given to the faithful, then should not the vision be held back, so that a space is left for faith and hope? If the meek are promised the inheritance of the land of blessedness, *Matthew 5:5* then is there no reason to endure the brazen persecutors in this land of testing? If love for God (that we might become worthy of Him) must become greater in us than all other loves, then are we not indebted to Him for His lessening our burden of debt by making our enemy the passing world that is so difficult to stop loving?

Come, O brave and wise man who imagines that he can judge the Judge of the world, come, tell us how you would have acted otherwise? "I would have given away even my earthly goods, but only to those who are worthy of heavenly ones." Be silent: you are only a man. Your thoughts, your desires accuse you. This is not the will of the One Who makes His chosen ones partakers of the *2 Peter 1:4* divine essence. He desires us to have divine joy—the joy of transforming evil into good, of changing obstacles into means, and of never having a need for the earth on our path to heaven.

The wise man retorts: "But at the very least, does not Christian love force us to desire that those who are not of this world be taken out of it, lest they are endangered by touching its impurity?" O, this is a Christian love, indeed, but it is not Christ's love. You love Christians; Christ loves Christians and all mankind. You do good to the faithful; He takes care of all. You want to keep those that are His; But He will acquire through His own even those who are not His. He surrounds light with darkness so that, little by little, as much as possible, He might illumine the darkness as well. He allows the sons of the light to intermix with the rejected sons, so that He might give even those a chance to *receive the love of the truth, that they might be saved.* If the kingdom of light separated itself so completely that not a single spark ever fell into the kingdom of darkness, then what would the world be, if not hell itself? What would happen to those unfortunate ones whom Christ now does not count among His own—for they have not yet crucified their flesh with its passions and lusts—but who are not yet deprived of the hope of correction?

Let us imagine, for a moment, the possibility of such a complete separation of the sons of the kingdom from the sons of this age. For example, let us suppose that Christ suddenly appeared in this church, as He did once in Jerusalem, and found here, as there, *those who bought and sold,* those who sell Pharisaical piety and buy the glory of being zealous servants of God, those who sell pomp and buy the wonder of the frivolous, those who sell a false majesty to the gaze and buy delusion for the hearts of the foolish, those who offer as sacrifice to God a few triumphant moments and want to pay off an entire life of sin with them. Christ would immediately cast out all of these from the church as He did from the Temple, He would have cast them out from the community of the truly faithful forever, lest they make a house of prayer a market of abominable purchases. What hope would then remain for these exiles? Repentance? But who would teach them of repentance? Who would assure them that it is still possible? Who would uphold them in the constant work of repentance? Without instruction, without inspiring words, amidst all the temptation that constantly move the waves of the sea of life, they would have been completely lost for the kingdom of God, and it would have been lost for them.

But today, if their conscience is asleep, then it is awakened by instruction. When instruction doesn't work, an example of virtue might inspire them to follow. Shame corrects; Decorum itself, which forces imitation, to a certain degree, in acts of piety, is a kind of instruction in virtue. For this reason, the Sower of the heavenly seed commanded His slaves to delay the separation of the wheat from the tares, until they all come to fruition: *Let both grow together until the harvest.* *Matthew 13:30*

It is true that sometimes the tares grow too large and leave little room for the wheat, but let us not be fooled by empty superficiality. Let us not envy the fatness of the tares, for that fat will soon be fuel for the fire. As sorrowful as it is for the flesh to hear that the kingdom of Christ is not of this world, it would be equally base to envy this evil world. The world does not reign; It is enslaved. If we were to exclude from it those who prefer the calling of Christian to all other callings, then it would be left only with slaves—slaves of avarice, slaves of gold, slaves of the stomach, slaves of sensuality, and all together slaves of self-love. Why else do all of them rush from acquisition to acquisition, from pleasure to pleasure, from honor to honor, if not because each of them senses all too well that his current state is a state of slavery?

Turn away, faithful soul, from the vain world. Turn toward your consolation, and in the secret place seek the quiet, serene kingdom of God within yourself. *The Kingdom of God is within you.* *Luke 17:21* Living faith, firm hope, pure conscience, angelic love—of these is the kingdom of God. Here Christ is conceived, born, lives, and reigns a second time. In this divine kingdom there are no dangers, no hunger, no thirst, for our King feeds His servants with *hidden manna.* Here there is no sorrow or despair, for He is joy. *Revelation 2:17* There is no sickness or death, for He is life. There is no persecution or oppression, for *where the Spirit of the Lord is, there is liberty.* *2 Corinthians 3:17*

The spiritual breathing of this Spirit, which sweetens the air of the soul, pours into it the sweet savor of peace. The heart—this great and vast sea, so often agitated by storms, filled with countless monsters of the deep, attacked by the dragon of the abyss—breaks its waves against the cliff of constancy, and in its meek striving, it expresses a single desire: *I shall be satisfied when Your glory is revealed.* Here there always a clear sky. The clouds of doubt do not cover the light of God, nor does the thunder of His wrath shake the inner hearing. The field of activity is covered with golden wheat. The more the warmth of love fills them and helps them grow, the more humility bows low. What a vision! Behold a new heaven and a new earth! Behold this small world that contains within itself the most exalted beauties of the great world!

All this is the beginning of blessedness. Eternity comes soon! Now it is moderate, but soon it will be without limit! This is the dawn of morning; Soon will the day with no evening come! This is the half-night vigil; Soon the bridal feast will begin!

Let it come, *Thy kingdom come,* O King of glory, O Bridegroom of immortality: First Your kingdom in our hearts, then our hearts in Your kingdom. Your Spirit intercedes for this with unutterable groanings. The Church, Your bride, calls out for this, and they both incite us to approach You, in spite of all obstacles. *And the Spirit and the bride say, 'Come!' And let him who hears say, 'Come!'* Amen.

36

God's Rights Over Us

Homily on the Entry of the Mother of God into the Temple (spoken in the house church of Prince Alexander Golitsin consecrated to the life-giving Trinity, 1814)

> "Listen, O daughter, behold and incline your ear, and forget your people and your father's house; For the King desired your beauty, for He is your Lord. And the daughters...shall worship Him."
> (Psalm 44:11-13)

Wondrous is God in His judgments, in that He blesses His own with a most exalted and inconceivable blessedness, having decided before the ages to unite His nature with human nature in the person of His only begotten Son. Then He extended this union to the whole Church, which, by the law of incarnation, is His body, so *that in the dispensation of the fullness of the times He might gather together in one all things in Christ*, and, finally, so that *God may be all in all*. Even though this great decision of the pre-eternal Counsel—or, as the apostle has it, this *mystery which has been hidden from ages and from*

1 Corinthians 15:28

Colossians 1:26

generations,— has to this day been revealed only to the saints, still bearing *seven seals* on itself, it had been revealed from time immemorial by the Holy Spirit to His prophets, and through them to all mankind, during the time when its gradually increasing revelation must correspond and aid its gradual fulfillment.

Revelation 5:5

Thus, one of the prophets—seeing mankind already passing the days of its childhood and mentorship under the Law and coming close to an age when it would be capable of being betrothed to God and give birth to an ageless babe—describes the Son of God as a king walking to his wedding. The prophet assumes the position of the best man in this prophecy, and it seems that he impatiently tries to convince human nature not to delay this blessed union through treachery and lack of submission, but rather to embrace it with complete sincerity and faithfulness. *Listen, O daughter, behold and incline your ear, and forget your people and your father's house; For the King desired your beauty."*

Psalm 44:11-13

But this prophetic voice sounded for a long time in the Church as though in a barren desert and evidently found no ready ear to hear its call. Mankind had no boldness to triumphantly go out to greet the divinity. What would have happened to us if the heart of the blessed virgin Mary did not open to the unutterable voice of the incarnation, if her limitless fidelity to the will of God had not answered the heavenly messenger *Behold the maidservant of the Lord! Let it be to me according to Your word?* She committed herself totally to the desire of the King of Kings, and the betrothal of God with man occurred for eternity.

Luke 1:38

It is from this vantage point that we can see, O Christians, how such a seemingly quotidian event—the entrance into the Temple and consecration to God of a three-year-old girl—becomes the object of the Church's universal celebration. This event is a kind of inception for her betrothal to the Holy Spirit and so, in a certain way, is the initial pledge of mankind's betrothal to God. True, this mystery must still be hidden for a time, like the future flower hidden in the seed, but providence, in order to demonstrate the rightness of its ways, often preceded its actions with certain meaningful events that instruct us of the future. And so, pious tradition tells us that during this actual entrance of the most holy virgin into the temple, she was accompanied by the singing of these exact prophetic words: "Hearken, O daughter," and so on.

Today, in the days of the completion of ancient oracles and foreshadowing, do you desire to see more clearly the glory of this present celebration? Then listen to the words of the prophet: *The virgins, her companions who follow her, shall be brought to You.* Can you not see that the bringing of the most holy virgin to the king of kings is the beginning of a great triumphant procession in which all pure, chaste souls will follow Her? Today's feast, in the Church's intention, is part and continuation of that great procession, and all who desire to take part in this feast must join it, having put on the qualities that are in accord with the image of the great leader of this procession. *Psalm 44:15*

Lest we Christians remain simply indolent viewers of someone else's feast, let us speak now to our own souls with this prophetic word: *Listen, O daughter, behold and incline your ear, and forget your people and your father's house; For the King desired your beauty, for He is your Lord. And the daughters...shall worship Him.* *Psalm 14:11-13*

First of all, admit, O Christian soul, the eternal law by which you belong to the King of Kings, so that you can be led to Him with submission and love: *The King desired your beauty, for He is your Lord.* *Psalm 44:11*

In a human kingdom, it would seem strange if someone in the king's own house, in the king's own presence, began to question that king's right to rule over his subjects. But is it not exactly this kind of brazenness if we, in this house and in this invisible presence of the King of Kings doubt the eternal law of His lordship over us? But what can we do with people who revere human majesty, but *reject authority, and speak evil of* the glory of God? *Jude 1:8*

So many proud thoughts, so many self-willed desires, so many deeds accomplished in forgetfulness of God—do these not speak more loudly that the *tongue that speaks proud things, who have said... who is lord over us?* Oh, if only we might calm, at least a little bit, this distressing wailing through our confession and perception of God's lordship over us!

Psalm 11:4

God is our Lord by the right of creation, our Lord by the right of His image in us, our Lord by the right of His redemption of us, our Lord by the right of His constant preservation and grace-filled providence.

God is our Lord by the right of creation. If we consider the house that we build with our hands, or the garden that we plant, to be our own, then does not God, in comparison, have a much greater right to determine everything that we have or that we are? If the work of our hands can compete with us over our lordship over them, like some of us seem to want to compete with God concerning the limits of His lordship over us, then it would be as though our house spoke aloud and said that we did not create the wood and stones in which we live, or our garden said aloud that we did not grow the fruits that we gather. But what, O man, *do you have that you did not receive?* Reject, at least for a minute, the gifts of the Master whose authority you call into question. Return that which you received. And what will you have left? Nothing, and worse than nothing: Sin that destroys the creation of God!

1 Corinthians 4:7

God is our Lord by the right of His image in us. As we put our seal on things to prove our ownership, or on those that we desire to hide from others, so God sealed mankind with His image, as His property, so that no other being would dare assume ownership over us. He sealed us like a manuscript that no one other than the only begotten Son of God may open. Though mankind destroyed this holy seal and uncovered the hidden mystery of the knowledge of good and evil and sold God's property for the price of sin, still, human nature preserves certain leftover elements of the divine seal, certain remnants of the image of God, which are preserved so that by these signs mankind might once again be assimilated to God and sealed for Him alone. In incorrupt man, the image of God was the source of blessedness, and in fallen man it is the hope of blessedness. It is the very foundation of human nature, which, though covered in dust and hidden in earth, still supports the entire building. In order to better understand our relationship to God through His image in us, let us imagine the form of a body that leaves a shadow behind it on the earth. What would this shadow be if there were no body or light? This is exactly what the man of dust is without the power and light of God!

God is our Lord by the power of His redemption of us. Sometimes, in order to make sure we keep ownership of some favorite object that someone else is trying to claim as their own, we might even agree to acquire it a second time by buying it. In effect, we unfairly sacrifice something we already own just to preserve something that we love more. Similarly, the endless love of God miraculously increases its hold over us in the unparalleled work of our redemption. Man did not want to belong to God; He stole himself from God; He rejected the lordship of God; He imagined that he might be his own lord and god. And the blasphemer and calumniator (man) is accused by impartial justice, condemned, and convicted to eternal death. But love still does not want to lose man. It enacts its plan to take him from hell and to once again assimilate man to himself even more than before. He *redeemed the criminal from the curse of the law*, and how? By becoming Himself a curse. He acquires the one sold under sin a second time, and by what price? *You were not redeemed with corruptible things, like silver or gold...but with the precious blood of Christ, as of a lamb without blemish and without spot.* Oh, what an inconceivable lordship of love that offers itself in order to own us, and He acquires us for a single reason: To give us everything! O Christians! The

Galatians 3:13

2 Peter 1:18-19

Lord could not have done a greater thing for you than making *you...not your own.*

1 Corinthians 4:19

God is our Lord by the right of His constant preservation and grace-filled providence. Calling man up from nothing, increasing him by making him the image of God, raising him up from a fallen state—these comprise, according to the sons of man, the ancient rights of God to rule over us. However, we can honor these rights more by pious remembrance than by actually sensing their power and action in us. But what does the Son of God say? *My Father has been working until now, and I have been working.* For the eternal, there is no past, everything is always the present. Everything exists solely by the constant activity of He Who Is. Man can sometimes leave his work behind, for he does not create, but only reforms what has already been made. However, if God turned aside His gaze from His creatures for a moment, nothing would be left of them. *When You turn Your face away...they shall die and return again to their dust.*

John 5:17

Psalm 103:29

Do we have to go far to find you, O Lord? If we merely continue existing, then this is ample proof that Your face is directed toward us. Does a pure desire animate our hearts? Do we do good deeds? You *work... [in us] both to will and to do for [Your] good pleasure.* Does any good thought arise? We are not *sufficient of ourselves to think of anything as being form ourselves, but our sufficiency is from God.* Do any dangers pass us by? Are our sorrows softened by consolation? Are our temptations defeated? You *will not allow [us] to be tempted beyond what [we] are able, but with the temptation will also make the way of escape.*

Philippians 2:13
2 Corinthians 3:5

1 Corinthians 10:13

Oh, how would we wonder, O Christians, every minute, if we had enough wisdom to reveal the hidden signs of God's rule over us in all things, in all that happens to us and surrounds us! Prophet Elisha, trying to calm the doubt of his apprentice, who feared enemies, prayed in this way: '*Lord, I pray, open his eyes that he may see.*' Then the Lord opened the eyes of the young man, and he saw. *And behold, the mountain was full of horses and chariots of fire*

2 Kings 6:17

4 Kingdoms 6:17

all around Elisha. Even in our own time, if faith opened the eyes of our spirit, we would see around ourselves all the heavenly powers raised up for our protection and to help us against the kingdom of darkness. Yes! All the heavenly powers! For *are they not all ministering spirits sent forth to minister for those who will inherit salvation?* Even one who dares not to believe anything other than the evidence of his eyes, if he constantly watches all events, he will not long await a moment when, having sensed His closeness, he will be forced to confess the truth of the omnipresence of God's and Christ's lordship over all. Like Thomas, he will exclaim, *My Lord and my God!* *Hebrews 1:14*

John 20:28

Is our intimate Lord and Master—Who is as powerful as He is generous—not justified in demanding whatever He wishes of His slaves, whose fate is in His hands, and who *in Him...live and move and have our being?* What yoke that He lays on our shoulders do we dare to call a burden to our freedom? What payment that He demands is not appropriate to His rights over us? What sacrifice is sufficient for Him? If He told us that He desires to take back everything that He ever gave us, what could we possibly answer Him, except for this: My Lord, Thy will be done, for we had no right to even a crumb of Your gifts, not even to a single moment of existence? *Acts 17:28*

But God does not lay any burdensome yoke on us, only an easy and light one. He seeks no payment from us other than our hands extended to receive His gifts. He does not want sacrifices or whole burnt offerings, for He satisfied Himself for our sake through the eternal sacrifice of His Son. And this Son of His, Who paid such a price to acquire the right to rule as our King, only rules over us for our own sake, and His endless lordship—we dare say this because it praises His goodness—is only an endlessly varied service to His own creatures. *Matthew 11:30*

Finally, what does the King desire of His slaves? His chosen mouthpiece says this to our souls: *The King desires your beauty, for* *Psalm 44:12*

He is your Lord. Your Savior desires to betroth Himself to you *in righteousness and justice, in lovingkindness and mercy. As a bridegroom rejoices over his bride, so the Lord* desires to *rejoice over you.* Can you possibly argue against such a blessed desire of your Lord?

And so, *Listen, O daughter, behold and incline your ear, and forget your people and your father's house; For the King desired your beauty, for He is your Lord. And the daughters...shall worship Him.* Learn, O Christian soul—this is the second part of the prophetic declaration—learn fidelity, which will bring you into the good graces of the King of kings, as the only desirable beauty in us who have no personal beauty whatsoever.

Listen, O daughter, and see. But the prophet does not explain what must be listen to or where we might see the beloved Bridegroom of souls. This could not have been spoken definitively once for all mankind. Sometimes the Lord appears and speaks to the soul when it does not expect Him: *I was manifest to those who did not seek Me; I was found by those who did not ask for Me. I said, 'Behold, I am here,' to a nation that did not call on My name.* But sometimes He remains silent and is not found by the soul that seeks Him and calls for Him: *I will rise now and go about the city...I will seek him whom my soul loves. I sought him, but did not find him.* But do not despair at this, O daughter of His mercy. You must only "listen," constantly to every sign of His presence, and seek out all His paths, *and when you find Him, call upon Him when He draws near to you.*

Listen, O daughter, behold. Only two senses out of five are left you by the declaimer of the will of the King of kings. Begin to leave, like Lot, these five cities, which must soon be destroyed. Leave the domain of the senses, rejecting first those that are more gross and fleshly. *Do not touch, do not taste, do not handle* in desire and pleasure and satiety, but only in need and to satisfy the weakness of the flesh. Those who are over-filled with pleasures of the senses sleep at the door of the bridal chamber of the heavenly Bridegroom and will not hear His voice. The oil in their lamps is disappearing, and they will not see His face.

Listen, O daughter, behold and incline your ear. Pay attention! There are many pleasant sounds that affect the inner hearing, but not all of them are *the sound of the Lord God walking in the garden in the cool of the day.* After all, in Eden even the serpent was given the power of speech. There are many beautiful views that attract the spiritual gaze, but not all of them are the light of Christ, and *Satan himself transforms himself into an angel of light.* You must come to know where to turn your gaze, lest you be deluded by phantoms: *Incline your ear,* or, better yet, *incline,* with David, *my heart to Your testimonies. Do not be carried about with various and strange doctrines. We have the prophetic [and apostolic] word confirmed, which you do well to heed as a light that shines in a dark place.*

Psalm 44:12
Genesis 3:8
2 Corinthians 11:14
Psalm 118:36
Hebrews 13:9
2 Peter 1:19

Having begun our spiritual journey to the heavenly Bridegroom and having preserved our faithfulness to Him from all delusions of the senses and the mind, we may still be long prevented from approaching Him by the passionate attachments of our hearts. But we must also tear apart these bonds: *Forget your people and your father's house.* "But is this even possible?" asks the passionate soul. Do the newly betrothed husband and wife ask the same question when the same God commands, by the law of matrimonial love, that *a man shall leave his father and mother and be joined to his wife*? Is not the loving heart a keeper and preserver of just as strict a law at that moment? Can love for God not do as much as love for a fellow creature? Should not the former be incomparably stronger than the latter? If one kind of created love can be sacrificed for the sake of another, higher creaturely love, then can we offer a lesser sacrifice to the love of God than all the lawful loves that we offer to ourselves and to our fellow creatures? And can the divine Bridegroom offer any smaller demands of those who wish to be betrothed to Him than this: *If anyone desires to come after Me, let him deny himself* ? *He who loves father or mother more than Me is not worthy of Me. And he who loves*

Psalm 44:11
Genesis 2:24
Matthew 16:24
Matthew 10:37

son or daughter more than Me is not worthy of Me. There should be no obstacle, no intermediary, no shadow falling between Him and a soul. *My beloved is mine, and I am his,* cries the soul.

    Blessed are you if you understand and cry out this song, O Christian soul. Then the King will desire your beauty, and He will reveal to you the hidden treasures of His love. *I love those who love me.*

    But be careful, O daughter of good will, lest you trip on the last approach to your King. Look with trepidation at the glory that He promises you, and think that you can in no way deserve it, but you can lose it for eternity with the smallest infidelity. Remember the final instruction of the Bridegroom's best man: *And you shall worship Him.* Pray constantly to the One *Who satisfied your desires with good things,* and when He *crowns you with mercy and compassion,* then fall at His feet in humility. As the blessed one said, "May your loving heart be covered with the fear of the Lord, in humble-mindedness, lest, as it is raised up, it fall away from the all-generous One."

    Through this true path and constant striving from the world to God, from darkness to light, may the virgins of our souls be led to the king of heaven, O Christians, following after the footsteps of the most blessed virgin who enters the Temple today. May they be led at the proper time into the uncreated and eternal *temple of the King* through His grace, and mercies, and love for mankind. Amen.

37

The One Thing We Need

Homily on the Nativity of the Mother of God
(1806-08)

"One thing is needed." (Luke 10:42)

Nothing is so typical in the world as complaints about a life full of cares. If all the groanings of all busy hearts in all the world were united in a single moment, our ears would hear a terrifying storm of noise! When fulfilling our physical needs—food, clothing, spiritual formation, and our social obligations—do not present us with too great a labor, then our imagination begins to get fruitful in coming up with new worries of the mind. These include a thirst for riches, glory, and pleasure, and they so divert us that even the most lazy person ends up having as many worldly cares as the most assiduous worker.

O frivolous mortal! You are as fretful as Martha, and you count thousands of needs. Through the noise of these cares, which, so to speak, root about in the confusion of your though, can you allow into your soul the voice of truth that desires to calm you down: *One thing is needed?* As for You, O Virgin who gave birth to the Lord of the Sabbath, for your sake we rest from our cares, if not for a complete Sabbath, then at least for this one hour of our day. O mother of the New Noah, who *will comfort us concerning our work and the toil of our hands, because of the ground which the Lord has cursed,* send down peace on our hearts through your active mediation, so that we might truly sense how this peace alone can calm us from our countless cares.

We human beings have a strange and calamitous quality to our desires—they rarely, and only for a short time, remain within their proper boundaries. He Who has "set a boundary" on the waters, *that they may not pass over, that they may not return to cover the earth,* it seems, has not set a boundary for the striving of the human heart. These desires extend from object to object with such irrepressible speed, like a rock dropped into the ocean creates ripples that move outward, swallowing each other in their haste. Sometimes, when we have done all that we need, we find that activity to be too limiting, and begin to extend outward into the impossible. At first, we seek the most necessary things, then we think of what is beneficial and pleasant, and finally that which is excessive begins to seem necessary to us as well. The slave groans in his lack of freedom, but the freeman complains that he has no slaves. Mountains of gold are insufficient for avarice; Thrones are too low for ambition; Palaces cannot contain the breadth of human desires, but neither can a hut.

But let not this rebuke fall only on the self-willed and the inexperienced among you. The hunger of desire is insatiable because its food doesn't satisfy and is not natural to the human person. Can desires be constant and moderate if their object is subject to constant change and diminution? *And the world is passing away, and the lust of it.* Can one be calm and not seek always for something greater if that which is acquired never satisfies, or even deludes? Pure spirit and crude matter, eternal life and momentary pleasure—what similarity can these have? The world is a spinning wheel; Our soul is the image of the triune divinity. A circle placed inside a triangle cannot extend to fill the entire space of the triangle, and so the whole world can never fill the soul of a human person, and I do not dare to claim to know whether this is wrath that punishes or a wrath that instructs.

The work of mercy is that man is placed amidst these dangers, and we must admit that in this state, we are both punished and instructed. It is our punishment, because the child-loving Father will never imprison His children in the country of famine and drought without good reason. It is our instruction, because the most wise Creator could not create famine if he did not first create food; Consequently, every groan of deluded and insatiate desires is a secret instruction to us that man is not for the world, though the world is for man. Everything we acquire here is only a waste of time; There is only one need that is everywhere revealed, but nowhere can be satisfied, and so it demands our entire attention: *One thing is needed.* Luke 10:42

This fact is inspired by every person's rational mind, but our reason is no longer capable of guiding us, a fact made very clear by Revelation, which takes over the instruction where reason loses its strength. There is only one thing, says Revelation, that comprises the constant, essential need for man—the kingdom of God, or grace-mediated union with God. Man once had this incomparable joy, but from the moment that he, the ingrate, turned away from his single joy and fell into the multiplicity of created joys, the world in which he, outside of God, wanted to establish his own lordship, became his prison, and every object of that world became a tool of imprisonment. In vain do you now seek fine tastes in the fruits of the ground, for sooner or later your eyes will be opened, and these fruits will be bitter in your mouths, for after the forbidden fruit was torn off, only curses grow on this earth. Only one thing is needed: To acquire the kingdom of God, to restore one's inner union with God through faith, love, and hope. Then, even the physical world will give you all manner of benefits and pleasures, for everything will turn into the gifts and blessings of the Heavenly Father: *But seek first the kingdom of God and His righteousness, and all these things shall be added to you.*

Matthew 6:33

Providence showed the first example of this kingdom in circumstances in which it was the least likely to happen. The physical world was amazed that the heavenly world rejoiced, looking at mankind. For people complained to the whole world that they *both hunger and thirst, and ...are poorly clothed, and beaten, and homeless, being destitute, afflicted, tormented,* but the angels at the same time triumphantly insisted that mankind was *as poor, yet making many rich; as having nothing, and yet possessing all things.*

1 Corinthians 4:11
Hebrews 11:37
2 Corinthians 6:10

Truly, what can the one who obtains God lack? All his thoughts are of God. All his desires consist of taking pleasure in God. His only action is to love God. His only goal is to please Him. Thinking of God is his food; Eternity is the field of his glory; Heaven is his treasure. From this spiritual height, he extends his gaze to his physical state and the so-called good things that comprise our cares. And so, he sees everything differently than the timorous children of the world. Power, he thinks, is not for the powerful, but for the oppressed, for he has nothing of flattery in him, no pleasure except to do good. He considers money (other than what is necessary for life) to be the property of the orphaned and the poor, and if heaven did not will to give him these riches, then that is because heaven wants to keep temptations away from him, or because someone else's hands are better suited to distribute that money. He thinks that luxuries are more of a burden than a decoration; Pleasures of the senses are more a pledge of future diseases or shame, and the less he indulges in them, then the easier it is to preserve himself from dangerous excess. Poverty, misfortune, insult, persecution—these he considers to be the gifts of providence. May the name of the Lord be blessed!

Oh, why do we not all think like this? Why do we instead spend the few short days of our life by foolishly burdening ourselves with a year's supply of extra food, or by picking up some shiny trifle from the earth and putting it on our backs as a pointless yoke, or by choosing a road covered in flowers, even though it clearly leads to a cliff edge, or by instead skirting the edges of cliffs and defiles. What a variety of self-torture! Why do we not instead think of the only One who might make our journey easier?

Come to Me, all you who labor and are heavy laden, and I will give you rest, said the Lord. *I am the way, the truth, and the life.* This is the one thing needed for everyone. Amen.   Matthew 11:28   John 14:6

The Virgin's Humble Wisdom

Homily on the Annunciation of the Mother of God
(1825)

"But when she saw him, she was troubled at his saying, and considered what manner of greeting this was." (Luke 1:29)

This Virgin was so deeply plunged into her solitude, was so distant from any human converse, that the presence of an angel (who is also a virgin) brought her into confusion: *She was troubled...* But now, she opens the door to her chamber, allowing entry into it both to virgins and those who live in matrimony. She accepts countless greetings not only from the bodiless ones (or those who are like the bodiless in their purity) but also from people who have impure mouths. And now, not only is she no longer troubled, but she consoles those who are troubled, not only is she no longer distant from joy, but she fills those who approach her with joy, not only is she no longer in fear before grace, but with boldness she grants grace to her petitioners. What a change! She was unapproachable to anyone when she was only a *maidservant of the Lord*, but she is approachable to all now, when she is the *Mother of the Lord*. *Luke 1:38*
Luke 1:43

Let us take advantage of this ease of access. Let us approach, not only to see the glory of the once-obscure Virgin and to be filled with the sweetness of this vision, but also to know, as much as possible, how such a great glory came about from such profound obscurity, and to take at least a few seeds from the fruits of the *enclosed garden* of the bride of the Holy Spirit for the spiritual garden of our own souls. *Song of Songs 4:12*

Come all you virgins, and accept from the Virgin Mary the confirmation of your struggle, gazing at her unutterably exalted dignity, her virginity, for she bears God within herself.

Come all you who live in the matrimonial state, and those who are yet betrothed, but not yet united with the blessing of matrimony, for all human unions would only have produced the children of wrath and inheritors of hell if the Virgin Mother had not given birth to the Son Who would give them new birth as sons and inheritors of God.

Come, all you who love solitude, and learn from the contemplative Mary that the heart of solitude is humble contemplation of God, and without this kernel, our solitude is often nothing other than empty stubbornness or even cruel hatred of others, a nest of evil thoughts and the abode of a spirit of madness.

Come, all you who love gatherings, and be reminded that visitations to the soul of heavenly powers occur not in the vanity of earthly work, not in the pleasure of large assemblies, not in the noise of pointless conversations, but the word of God is sown in the heart.

But how can we possibly show you all the fruits of Mary's vineyard in such a short time, that is, how can we demonstrate for your instruction all her perfections and virtues? Thus, we will limit ourselves this time only to one that might seem small. On this branch of the Gospel one can see, like a full and ripe bunch of grapes that bow down to the earth, her virtue of humble wisdom and wise humility.

But when she saw him, she was troubled at his saying. The presence of the heavenly messenger, who brings with him the presence of the Lord to the Virgin Man, should be grace, joy, and a blessing. After all, he said to her, *Rejoice, highly favored one, the Lord is with you; Blessed are you among women!* The presence of such a messenger, however, does not give her joy, but rather distresses her. Why? Was it because she did not recognize the heavenly messenger and thought at first that he was a human stranger? But if the appearance of an unknown man would have distressed her, then his meek and pious words should have immediately calmed her. But the opposite is true: *She was troubled at his saying.* Or was she shaken by the appearance of an exalted heavenly being, which is never easy for weak and mortal human nature, as we see in the examples of Daniel and John? But her purity, unparalleled among those born of Adam, made her capable like no one else of receiving heavenly visitors. And Orthodox pious tradition tell that this would not have been her first encounter with Gabriel. And so why was this young, but already experienced, converser with the divine distressed by the words of the angel?

Let us delay the answer to this question, and let us instead remember the tradition that the Virgin Mary, previously visited by the archangel, was reading and coming to understand the prophecy of Isaiah: *Behold the virgin shall conceive and bear a Son, and shall call His name Immanuel.* This tradition lets us know for certain what the Gospel only hints at: That her spirit was already filled with the reading of the holy Scriptures, and not only with the milk, but the solid food of divine wisdom. And since that was the case, then was it not easy for her to understand that these new and triumphant names—highly-favored, blessed among women—in the tongue of the angel who never lies could mean nothing other than a greeting to the Mother of Immanuel? That being the case, then would it not have been easy for the angelic greeting not only to bring her joy, but spiritual ecstasy? And so why, on the contrary, did it distress her?

Now is the time to resolve this dilemma. Everything makes it clear that there can only be one answer: The profound humility of the most exalted Virgin. Wisdom and faith spiritually showed to her the image of the mother of Immanuel, that is the Mother of Christ, in the prophecy of Isaiah, and her love and humility then also inspired her with a desire to see this majestic mother in the flesh, and to be her slave. But that same humility did not allow Mary to see that image applied to her own self, even when the words of the angel, as it were, placed a mirror before her face. She heard the greeting that raised her above all other human beings, but the constant striving of her soul, then and before, was to constantly humble herself before all others. Thus, just as pure water shakes and moves from the blowing of a soft wind without losing its purity, but becoming more animated with the movement, so the pure soul of Mary was disturbed by the words of the heavenly spirit, but did not lose the purity of her senses. Instead, her confusion became the cause of even greater spiritual progress in her life in God.

The results of this confusion also prove to us that Mary's spiritual distress was not in any way false or impure, that it was not the result of cowardice or doubt in God's protection during dangers, nor was it a proud flutter of the heart or a battle against the delusive seduction of the angel's praise. Cowards and doubters don't think; Those who are seduced by praise cannot remain silent, but either answer the praise with a kind word or speak falsely humble words to seem to deflect the praise, while actually hoping to increase it. We see nothing like this in Mary. Her confusion does not deprive her of her spiritual courage, nor does it take her out of her customary state, nor does it steal from her cursory words, nor does it prevent her from silently contemplating what she heard: *She was troubled at his saying, and considered what manner of greeting this was.* *Luke 1:29*

These were her reactions at the suddenness of the event. She was not carried away by her confusion, nor did she allow herself to doubt or become afraid, nor did she hurry or act puffed up or exalt herself. She closed herself off from her imminent glory with her usual cover of humility, and at the same time, she had the ability to hide her humility from others and herself even through her silence, lest even a humble word betray the true spirit of humility. Finally, against this unexpected occurrence, she had as a ready medicine her ability to calmly think. What is the source of this disposition and this manner of action in Mary? Is it not the indomitable strength of wisdom and advanced spiritual progress?

And so, we see that in the spiritual vineyard of the Bride of God, one of the most glorious plants was wisdom, and the earth that held the root of this wisdom and the power of this spiritual flower was humility, and the tool with which she cultivated the ground of humility and protected it from weeds was again wisdom. She who was to become the Mother of the self-emptying Word of God had humble wisdom and wise humility to an advanced degree. Her great wisdom was protected from pride and brazenness by humility, and her humility was cultivated by wisdom in such a way that there would be nothing base in it, and that it would be unassuming, pure, and simple.

Let us take this example of the vineyard and apply it to ourselves. If we desire the garden of our souls to be filled with unfading flowers and to bring forth fruits of eternal life, then we must labor in such a way to acquire humble wisdom and wise humility. Whoever wants to grow his wisdom without humility wants his flowers to grow without soil. And whoever wants to be content with humility without wisdom wants to have uncultivated soil when it could be very fruitful.

What is it that produced so many opinions about the truth, which is one, so many arguments, so many delusions? What produced sects within philosophy, heresies within the Church, and false wise men in society, godless people in the kingdom of God, and the devil amid the angels of light? What? False wisdom, not true wisdom, because it lacked the necessary humility. False wise men of this earth have tried to cultivate their garden in the air, not in the earth, and the devil planted it in fire, that is, they imagined that frivolity and pride might made for good soil to cultivate wisdom. But if false wisdom without humility brings you close to the devil, then, on the contrary, by departing from wisdom, to whom does mankind come close then, except to irrational beasts?

If, O Christian soul, you hear a voice that greets you with some kind of success in the works of the spirit, or with some kind of progress, even if it is the result of grace, do not hurry to rejoice. I rather desire you to have the confusion of Mary, that is, her humility, so that the spirit of flattery not carry you to a height under which there is nothing but the abyss.

If, on the contrary, you are told that striving toward spiritual progress is delusion, that love for wisdom is brazen proud-mindedness, that contemplating the faith, learning the law of God, reading the word of God is either unnecessary or even dangerous, then listen carefully: Does this sound like the voice of an angel giving spiritual instruction or a heavenly sermon? Compare this with the true and pure voice of the prophet: *Blessed is the man...[whose] delight is in the law of the Lord, and in His law he meditates day and night.* Compare it with this teaching of the divine Teacher: *Search the Scriptures.* Compare it with the words of the apostle: "Let the word of Christ dwell in you richly in all wisdom, teaching and admonishing on another." (Colossians 3:16) Compare it with the example of Mary: No one forbade the young Virgin to read the book of Isaiah the Prophet and to contemplate the image of Immanuel.

No! Christianity is not foolishness or ignorance, but "the wisdom of God in a mystery, the hidden wisdom which God ordained before the ages for our glory, and in which our spiritual

Psalm 1:1-2

John 5:39

1 Corinthians 2:7

progress will glorify God the Father, the Son, and the Holy Spirit, for all ages. Amen.

39

The First Resurrection

Homily on the Dormition of the Mother of God
(1825)

St. Dionysius the Areopagite was present at the burial of the Mother of God, and we can partly discover what occurred there from his writings:

> For, amongst our inspired hierarchs (when both we, as you know, and yourself, and many of our holy brethren, were gathered together to the depositing of the Life-springing and God-receptive body, and when there were present also James, the brother of God, and Peter, the foremost and most honored pinnacle of the Theologians, when it was determined after the depositing, that every one of the hierarchs should celebrate, as each was capable, the omnipotent Goodness of the supremely Divine Weakness. (On the Divine Names, Book 3)

According to St Maximos the Confessor, the name "supremely Divine Weakness" refers to the willing condescension of the Son of God into human nature (except for sin). For, because of this willing condescension, He endured even a death on the cross, and bore our weaknesses on Himself. It is pleasant even to this day to recognize the one, holy, catholic, and apostolic Church, by the way, in the unity of its holy and apostolic rites. After so many centuries from the day of the Dormition of the Mother of God to this very day "many of our holy brethren gather together." In emulation of this divine procession in Sion or Gethsemane, today we also offer to your contemplation the image of her life-giving and God-accepting body, as it was on the day of her burial. "Every one of the hierarchs should celebrate," or, in other words, glorifies in word and in hymn the "omnipotent Goodness" of the Son of God in His salvific incarnation, for He laid a path through weakness and death to divine glory.

Oh, if only we might today hear one of these hymns that were uttered to the Lord and His mother by the assembly of the apostles, inspired by the Holy Spirit! But St. Dionysius only tells of them, but does not share their content.

However, I hear at least a series of hymns that are appropriate for today's event, spoken by the mouth of the foster-son of the most pure Virgin and her nearest servant in her life and burial. St John exclaimed, *Blessed and holy is he who has part in the first resurrection.* [Revelation 20:6]

Who other than the Birthgiver of the Author of our resurrection has a better right to be first to partake in that resurrection? And tradition does tell us that she, like her Son, left only her burial shroud behind her in the tomb three days after her burial. And so, first of all mankind she is *blessed and holy*, the Virgin Mother, for she was first *who has part in the resurrection* of her Son and God. [Revelation 20:6] But what is the "first resurrection" that many can partake of? Let us seek an answer to this question, not out of idle curiosity, but to glorify the Resurrector and to instruct ourselves.

Every day, we announce the resurrection to ourselves and to each other when we repeat the words of the Creed: "I look for the resurrection of the dead." Moreover, we assume that this refers to the one universal resurrection of the dead. But if that were true, we could not say, *Blessed and holy is he who has part in the first resurrection*, for in the universal resurrection not only the saints, but the sinners, not only the blessed, but the condemned will arise from the dead. As the Author of our resurrection Himself said, *The hour is coming in which all who are in the graves will hear His voice and come forth—those who have done good, to the resurrection of life, and those who have done evil, to the resurrection of condemnation.*

Revelation 20:6

John 5:28-29

So, what is this resurrection announced by the seer, which will belong exclusively to the blessed and the holy? It is called "first;" Consequently, it is not the only resurrection. If we do not find the first resurrection, we will seek another, or the final one. Perhaps it will help us find the first?

Everyone who sees the Son, said the incarnate Son of God, *and believes in Him will have everlasting life; And I will raise him up at the last day.* We have found the final resurrection. It is the final one because it must occur on the last day of this passing world. From this limit, we must by necessity return back in time to seek the first resurrection. Is it distant? Doubtless, it is no more distant than the day of the resurrection of Jesus Christ Himself. For, as the apostle said, *Christ is risen from the dead, and has become the firstfruits of those who have fallen asleep. In Christ all shall be made alive. But each one in his own order: Christ the firstfruits, afterward those who are Christ's at His coming. Then comes the end...*

John 6:40

1 Corinthians 15:20; 15:22-24

Thus, the first resurrection, the resurrection of the blessed and holy, should be sought between the day of the resurrection of Christ and the final day of the world. But where is it? Truly, is not the taking of most holy Virgin's body to heaven, like the resurrection of Christ, the first example of this first resurrection? If the mother of the Author of our resurrection follows him into resurrection three days after her own Dormition, then is it not possible that some others, who are especially holy and worthy of blessedness, such as those who gave their life for the name of the Giver of resurrection, might, over the course of the centuries, but before the universal resurrection, receive a certain preliminary, specially chosen participation both in the resurrection and in the glory and blessedness that are appropriate to it? How clear, then, appear the words of the seer: *The souls of those who had been beheaded for their witness to Jesus and for the word of God...lived and reigned with Christ...but the rest of the dead did not live again.... This is the first resurrection.*

Revelation 20:4-5

But *who has known the mind of the Lord? Or who has become His counselor?* Man, who does not know what the coming day will bring, can he grasp for knowledge of that which the ages will give birth to, pregnant as they are with mysteries of God's judgments? *Do not seek things too difficult for you, nor examine what is beyond your strength. Think about what is commanded you, for you do not need what the Lord keeps hidden.*

Romans 11:34

Sirach 3:20-21

And so, I bow my head to the wise teacher. I leave behind this testing of the mysteries of the future, for truly it is not as necessary for us to know them truly than it is dangerous for us to be deluded by incorrect knowledge. I seek to think only about what is commanded.

Blessed and holy is he who has part in the first resurrection. Is there anything here that is commanded? What about holiness? Did not God Himself command it, saying, *Be holy, for I am holy* ? And what about blessedness? Are we not commanded to seek it under the name of God's kingdom? But since the seer declares those who partake of the first resurrection to be blessed and holy, then should we not be worried that whoever does not partake of the first resurrection should have no hope of any blessedness at all? This forces us to ask the question a second time, this time out of care for our own eternal fate: What is the first resurrection?

Revelation 20:6

1 Peter 1:16

Resurrection refers to being raised from the dead, for whoever is alive has no need of resurrection. Therefore, to properly understand what resurrection is, we must first understand properly what is death. And so, what is death? Is it the parting of the soul from the body? This is the usual definition in human language, but it is foreign to Christian language and to the word of God. It is foreign to Christian language because do you not yourselves call today's feast the "falling asleep" of the Mother of God? To say that we celebrate the death of the Mother of God would sound crude, as though it were a bad translation from another language, almost insulting to the Christian ear. It is also foreign to the word of God. For example, Adam was told, *But of the tree of the knowledge of good and evil you shall not eat, for in the day that you eat of it you shall surely die.* And yet, Adam continued to live, even after eating the forbidden fruit, for nine hundred and thirty years. Will we then say that the word of God was not fulfilled? If, on the other hand, as everyone must admit, the word of God was in fact fulfilled and to the letter, then does this not reveal to us that death, according to the logic of the word of God, is completely not that which we imagine it to be when we see the body lying still, without the soul? True death was born on earth on the day of the first sin and from that day, it lived with Adam, cooperating in all his acts and in the birth of his children, which is why it multiplied together with the human race.

Genesis 2:17

And so, what is death? To answer this according to the wisdom of the word of God, it is better still to use this question: What is life? For death is merely the cessation of life. And so, come, let us know life in its source. The Theologian said, *In Him was life, and the life was the light of men.* Life is contained in God the Word, and this life is the light of mankind. Communion with the life that is essential to the Logos and His light is the true life of man. It is an active state of light, calm, freedom, power, purity, and incorruption.

John 1:4

Consequently, separation from the life of God the Logos and separation from His light is the true death of a person. This is a state of darkness, sorrow, anxiety, weakness, impurity, and finally, corruption.

Consequently, a renewal of communion with the life of God the Word, and a return to His light, is the true resurrection of man, in which the blessed and the holy participate.

The final resurrection of the unrighteous in their bodies of condemnation is not true resurrection, for they rise up not for communion with the life of God the Word and His light, but for a renewed separation from Him: *Depart from Me, you cursed, into the everlasting fire prepared for the devil and his angels.* These are resurrected for a second death.

Matthew 25:41

Revelation 21:8

The final resurrection of the righteous with their bodies of glory is the true resurrection, but it is not the first resurrection, but the final one. It is the triumphant revelation in the bodies of the righteous of the preliminary, secret, spiritual resurrection, just as physical death is only the visible manifestation of the final, invisible, spiritual death. The power of the final, bodily resurrection is contained within the preliminary, spiritual one. The final bodily resurrection of the iniquitous therefore is not the true and blessed resurrection, for they had no preliminary, first, spiritual resurrection.

Therefore, "'Blessed and holy is he who has part in the first resurrection," that is, the spiritual resurrection.

1 Thessalonians 4:3

And so, do you desire that *the will of God, your sanctification"* be accomplished in you? Do we labor to acquire this blessedness? We must both desire and labor to participate in the first resurrection, in the spiritual resurrection, through the mortification of the flesh by rejecting its pleasures, through faith in the Resurrector and love for Him, through our constant turning toward Him and opening our hearts and minds to Him to accept His rays of light and life, for He is the life-giving Sun of the spirit.

Philippians 3:11

This is how the apostle acted when with care and assiduity, as though vacillating between fear and hope, he said, *If, by any means, I may attain to the resurrection from the dead.* And this is how he recommends that we act also, when he exclaims, *Awake, you who sleep, arise from the dead, and Christ will give you light."* From what sort of sleep is he awakening us, and to what sort of resurrection is he calling us? It is not an apostolic work to awaken someone from a purely physical sleep; But neither is it the work of an apostle to call us to the final resurrection of the body, for then *the Lord Himself will descend from heaven with a shout, with the voice of an archangel, and with the trumpet of God. And the dead in Christ will rise first.* Consequently, the apostle wants to awaken us from the sleep of sensuality, from the death that invisibly infects and poisons our entire life of the body. He wants to inspire us toward the first resurrection, the spiritual resurrection. *1 Thessalonians 4:16*

Some people who know no other form of life than the one of flesh and blood might find this teaching to be strange. A strange teaching that transforms the entire world of living people into a cemetery filled with animated corpses and recommends that these dead people take care for their own resurrection! Yes! Indeed, this teaching truly is strange for those who, according to the apostle, *walk in the futility of their mind, having their understanding darkened, being alienated from the life of God, because of the ignorance that is in them, because of the blindness of their heart.* *Ephesians 4:17-18*

But can this teaching seem strange to one who finds nothing strange in the teaching of the Lord Jesus? Did He not transform the holy city into a cemetery, and the honored and multitudinous assembly of pharisees into an assembly of moving tombs when He called them "graves which are not seen" (Luke 11:44) and *whitewashed tombs which indeed appear beautiful outwardly, but inside are full of dead men's bones and all uncleanness.* Or when His beloved disciple saw with his spiritual eyes and said that *He who does not love his brothers abides in death.* This is clearly evident to anyone, for there are so many people that do not love their brothers, that is, do not love someone. Think, then, how many animate corpses there are walking around, seeming to be alive! *Matthew 23:27* *1 John 3:14*

Whoever sleeps is not conscious during the time that he sleeps. But while he dreams a dream, he believes himself to be awake, and only after he awakes does he realize that he was sleeping and imagining things. In the same way, those who are dead in their sins are not conscious in this state that they are dead. They think that the life of their fleshly and sensual dreams is true life. Such people need the words of the Gospel, the power of grace, to awaken or to rise again into the spiritual life, and only then can they know just how deep was their sleep, how false their dreams, and how truly they were dead and far distant from any kind of true blessedness. And so, if this teaching seems strange or disturbing to some, then I remind you that we all are also placed here, in emulation of the apostle, to call and awaken the sleeping and dead: *Awake, you who sleep, arise from the dead, and Christ will give you light.*

<small>Ephesians 5:14</small>

If this teaching seems strange, this only shows just how far the Christian world has gone from the true spirit and wisdom of the teaching of Christ, which is also the teaching of the saints and blessed ones, who learned it from Christ. Let us call to witness one of the greatest of these.

"True death," said St Makarios the Great, "is found and hidden inside the heart, and man dies internally. If anyone passes from death to life in the inner man, then truly he will live for all eternity and will not die." (Homily 15:37) In a different place: "This body is a likeness of the soul, and the soul is a likeness of the spirit. And just as the body without a soul is dead, incapable of doing anything, so also the soul is dead without the heavenly soul, the divine spirit, unable to do anything beneficial without the Holy Spirit." (Homily 30:3) And another place: "If your soul communes with the Spirit of God, and the heavenly soul enters into your soul, then you will become a complete man, an inheritor and son of God." (Homily 32: 6) and another place: "In the general resurrection, even the bodies of those whose souls mystically were raised up in advance" (this is the first resurrection) "and were illumined with heavenly glory, will rise up together with their souls" (this is the final resurrection) "and will be glorified and illumined." (Homily 34:2)

St Makarios concludes thus: "Let us pray also that with the power of God we might also die to the age of dark wrath, that the spirit of sin be destroyed within us, that we might accept the soul of the Heavenly Spirit, and that we may pass from dark wrath to the light of Christ, and find rest in the blessed life for all ages." (Homily 1:9) Amen.

40

Walking Behind the Virgin

Homily on the Entry of the Mother of God in the Temple
(1825)

"The virgins behind her shall be brought to the King."
(Psalm 44:15)

What does the divine prophet see? Who is this King? Who are the virgins? Why are they being brought as a group to the King? Whom are they following?

The King is Jesus Christ, Whose kingdom, it must be said, is not of this world. The virgins are pure souls who have come to love Jesus Christ so much that they are no longer attached to anything in the world with physical love. They are brought to the King to receive the kingdom of heaven, to not only belong to this kingdom as its servants, but also so that it might belong to them as to king's daughters, as to brides of the king, as to a queen. They are led by the great bride of the King: the Church, and this great assembly of the Church is itself led by the chief bride of the king, the grace-filled Virgin Mary.

SERMON 40: WALKING BEHIND THE VIRGIN

Today's feast of the most holy Virgin's entry into the Temple of the Lord is, in a certain way, a triumphant revelation of this procession of virgins to the King. For this reason, it is appropriately chosen as the patronal feast of one of the churches here in this convent of virgins who have dedicated consecrated themselves to God. Let them see themselves in this feast as in a painting or a mirror, being led by their divine (and yet intimate) guide and sincere patroness, who today begins the path to her most exalted perfection, and little by little may they come to know and come to follow her footsteps, walking *behind her*. Let them learn, as those who prepare themselves for being led to God, let them arouse themselves with the thought of coming near to Him, even uniting themselves with Him. *Psalm 44:15*

We can find a short description of this path of the soul being led to God in the same psalm of David, from which I took the first words of this homily. This description is provided to us by St. Basil the Great.

The beginning of the path that leads the soul to God is expressed by the Psalm in the following words: *Hearken, O daughter, and see, and incline thy ear: And forget thy people and thy father's house. And the king shall greatly desire thy beauty, for he is thy Lord, and him they shall adore.* *Psalm 44:11-12*

In his interpretation of these words, St. Basil says, "He summons the Church to hear and observe the precepts...Observe well, he says, the creation, and aided by the order in it, thus ascend to the contemplation of the Creator. Then bending her lofty and proud neck, he says: 'Incline thy ear' to this teaching in order that you may forget those depraved customs and the lessons of your fathers. Therefore, 'forget thy people and thy father's house.' For, everyone *who commits sin is of the devil*. Cast out, I pray you, he says, the teachings of the evil spirits, forget sacrifices, nocturnal dances, tales which inflame to fornication and to every form of licentiousness. For this reason have I called you my own daughter, that you may hate the parent who previously begot *1 John 3:8* you for destruction. If through such forgetfulness you erase the blemishes of your depraved learning, assuming your own proper beauty, you will appear desirable to your Spouse and King. 'He is thy Lord, Him they shall adore,' that is, every creature."

Later in the same psalm, the perfection of approaching God is depicted in the following words: "All the glory of the king's daughter is within, invested and adorned with golden borders. After her shall virgins be brought to the king.

Psalm 44:14-15

In his interpretation of these prophetic words, once again St. Basil says this about the Church: "After she had been cleansed of the former doctrines of wickedness, and was heeding the instruction and forgetting her people and her father's house, the Holy Spirit relates what pertains to her. And since He saw the cleanliness deeply hidden, He says, 'All the glory of the king's daughter,' that is to say, of Christ's bride, who has become henceforth through adoption a daughter of the king, 'is within.' The assertion urges us to penetrate to the inmost mysteries of ecclesiastical glory, since the beauty of the bride is within. He who makes himself ready for the Father who sees in secret, and who prays and does all things, not to be seen by men, but to be known to God alone, this man has all his glory within, even as the king's daughter. And the golden borders with which the whole is invested and adorned are within.

Colossians 3:9-12

"Seek nothing with exterior gold and bodily adornment; but consider the garment as one worthy to adorn him who is according to the image of his Creator, as the Apostle says: *Stripping off the old man, and putting on the new, one that is being renewed unto perfect knowledge according to the image of the creator...and he who has put on the heart of mercy, kindness, humility, patience, and meekness,* is clothing within and has adorned the inner man. Paul exhorts us to put on the Lord Jesus, not according to the exterior man, but in order that our remembrance of God may cover over our whole mind. But, I believe that the spiritual garment is woven when the attendant action is interwoven with the word of doctrine. In fact, just as a bodily garment is woven when the woof is interwoven with the warp, so when the word is antecedent, if actions in accordance with the word should be produced, there would be made a certain most magnificent garment for the soul which possesses a life of virtue attained by word and action. But, the borders hang down from the garment, these also are spiritual; therefore, they too are said to be golden. Since, indeed, the word is greater than the deed, there is, as it were, a certain border which remains over from the woven robe according to the actions. Certain souls, since they have not accepted seeds of false doctrines, follow the spouse of the Lord and because they are following His spouse they will be led to the King. Let those also who have vowed virginity to the Lord hear that virgins will be led to the King, but virgins who are close to the Church, who follow after her, and who do not wander away from the ecclesiastical discipline."

If we can add our own, still puerile word, to this spiritually wise teaching of a truly great teacher of the Church, I will only add that not only those who promised virginity to the Lord, but all souls who promised and accepted union with Christ and adoption as sons through baptism should hear how the Holy Spirit calls them to follow the Church and approach Christ the King, and how He instruct us in this path, what perfection in approach to God we must achieve, and what blessedness in this approach we may obtain.

Hearken, O daughter! Listen, O Christian soul. For the same word that calls the Church of Christ in general also calls each individual Christian soul. Listen to what God tells you in His Scripture, or in a word of instruction, or in the voice of your own conscience. Listen carefully and preserve what you hear; do not allow the word of truth and salvation to enter one ear and fly out the other. *Psalm 44:10*

Hearken, O daughter, and see! A Christian soul can not only hear the God Who calls, but can also see Him. Or did I just tell a false- *Psalm 44:10* hood? If someone wants to doubt, let him doubt, but without a doubt I have spoken truth, as the prophet himself said and wrote: *I have set the Lord always before me.* So also should you labor to see Him Who Is—by your reason through the created things that are outside you, and by your spirit in your own heart. You will always hear, understand, and preserve the word better when you see before your eyes the one who speaks.

And incline thine ear. Listen to the salvific teaching with humility. Even if God speaks from on high, still, only the humble hear him clearly and faithfully recognize His voice. The voice of grace is quiet, while the world is loud. With all your strength tear away and guard your inner hearing from created things, and instead direct the attention of your spirit to God.

Forget thy people and thy father's house. This forgetfulness is not lack action in memory, but in the heart. For example, if a person speaks to us as though he knows us well, we can rebuke him if he did not visit us or did not show some other signs of heartfelt connection. Those who promise virginity to the Lord, and for that reason clearly separated themselves from their own family to shut themselves up in a place together with others like them, act in a way even more appropriate to the One Who called them when they also guard their hearts from attachments to the world and their family, when they rarely even step beyond that blessed wall. For it is true that until they have forgotten what lies beyond that wall, they will not find Him Whom they seek within the wall. First you must *forget thy people and thy father's house,"* and only afterward *the king shall greatly desire thy beauty.* But no matter what house you inhabit, no matter what family you belong to, O Christian soul, you must forget thy people and thy father's house, you must leave behind your sins in which you were born, you must hate and reject the works of the devil, and cease to love anything in the world as much as you love Christ, or rather, love nothing in the world other than Christ the Beloved.

And the king shall greatly desire thy beauty, for His is thy Lord, and him they shall adore. When you will cease to desire the vanity of created things, then the King of heaven will desire your beauty. And when you thus will come to know in Him not only the Lord of all, but *thy Lord* in particular, then you will no longer have to force yourself to bow before Him, as you must at the beginning of this ascesis, but you will do this freely, with joy, with exaltation, you shall adore Him, not only as a slave of the Lord, fearfully, but even with bold adoration, as a bride for her groom, as the daughter of the king for the king himself. Then you will not labor to please Him with virtues, so much as He Himself will invest and adorn you with them, as with the garments of a bride, as with the ornaments proper to the daughter of a king.

Will this external word dare to enter even deeper into the bridal chamber of the Bride of Christ, to bring out from there at least a part of her glory for the eyes of those outside it? No! At the very least, until the great judgment and the revelation of the sons of God and the kingdom of glory, "all the glory of the king's daughter is within." Let us end with these words of St Basil: "These words encourage us to enter into the sanctum of the glorious mysteries of the Church, for within is the beauty of the bride." Amen.

41

Lessons from the Miracle at Cana

Homily on the Day of the Mother of God, in Honor of Her Icon of Tikhvin (1834)

"When they ran out of wine, the mother of Jesus said to Him, 'They have no wine.'" (John 2:3)

Hearing these words, some might think: What an insignificant word precedes the first miracle! But if you are one of these people, then I have the pleasure of reminding you, and proving to you with this example, that in the mouths of the saints there are no insignificant words, and in the divine books, nothing unimportant is ever written. Be attentive. Let us open up this kernel of the word of life, and inside we will find food for our spirit.

Remember that these words of the most holy Mother of God were spoken to Her divine Son in Cana of Galilee at a wedding feast to which both Jesus and His mother were invited. You remember also that what follows is a miraculous transformation of water into wine of such high quality that the steward of the feast was amazed. Finally, remember that *This beginning of signs Jesus did in Cana of Galilee, and manifested His glory; and His disciples believed in Him.* Without delving deeply into the whole event, whose importance is clear from the fact that the disciples believed in Him, I will limit myself to the thoughts and instructions that are contained in this single phrase of the Mother of God that I have already offered.

John 2:11

First of all, these words prove to us that the Lord Jesus had already performed miracles before any that were described in the Gospels. This is not contradicted by John's remark that this is the first of signs, for it is the first of the signs in which Jesus "revealed His glory," that is, in which He gave other people an open way of recognizing Him as the Son of God and Savior, but this does not mean that it was the first miracle He ever performed. After all, what do the Theotokos's words mean: *They have no wine?* It is not a simple declaration of fact, but a humble request for help, and it can only be a request for miraculous help, since they were poor and could not have purchased wine on behalf of the bride and groom. This interpretation is further supported by Jesus' next words: *My hour is not yet come.* That is, it was not yet the time for open miracle-working. It is further supported by the miracle itself, when Jesus finally submitted to His mother's intercession. But how could she have thought to ask for a miracle if she did not know in advance that she could receive it? In other words, how could she have asked for a miracle if she had not had previous experiences of His miracle-working? And Jesus' own words demonstrate His profound humility, which would have covered any previous miracles with obscurity, not allowing for a possibility of self-glorification before the proper time, even before His dear ones.

John 2:3

John 2:4

Thus, we must conclude that the Mother of the Lord had seen miracles performed by her Son even before Cana of Galilee, similar to the one that she asked for. This is not merely the conclusion of an inquisitive mind, but it is beneficial and instructive example. It lets us know that in addition to the miracles that revealed the glory of Christ, that is, the open, triumphant ones that served to spread and confirm the true faith throughout humanity in general, there are also miracles that reveal only the extreme love that the Savior has for mankind, miracles that condescend to specific needs, weaknesses, and sorrows of certain people, for the cessation of their temptations and for the confirmation of their faith and hope in Him. After all, sorrows, weaknesses, and needs persist to this day, and so we must conclude that our Lord will not refuse even today to help us to weather those storms, even in miraculous ways when natural means are not sufficient. All that we need to do is run to Him with complete zeal and with a pure desire.

Secondly, these words of the most holy Virgin reveal her own special love for mankind and her readiness to help us in our sorrows. If the lack of wine had not been addressed at the wedding, this would not have been a terrible calamity. Perhaps there would have been a bit of embarrassment for the hosts and a certain disturbance in the feast itself. If these small troubles touched the heart of Mary with compassion and incited her to approach, with the key of a mother's love, the limitless treasure trove of love from mankind hidden in her divine Son, then should we not expect that serious calamites will only incite her intercession even more strongly?

A wedding feast is a rather foreign thing for one who was ever-virginal, and if still she attended not without attentiveness, but with compassion, with a desire to participate in resolving the difficulty, with readiness to help, then is it not natural for her, with loving attention, with empathetic participation, with grace-filled aid, to reveal her presence wherever she is called upon in reverent prayer, wherever she is accepted as ever-virgin and Theotokos, especially considering that her motherly intercession can no longer be limited by the rebuke of her Son concerning the time not being right, since now *all authority has been given to [Him] in heaven and on earth* ?   Matthew 28:18

Thirdly, these words of the Mother of God allow us to understand her power to intercede for us before her Son and God. At first, her intercession on behalf of the needy hosts of Cana seemed to be fruitless. The Lord found her request of a miracle to be untimely, and the situation seemed to have so little to do with either Himself or her, that He spoke to her as though she were not His mother: *Woman, what does your concern have to do with Me? My hour has not yet come.* But as stern as the word was, the deed was equally compassionate. The beginning seemed not very hopeful, but the conclusion was extremely successful. By His stern word, the Lord instructed us, through His mother, that we should not boldly ask for miracles to fix difficulties that have little significance, especially if a bit of patience would have been more than enough to resolve the problem. However, His compassionate deed also showed how the sternness of His justice can be softened by the meek intercession of His beloved Mother, and how her powerful intercession acquires His mercies for us, even when we don't deserve them.   John 2:4

Fourthly, these meek words of the most holy Virgin that we examine today, which were quickly sealed with silence, offer us a model for humble prayer and proper attention to the paths of God. How quiet and almost voiceless is her request! She doesn't say what she wants, and she doesn't even indicate what she would like Him to do. She doesn't say, "Perform a miracle: This is what I ask; I demand it of you." She makes not the slightest hint to her right to demand anything of Him as His mother. She only describes a need: *They have no wine*, and immediately is silent. It is as if she continued the conversation only in her thoughts: "Here is a need, and I cannot conceal that I feel sorry for them. But should we help them, and how, this I do not dare to say aloud. I await Your word, to which I am always obedient."   John 2:3

And after, when this humble request of hers seemed to be answered unfavorably, the Mother did not complain to her Son, nor did she contradict Him. She did not insist that it is always the proper time for works of mercy, that any human need should never be ignored, especially by the Creator and Savior of mankind. She revealed no sign of impatience or self-will; In silent submission she offered Her intercession to the will of the One in Whose limitless goodness she believed completely. Experience shows that this humble trust in the will of God is stronger the more pure it is in its intention. It is much more powerful than the vain busyness and restless rushing-about of man's self-will.

This small examination of a short word of the great Mother of God should not allow us to remain fruitless, O brothers, in our attentiveness to ourselves. In our needs, weaknesses, sorrows, temptations, let us run with hope to her powerful intercession before her Son and God, the easier to open the treasures of His limitless goodness, which are closed to us because of our unworthiness. But at the same time, let us strive to preserve that purity of intention, that humility of prayer, that unassuming fidelity to the judgments of God that is so beautiful demonstrated by the most holy Virgin.

Pathetic are those who close off the life-giving source of grace because of their lack of faith. But no better are those brazen fools who think to open the sluices of that source by their own efforts, to direct its flow according to their own will. The supreme will of God cannot be bent under the low yoke of human willfulness, but when the will of man offers itself, in faith and hope, as a whole burnt offering to the will of God, then the treasures of grace are opened, prayers are answered, miracles increase, God is glorified, and man is saved. Amen.

42

Heart-Attention to God's Word

Homily on the Dormition of the Mother of God
(1843)

"But Mary kept all these things and pondered them in her heart."
(Luke 2:19)

If the death, or the remembrance of the death, of a typical man of virtue leads us to remember his virtues, and we contemplate them on this day, talk of them with each other, thereby glorifying the one who has passed on as well as giving ourselves consolation and incitement to doing good, is it not so much more appropriate for us to do the same today, when we triumphantly remember the blessed Dormition of the most holy Mother of God? In her, without a doubt, we can contemplate the fulfillment of all virtues, because He Whose virtue covers the heavens and fills the earth abode in her worthily and, of course, never left her abandoned. But since we could not possibly speak or think of all her virtues, for they are too many, I will instead take as the subject of our discourse today only one of her virtues, which the holy evangelist Luke expressed in the following words: *But Mary kept all these things and pondered them in her heart.* This virtue is heart-deep attentiveness to the words of God and to the deeds of God's providence. Examining this virtue in the person and life of the most holy Theotokos can lay the path to a teaching concerning this virtue in our own lives.

St. Luke, in the beginning of His Gospel, described the miracles that announced the incarnation of the Son of God; The angelic prophecies of the coming birth of the forerunner of the Christ from a barren woman and of the birth of Christ from a virgin; The ecstatic prophecies of St. Elizabeth, the Virgin herself, and St. Zechariah the father of the forerunner; The appearance of the army of worshipping angels to the shepherds who pointed out the newly born Savior in a sign that was most unexpected (*You will find a Babe wrapped in swaddling cloths, lying in a manger*). St. Luke, having mentioned the amazement of all who heard this news from the shepherds, finally concludes: *But Mary kept all these things and pondered them in her heart.* This repetition of the same phrase shows that it was not a slight, incidental mention, but a very important thought that powerfully occupied the holy writer, and which he wanted to profoundly impress upon the readers and listeners of the Gospel.

What did he want us to understand in this repeated phrase? Did he perhaps want to anticipate and resolve the question of his source for these first events in the life of Christ, which naturally would have been talked about at that time in Bethlehem and Jerusalem, but naturally would have also been largely forgotten during the many years of Jesus' quiet life in obscure Nazareth? Did he perhaps want to show us that Mary was the source for his account, the witness of their truth? No, I do not think so. The Holy Spirit was an endless source and a true witness to the truth of the Gospels; Therefore, the evangelists did not care to point out the source for their account or to condition their veracity on the trustworthiness of extraneous sources.

Thus, what was the purpose that St. Luke had in twice repeating that Mary kept the words of the judgments and life of Christ in her heart? I think that his goal and thought was to open for us a door into her soul, which is the door to heaven, to reveal the glory of the daughter of the King, which is hidden *within*, to lead us to the sanctuary of the heart of the most holy one, to show us in what way He Who abode in her womb for a short time continued to abide within her in a different way for the rest of her life. How? Through the attentiveness of her heart to the words of God, through her heart-deep attention to the works of God. *Mary kept all these things and pondered them in her heart.* *Psalm 44:14*

Luke 2:19

These things she contemplated included the prophecies and words spoken concerning Christ and the Savior, as well as the events of His earthly life, which were arranged by a special providence of God. Often God speaks to man through His works, just as a person speaks to another person with words. Mary heard many words concerning Her Son as the Savior of the world, read the words of His glory in the miracles surrounding Him, and her attention focused on His own works and actions that revealed divine wisdom and power. These words were various and many, often unreadable in their exaltedness or their unusual nature, and sometimes they were sorrowful and threatening. When all words cease, how easy do we forget most of them! How difficult it is to preserve exactly, unforgotten, all the variety and all the wonder! How often, on the contrary, do we try to forget the unpleasant or the terrifying! How often is our memory of exalted words and events damaged by unlimited inquisitiveness or brazenness to try to plumb the mysteries of providence and to explain the words of God's wisdom in terms of human reasoning!

The Virgin preserved herself from all this by her good attentiveness: Without loss, without change, she faithfully *kept all these things in her heart*. How? Did she write them down in a book? Did she put them into some treasure box, unknown to anyone else? No, she knew how to find a better hiding place than all these. The *Luke 2:19* first book in which the words of the Gospel were written was the heart of the most blessed Mary. It was the treasure box of the riches of Christ, for *Mary kept all these things and pondered them in her heart.* In a heart that believed God, in a heart that loved the only begotten Son of God and her own Son, she placed the words of the mystery and the glory of Christ, and no forgetfulness could steal from it, because her love did not allow for forgetfulness, no curiosity or self-styled reasoning could crawl into it, for her faith was not inquisitive. The words of Christ were living words in Mary's heart, because their subject was Christ, Who is the light and the author of our life, because out of a diligent heart *spring[s] the issues of life,* because love itself is life. And after the One Who descended into her by incarnation passed from her through birth, she could still say, *Christ lives in me.*

After examining these words of the evangelist, his silence is also worthy of contemplation. During the early events of the earthly life of Christ, he twice notes that the mother of the Lord *kept all these things and pondered them in her heart.* But later, during the entire rest of his Gospel, he does not repeat this comment and does not take pains to explain how the life of the Lord Jesus affected the life of His mother. What does this mean, that after a certain excess in words, he concludes with a miserly silence? Lest we imagine the holy writer as though he disagreed with himself, we must assume that in these two phrases, he already gave us the key to the entire life of the most holy Virgin, and he considered this to be enough. In actual fact, if we were to ask what the Mother of the Lord did when the Lord Jesus preached, worked miracles, suffered, died, resurrected, and ascended, only one answer would be sufficient: *Mary kept all these things and pondered them in her heart.*

This phrase explains also what is especially hard to understand in her unparalleled life. For example, how could she accept the most exalted annunciation of the incarnation without doubt or pride? She could because even then, she kept the words of prophecy concerning the coming of Immanuel and pondered them in her heart. How could she pass through the difficulties, dangers, terrors that surrounded the birth and childhood of her Son? Without a doubt, she did this with unbreakable firmness and hope, because she kept in her heart the words of promise concerning Him. How did she bear the separation when He left home to preach salvation to mankind, walking straight into the jaws of personal danger? Without a doubt, she did so with hope, because she kept in her heart His own words: *Did you not know that I must be about My Father's business?* How was she not killed by the sword of sorrow that pierced her during the hours of the suffering and death of Her Son and God? She remained alive because she had already felt the sting of this sword when it passed from the lips of Simeon the God-receiver, when she prepared her heart to accept the wound of the deathly word and to be raised up again by the words of resurrection. How did she remain alive when the ascension of the Lord hid the One who was her only reason for living? In her heart, Christ and His words continued to live, and she lived a life of faith, love, and hope, until she could pass through the road that we call death into His life of love, blessedness, and glory.

Luke 2:49

I called the life of the most holy Mother of God unparalleled compared to the rest of humanity, because the mystery of the Theotokos is not repeatable and not communicable to others. However, does that mean that we cannot possibly emulate her? That we can converse with her only about her glory, which was never necessary for her, and not to our own instruction or our benefit? God forbid. Good cannot be without benefit to others. Virtue cannot be fruitless. Does the example of holiness cease to be instructive for holiness only because one is higher than another? Mary's keeping the words of God in the heart, her maintaining a pious attentiveness of the heart—the Gospel offers us this not only for our piety and wonder, but for our instruction and emulation. The God Who seeks our salvation is not silent for our sake, brothers.

How abundantly does He extend to us His words of salvation? How does He pursue us with these words, so to speak, through His Gospel, through the mediation of His Church and the example of the saints and the righteous ones? When you stand in church, the words of psalmody constantly assail your ears, the words of prayer, the words of the mystical work, the words of the divine writings, the words of spiritual instruction. All these are the words of God, words that call, instruct, and arouse us to our salvation. But even when we sit at home, we can also have near us the holy books. All you must do is open one of them, and the words of salvation will rush into your heart. When you see one who truly prays or who does good deeds of love for fellow man, know that these deeds speak the words of God to you, and so you must pray yourself, you must do good deeds yourself. If this is insufficient, God speaks to you with the lips of heaven and earth, and sometimes He even makes the vanity of the world speak important words to your soul. The positive effects of nature, beneficial chance occurrences during life, all these speak to you: Come to know the merciful God and gratefully please Him by doing good. Horrible, destructive, punishing events also call out to you: Come to know the just God and do not wait to propitiate Him.

After all this, I have the thought to ask: Can it be that there are so few who attend to the words of God and who are saved? I do not know myself, but He Who knows has said, *Many are called, but few chosen*. The incarnate Word of God often concluded His salvific words with the exclamation: *He who has ears to hear, let him hear*. Evidently, there are many who not only do not hear, but do not even have ears, that is, who do not attend with the hearing of the heart. And so, let us work on ourselves to have those ears and to hear with them. Let us learn the virtuous attentiveness of the heart. I do not speak at all about complete lack of attentiveness: If I speak, and you do not listen but rather pay attention to

Matthew 20:16

Matthew 11:15

something completely different, then clearly you will learn nothing from me, and will do nothing after I finish speaking. And the all-powerful word of God is powerless for him who is without attention and, as it were, simply does not exist for him. But there are also forms and degrees of attention.

You apply your ear to the word, and you direct your gaze to an object—this is physical attentiveness, but it is only the beginning, the lowest degree of attention. We must ascend that step to go up to higher degrees, but in terms of the words of God, whoever stops on this level of attention is still far away from salvific attentiveness. These are the people that Christ rebuked: *Having eyes, do you not see? And having ears, do you not hear?* You see with the eye, but you do not contemplate with the spirit. You attend to the external noises of the word, but you do not attend to the internal power of the word. Such people can listen to, or read, many prayers, but they pray little. They often encounter teaching, but they do not ascend to a contemplation of the truth, and they do not lead it into their lives. *Mark 8:18*

Then there is the attentiveness of the reason, when one deepens the vision of an object with thoughts, when one seeks the resolution of truth in a word that one hears. However, it is not difficult to see that this level of attentiveness, though useful for the words of God, are still not sufficient. Faith is not love of wisdom, piety is not a science, though there is a philosophy of faith, there is a science of piety. Whoever has a small light in the mind has not yet made his whole being a son of light. Human reason puts on airs, and a humble admission of ignorance is sometimes better than knowledge. Moreover, the truly salvific knowledge is acquired not only through the efforts of the mind, but much more through zealous prayer and a pure desire to be illumined from above. In the parable, the Lord compared the word of God to a seed, and those who hear it to the soil about to be sowed, and in explanation of the parable, He said, *But the ones that fell on the* *Luke 8:15 good ground are those who, having heard the word with a noble and good heart, keep it and bear fruit with patience.*

Thus, the attention of a good and kind heart—this is the truly beneficial and salvific level of pious attention. Therefore, do not be content with the fact that your ears are open to the word of God. Seek to also open the ears of your heart. Attend with the mind, but do not strain your inquisitive reason overmuch. Instead, arouse your heart with love for God and His words, and calm it in faith, fidelity, and humility. Do the same with the words of prayer; do the same with the words of instruction. Attend thus to the works of the providence that instruct you. And when grace-filled words allow your heart to feel inner peace and consolation, then actively and faithfully contemplate these words in your heart. Preserve the mystery of faith in a pure conscience, and keep a distance from distraction and busyness, lest you fall back into your old inattentiveness, *which has eyes to see but does not see, and ears to hear but does not hear,* in which you only approach God with your lips, but remain apart from Him in your heart.

Ezekiel 12:2

O God-blessed Mother of the incarnate Word, faithful keeper of the words of salvation! Ask of Him the grace for our own heart-attentive hearing, our own faithful keeping of the words of God in our hearts and lives, lest we remain outside the promised blessedness for those who hear the word of God and keep it. Amen.

www.ingramcontent.com/pod-product-compliance
Lightning Source LLC
Chambersburg PA
CBHW020517080526
44583CB00013B/634